The Web3 Revolution

Building the Future of Blockchain, DeFi, and the Metaverse

Hui Gong

Apress®

The Web3 Revolution: Building the Future of Blockchain, DeFi, and the Metaverse

Hui Gong
Institute of Finance & Technology
University College London
London, UK

ISBN-13 (pbk): 979-8-8688-0490-8　　　　　　ISBN-13 (electronic): 979-8-8688-0491-5
https://doi.org/10.1007/979-8-8688-0491-5

Copyright © 2024 by Hui Gong

This work is subject to copyright. All rights are reserved by the Publisher, whether the whole or part of the material is concerned, specifically the rights of translation, reprinting, reuse of illustrations, recitation, broadcasting, reproduction on microfilms or in any other physical way, and transmission or information storage and retrieval, electronic adaptation, computer software, or by similar or dissimilar methodology now known or hereafter developed.

Trademarked names, logos, and images may appear in this book. Rather than use a trademark symbol with every occurrence of a trademarked name, logo, or image we use the names, logos, and images only in an editorial fashion and to the benefit of the trademark owner, with no intention of infringement of the trademark.

The use in this publication of trade names, trademarks, service marks, and similar terms, even if they are not identified as such, is not to be taken as an expression of opinion as to whether or not they are subject to proprietary rights.

While the advice and information in this book are believed to be true and accurate at the date of publication, neither the authors nor the editors nor the publisher can accept any legal responsibility for any errors or omissions that may be made. The publisher makes no warranty, express or implied, with respect to the material contained herein.

　　　Managing Director, Apress Media LLC: Welmoed Spahr
　　　Acquisitions Editor: Malini Rajendran
　　　Development Editor: James Markham
　　　Editorial Assistant: Gryffin Winkler

Cover designed by eStudioCalamar

Distributed to the book trade worldwide by Springer Science+Business Media New York, 1 New York Plaza, Suite 4600, New York, NY 10004-1562, USA. Phone 1-800-SPRINGER, fax (201) 348-4505, e-mail orders-ny@springer-sbm.com, or visit www.springeronline.com. Apress Media, LLC is a California LLC and the sole member (owner) is Springer Science + Business Media Finance Inc (SSBM Finance Inc). SSBM Finance Inc is a **Delaware** corporation.

For information on translations, please e-mail booktranslations@springernature.com; for reprint, paperback, or audio rights, please e-mail bookpermissions@springernature.com.

Apress titles may be purchased in bulk for academic, corporate, or promotional use. eBook versions and licenses are also available for most titles. For more information, reference our Print and eBook Bulk Sales web page at http://www.apress.com/bulk-sales.

Any source code or other supplementary material referenced by the author in this book is available to readers on GitHub. For more detailed information, please visit https://www.apress.com/gp/services/source-code.

If disposing of this product, please recycle the paper

This book is dedicated to my son, Tianyi Gong.

Table of Contents

About the Author xiii

Acknowledgments xv

Introduction xvii

Part I: The Origins and Fundamentals of Blockchain 1

Chapter 1: Decrypting Blockchain Technology 3

1.1 What Is Blockchain? 3

    Blockchain vs. Internet 9

    Blockchain and AI 10

1.2 How Blockchain Works: Hash Functions, Encryption and Digital Signatures 12

    Hash Functions 12

    Encryption 14

    Digital Signatures 16

    Case Study: Creating a Bitcoin Address Using Python 18

1.3 Consensus Algorithms 21

1.4 Summary 25

1.5 Notes 25

Chapter 2: Bitcoin: The Pioneer of Digital Currency 27

2.1 The Birth of Bitcoin 27

    Satoshi Nakamoto and the Whitepaper 28

    The Genesis Block and the First Bitcoin Transaction 30

    Hal Finney's Legendary Story and Impact on Bitcoin 31

TABLE OF CONTENTS

    The Legacy of Bitcoin 32
    Technical Overview of Bitcoin 32
  2.2 How Bitcoin Works: Mining Mechanisms 34
    Understanding Bitcoin Mining 34
    Evolution of Mining Hardware 38
    Mining Pools 39
  2.3 The Challenges of Bitcoin: Security Concerns, Wallet Storage and the Issue of Scaling 43
    51% Attacks: A Theoretical Threat to Bitcoin's Integrity 43
    Block Size Debate and Bitcoin Forks: The Scaling Challenge 44
    Diverse Wallet Types 44
  2.4 Gold Jewellery: Ordinals (Inscriptions) 46
  2.5 Summary 50
  2.6 Notes 50

Part II: Ethereum: The Cradle of Smart Contracts 53

Chapter 3: The Rise of Ethereum 55

  3.1 Ethereum Virtual Machine 55
    Turing Completeness of Ethereum 57
    Ethereum As a Decentralised Computing Infrastructure 57
    The Development Journey of Ethereum 58
  3.2 Getting Started with Smart Contracts 61
  3.3 Introduction to Remix – Ethereum IDE 65
    Using Remix for Smart Contract Development 67
  3.4 Simple Smart Contract Examples 74
  3.5 ERC Standards: ERC20, ERC721, ERC1155 83
    A Brief Overview of ERC Standards 83
    Comparing the Standards 106

3.6 Summary 107

3.7 Notes 108

Chapter 4: The Pillars of Web3: Ethereum's Wallet, Faucet and Layer 2 Solutions 111

4.1 The Gateway to Web3: Crypto Wallets 111

    Setting Up and Using a Wallet: The MetaMask Example 114

    Ethereum Explorer: Etherscan 127

4.2 Dripping Resources for Blockchain Newcomers: Faucets 127

    Smart Contract Example – Faucet 129

4.3 Expanding Horizons with Layer 2 Solutions 134

4.4 Summary 137

4.5 Notes 138

Part III: Decentralised Finance (DeFi) and Applications 141

Chapter 5: The Rise of Decentralised Finance (DeFi) 143

5.1 Core Concepts and Applications of DeFi 143

    DeFi vs. TradFi (Traditional Finance) 146

    Decentralised Exchanges (DEXs) 148

    Lending Platforms 150

    Stablecoins 151

    Insurance 153

    Prediction Markets/Oracles 154

5.2 Analysis of Mainstream DeFi Protocols 156

    Uniswap 157

    Aave 161

    MakerDAO 163

    Total Value Locked (TVL) 166

TABLE OF CONTENTS

5.3 Risks and Challenges of DeFi 167
    Security Risks 167
    Regulatory Challenges 168
    Scalability and Interoperability 170
    Market Risks and Volatility 170

5.4 Summary 171

5.5 Notes 171

Chapter 6: Tokenised Real- World Assets (RWA) and Decentralised Physical Infrastructure Networks (DePIN) 175

6.1 Introduction to RWA 175
    The Blockchain As Ideal Infrastructure 177
    The Disruptive Impact of RWA Tokenisation on TradFi 178

6.2 Overview of DePIN 181
    Real-World Applications 182
    The Dynamics of DePIN Flywheel 185
    Scalability and Sustainability 187

6.3 Synergy Between RWA and DePIN: Opportunities and Complexities 189
    The Solana Edge in DePIN Projects 189
    Challenges 191
    Solutions 192

6.4 Summary 195

6.5 Notes 196

Chapter 7: Non-fungible Tokens (NFTs) and Digital Art 199

7.1 Understanding NFTs: Mechanisms and Market Dynamics 199
    Unique Properties and Underlying Technology 199
    Applications of NFTs 201
    Distribution Models: From Standard Mints to Dutch Auctions 203

Addressing Market Challenges: Inclusivity and Integrity 205
Market Dynamics 206
7.2 The Evolution and Future Trends of NFT Markets 207
Towards More Equitable and Transparent Distribution Models 207
Market Volatility and Liquidity Concerns 208
Beyond Digital Art: The Expanding Applications of NFTs 209
7.3 Creating and Trading NFTs: A Step-by-Step Guide 209
Step 1: Generate a Random Image with Python 210
Step 2: Upload the Asset to a Storage Solution 215
Step 3: Create Metadata Compliant with OpenSea's Standards 219
Step 4: Mint the NFT on the Blockchain 222
Step 5: List the NFT for Sale on OpenSea 235
7.4 Summary 238
7.5 Note 239

Chapter 8: DEX and Market Cap Management 241
8.1 How DEXs Work 241
Principles of Operation 241
Token Listing and Liquidity Pools 244
Decentralisation, Security and Governance 247
8.2 Tokens' Market Cap Management Strategies 248
Token Burn 248
Liquidity Provision 248
Partnership and Integration 249
Mechanism and Fiscal Policy Design 249
Algorithmic Market Making 249
Strategic Distribution 250
Monetary Policies: Burn-and-Mint Equilibrium 250

TABLE OF CONTENTS

8.3 Future Development of DEXs 250
    Integration with Traditional Finance 251
    Addressing JIT Liquidity and Sandwich Attacks 252
    TWAMM vs. CFMM 253
    Encouraging Liquidity Providers 255
8.4 Summary 256
8.5 Notes 257

Part IV: Advancing Web3: Integration, Innovation and Regulation 259

Chapter 9: Navigating the Future of Web3 and the Metaverse 261

9.1 Web3 and Metaverse: Foundations and Technologies 261
    Core Foundational Elements of the Metaverse 263
9.2 Economic Models and Opportunities in Web3 and the Metaverse 266
    Decentralised Economic Systems 266
    Value Creation and Distribution 268
    Collaborative Work and Innovation 270
    Tokenisation and Economic Incentives 272
9.3 Leading Platforms, Projects and Their Applications 273
    Decentraland: A Case Study in User-Governed Virtual Real Estate 273
    JPMorgan's Foray into the Metaverse: Onyx Lounge and Beyond 274
9.4 Future Directions: Challenges and Preparations 276
    Regulatory and Ethical Considerations 276
    Future Directions: Challenges and Preparations 277
    Preparations for the Road Ahead 277
9.5 Summary 278
9.6 Notes 279

TABLE OF CONTENTS

Chapter 10: The Integration and Evolution of AI in Web3 281

10.1 Blockchain Enhanced by Generative AI 281

10.2 AI and Web3 Synergy 285

    Decentralised Finance (DeFi) and Predictive Analytics 288

    Healthcare: Patient Data and Personalised Medicine......................290

    Education: Tailored Learning Experiences 292

    Governance: Transparent Voting Systems 294

    Supply Chain Management..296

    Environmental Sustainability 298

10.3 From Meme to Mainstream: AI's Expanding Role in Web3 Culture and Creativity 300

    The Power of Memes in Digital Currency Communities 301

    Generative AI's Role in Meme Creation and Evolution 301

    The 'Make It More' Trend and the Expansion of AI Memes.........302

    The Cultural Impact and Future Directions 302

10.4 Summary...303

10.5 Notes..303

Chapter 11: Legal Frameworks for Web3 305

11.1 Global Regulatory Divergence and Convergence in Token Definitions......305

    United States – Securities and Exchange Commission (SEC).....................305

    United Kingdom – Financial Conduct Authority (FCA)..................307

    European Union – Markets in Crypto-Assets (MiCA) 309

    Switzerland – Financial Market Supervisory Authority (FINMA).................310

    Singapore – Monetary Authority of Singapore (MAS) 312

    Hong Kong – Monetary Authority (HKMA).......................................313

11.2 Global Regulatory Strategies for Digital Assets 316

    The SEC's Regulatory Compass...316

    The FCA's Regulatory Blueprint 317

TABLE OF CONTENTS

    Navigating Cross-Border Regulatory Waters 317

    Convergence and Divergence in Global Regulation 318

    Future Horizons 318

11.3 Digital Asset Custody and User Protection 319

    The Essence of Digital Asset Custody 319

    Regulatory Approaches to Custody and Protection 319

    Case Studies in Regulation 320

    The Path Forward 321

11.4 Navigating the Future: Regulation, Innovation and the
       Standardisation of Web3 322

    The Emergence of Bitcoin ETFs: Bridging Traditional and
    Digital Finance 322

    The Innovation Horizon 324

    Navigating the Risks 325

    The Quest for Standardisation 326

    Future Projections 327

11.5 Summary 329

11.6 Notes 330

Index **333**

About the Author

Dr. Hui Gong is the Programme Director of the MSc in Banking and Digital Finance and a Lecturer in Decentralised Finance and Blockchain at UCL Institute of Finance & Technology, where he also leads the Blockchain and DeFi Lab. His academic journey, which includes a PhD from University College London, has been marked by an in-depth exploration of blockchain, cryptocurrencies, Web3, and the transformative power of these technologies. He has collaborated with leading financial institutions such as Credit Suisse, integrating artificial intelligence and blockchain into the core of quantitative finance and fintech innovations.

As the founder of the China-UK Blockchain Association and a former Special Advisor on Fintech and Blockchain for some All-Party Parliamentary Groups, he has actively contributed to both the Sino-British dialogue and policy discussions in these sectors. His extensive work with the UCL Centre for Blockchain Technology (CBT) and Westminster Business School has resulted in numerous publications on topics such as ICOs and Central Bank Digital Currencies (CBDCs). Dr. Gong continues to dedicate his experience and knowledge to advancing financial technology, teaching and sharing his expertise in blockchain, DeFi, Web3, and the metaverse at a crucial time of technological evolution.

Acknowledgments

In the journey of writing this book, my deepest gratitude goes first and foremost to those who have supported me and embraced blockchain technology amidst its many controversies. Having been in this industry for nearly a decade, my passion has thrived on the support of everyone who shares a 'consensus' on the transformative potential of this field.

A special thanks to Professor Harry Thapar, former Head of the School of Finance and Accounting, and Ann Thapar, former Course Leader of MSc Fintech with Business Analytics, at Westminster Business School. Their decision to hire me post my PhD in 2019 allowed me to pioneer courses on blockchain, including topics on tokenisation that were yet to gain full regulatory acceptance. My innovative curricula have been well received by students, enhancing my teaching journey. In 2023, Professor Francesca Medda welcomed me back to the UCL Institute of Finance & Technology, offering me the opportunity to continue educating on Decentralised Finance and Blockchain at UCL. Their forward thinking, coupled with the encouragement and enthusiasm of my students, has been pivotal in my path and instrumental in the creation of this book, which will serve as a resource in my future courses. Additionally, the 4btc Inscription community, which I formed while writing this book, and all its members have provided unwavering support, reinforcing my belief in blockchain's capacity to revolutionise and disrupt finance as a part of the Web3 revolution.

Lastly, I extend my deepest appreciation to my family for their selfless dedication and support. I hope this work not only guides beginners in blockchain and cryptocurrency but also sparks innovative thinking among them. This journey has been challenging, but it's the community of like-minded, consensus-driven individuals that has made it worthwhile. We believed, and therefore we have seen.

Introduction

In the ever-evolving landscape of digital innovation, *The Web3 Revolution* charts a comprehensive journey from the theoretical underpinnings of blockchain technology to its practical applications in today's digital world. This book is crafted not merely as a guide but as a bridge, connecting the intricate mechanisms of decentralisation, cryptography and smart contracts with their real-world implementations that promise to redefine the fabric of our digital society.

As we delve into the complex world of Web3, we explore how these technologies are not just technological advancements but transformative tools that facilitate a shift in power from centralised entities to individuals and communities. Each chapter systematically unfolds, starting from the fundamentals of blockchain technology as exemplified by Bitcoin and Ethereum, moving through the nuances of non-fungible tokens (NFTs), decentralised autonomous organisations (DAOs) and the burgeoning field of decentralised finance (DeFi).

This book aims to serve both novices and seasoned professionals in the tech industry by providing a clear, contextual understanding of how each piece of the Web3 puzzle fits together and why it matters. Through a blend of technical descriptions, industry case studies and real-world scenarios, *The Web3 Revolution* offers readers not just knowledge but a vision of the potential impacts and opportunities that lie ahead in this new digital frontier.

Embark on this journey to demystify the complexities of blockchain and discover the practicalities that make Web3 a revolutionary step towards a more transparent, secure and equitable digital future. Whether you're an entrepreneur, a developer, a builder or simply a tech enthusiast, this book is designed to equip you with a robust understanding of Web3 and Blockchain technology and inspire you to be a part of this transformative wave.

PART I

The Origins and Fundamentals of Blockchain

CHAPTER 1

Decrypting Blockchain Technology

This chapter delves into the foundational aspects of blockchain, exploring its origins, key mechanics and the transformative potential it holds for creating a transparent, efficient and secure digital world. As we unfold the layers of this technology, we invite readers to explore how blockchain is not just reshaping finance but also redefining the boundaries of technology and trust in the modern era.

1.1 What Is Blockchain?

The origin of blockchain technology is closely linked to Bitcoin, tracing back to 2008 when the concept of Bitcoin was first introduced. Bitcoin is not only a cryptocurrency but also runs on an innovative technology known as blockchain. This technology, evolving alongside Bitcoin, has now been widely applied in various fields.

The genesis of Bitcoin dates back to 31 October 2008, when a mysterious individual or team known as Satoshi Nakamoto released a groundbreaking document – the Bitcoin whitepaper.[1] In this whitepaper, Nakamoto proposed a novel concept of digital currency, challenging the existing financial system and revolutionising traditional monetary concepts. Then, on 3 January 2009, the Bitcoin network witnessed a historic moment as the first block, known as block #0, was successfully mined.[2] This block, commonly referred to as the genesis block or the original block, not only marked the official start of the Bitcoin network but also the first practical application of blockchain technology. This innovative application heralded a new era of digital currency and distributed ledger technology, laying the foundation for modern cryptocurrencies and blockchain technology.

As an innovative digital ledger technology, the core of blockchain lies in its ability to store and transfer data in a decentralised, transparent and immutable manner. In a blockchain, data is grouped and stored in structures called 'blocks', which are linked in chronological order, forming a continuously growing chain. Each block contains a series of transaction records and the cryptographic hash of the previous block, ensuring that once data is written to the blockchain, it is nearly impossible to alter or delete, thus preserving the integrity and complete history of data.

Decentralisation is another key characteristic of blockchain. Unlike traditional databases or ledger systems where data is stored in centralised servers or data centres, blockchain data is distributed across the entire network, with each node in the network maintaining a copy of the entire blockchain, shown in Figure 1-1. This distributed data storage significantly reduces the risk of single points of failure and enhances the system's resilience against attacks.

CHAPTER 1 DECRYPTING BLOCKCHAIN TECHNOLOGY

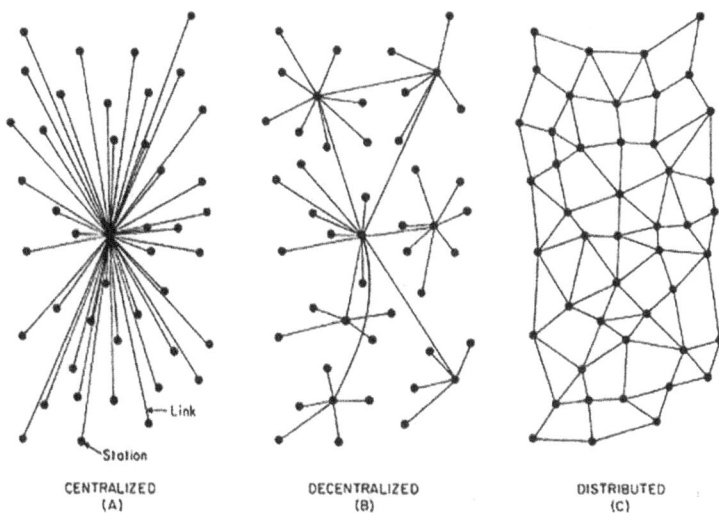

Figure 1-1. *Centralised vs. Decentralised vs. Distributed*
Source: https://berty.tech/blog/decentralized-distributed-centralized

This table provides an overview of the key characteristics and trade-offs associated with each type of system in terms of maintenance, stability, scalability, development and potential for evolution and diversity.

Table 1-1. *Comparison of Centralised vs. Decentralised vs. Distributed*

System Type	Centralised	Decentralised	Distributed
Points of Failure/ Maintenance	Single point of failure, easier to maintain	More points of failure than centralised but finite, harder to maintain	No single point of failure, hardest to maintain
Fault Tolerance/ Stability	Highly unstable if the central point fails	More stable than centralised, can survive central node failures	Very stable, single failures have little impact
Scalability/Max Population	Low scalability	Moderate scalability	Infinite scalability
Ease of Development/ Creation	Fastest to create, follows a single framework	Slower than centralised, need to sort out lower-level details	Slowest, complex resource sharing and communication required
Evolution/ Diversity	Low diversity, evolves slowly	Once infrastructure is in place, can evolve quickly	High potential for evolution once infrastructure is set

Furthermore, the transparency of blockchain technology is one of its defining features. In public blockchains, anyone can view all transaction records and block information, yet the identities of transaction participants remain anonymous or pseudonymous, as illustrated in Figure 1-2. This combination of transparency and privacy makes blockchain an ideal technology choice for sectors such as finance, supply chain management and healthcare.

CHAPTER 1   DECRYPTING BLOCKCHAIN TECHNOLOGY

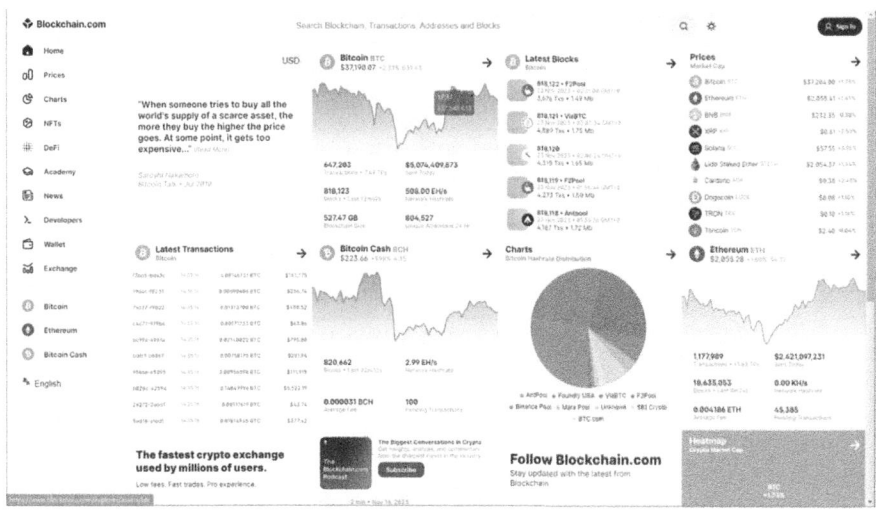

Figure 1-2. *Bitcoin Explorer*
Source: *www.blockchain.com/explorer (Accessed: 23 November 2023)*

To ensure the accuracy of transactions and the security of the network, blockchain networks typically employ a method known as the 'consensus mechanism' to verify and add new transactions. The most famous consensus mechanism is the proof of work (PoW) used by Bitcoin, where participants (miners) in the network must solve complex computational problems to validate transactions and create new blocks.

Hence, blockchain technology is not only designed to validate transactions and enhance the security of the digital ledger but also to mitigate critical issues such as the double-spending of cryptocurrencies and various fraudulent activities. Blockchain 1.0,[3] the initial iteration of this technology predominantly used in cryptocurrencies like Bitcoin, targets two fundamental problems:

- **Double-Spending Problem**: It uses a combination of peer-to-peer file sharing and public key encryption technologies to prevent the same digital currency unit from being used more than once. This is executed

7

within a trustless framework where transactions are recorded on a publicly accessible ledger and confirmed by a consensus among participants, thus eliminating the need for a centralised authority.

- **Byzantine Generals' Problem**: This refers to the challenge of achieving consensus in a decentralised network. Blockchain 1.0 addresses this through the proof-of-work (PoW) mechanism, where all participants agree on a verified truth without the need for a trusted intermediary. This is accomplished by miners solving cryptographic puzzles to validate transactions and add new blocks, thereby ensuring network agreement on the ledger's state.[4]

These foundational aspects underpin the robustness of blockchain against potential vulnerabilities and form the basis for its widespread application in various sectors beyond cryptocurrency.

Blockchain 2.0 represents a significant evolution from the original blockchain concept, marked by the integration of smart contracts into blockchain protocols. Pioneered by Ethereum, smart contracts are automated codes that execute when predefined conditions are met, enabling complex transactions beyond simple cryptocurrency exchanges. This advancement fostered the development of decentralised applications (DApps) and decentralised autonomous organisations (DAOs), expanding blockchain's utility into various domains such as governance and digital ownership, exemplified by non-fungible tokens (NFTs).

Blockchain 3.0 extends blockchain's application beyond financial sectors to diverse industries, emphasising sustainability, scalability and enhanced security. It integrates enterprise-level systems with blockchain, enabling industries like healthcare and supply chain management to utilise smart contracts for functions like medical services and logistics. Additionally, Blockchain 3.0 supports interoperability between different blockchain networks, as seen in Cosmos and Chainlink ecosystems. Technological innovations like proof-of-stake consensus models and Directed Acyclic Graph (DAG) algorithms in this generation of blockchains, exemplified by platforms like Cardano, Solana and Avalanche, address previous limitations by reducing energy consumption and significantly increasing transaction processing speeds.[5]

In summary, blockchain technology offers a novel, more secure and reliable method for digital transactions and data storage through its unique decentralised structure, immutable data recording, transparency and robust consensus mechanism.

Blockchain vs. Internet

The Internet revolutionised the way information is disseminated, enabling rapid, cost-efficient and seamless exchange of knowledge across the globe. However, it falls short in transmitting value due to inherent trust issues and centralisation, often requiring intermediaries for validation.

In contrast, blockchain technology is engineered to transfer value. It does so by providing a decentralised platform where transactions are not only transparent but also immutable, creating an environment where trust is established through cryptographic verification rather than central authorities. Blockchain's capability to transmit value is exemplified by its ability to facilitate the exchange of digital assets, execute smart contracts and ensure the authenticity and integrity of transactions without centralised oversight. This makes blockchain an ideal infrastructure for the digital economy, where value transfer is as critical as information exchange.

CHAPTER 1   DECRYPTING BLOCKCHAIN TECHNOLOGY

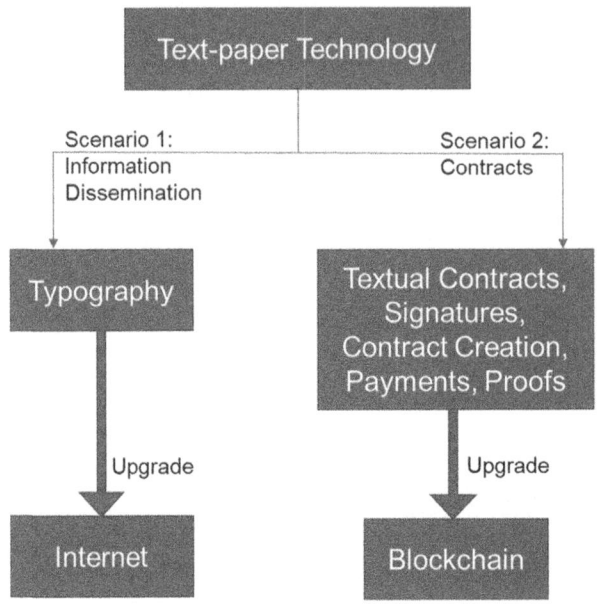

Figure 1-3. *Information vs. Value Transfer*

Figure 1-3 outlines the evolution of technology from text-paper to digital formats. At the top, 'Text-paper technology' serves as the starting point. From there, two paths diverge: one leads to 'Typography', eventually evolving into the 'Internet', symbolising the digital upgrade of text for information dissemination. The other path heads towards 'Textual Contracts, Signatures, Contract Creation, Payments, Proofs', which then lead to 'Blockchain', representing the digitisation of contractual and transactional processes. The diagram suggests that while the Internet evolved as the digital successor of typography for text, blockchain serves a similar role for transactions and contractual agreements.

Blockchain and AI

Blockchain and artificial intelligence (AI) are forging a strategic alliance that not only amplifies their individual strengths but also addresses fundamental societal and economic challenges. Blockchain's architecture,

CHAPTER 1 DECRYPTING BLOCKCHAIN TECHNOLOGY

celebrated for its security and immutability, establishes a bedrock for AI to function in a manner that is both transparent and verifiable, paving the path for 'decentralised AI' systems like SingularityNET. AI, in reciprocation, elevates blockchain's operational efficiency through intelligent optimisation of complex computations. This symbiosis further empowers individuals to take control of their data, facilitating personal data monetisation while disrupting the data monopoly held by tech behemoths. As AI algorithms evolve in complexity, the trust and clarity provided by blockchain become crucial in validating and understanding AI-driven decisions. Although still nascent and ripe with undiscovered possibilities, the convergence of blockchain and strong AI is a testament to their potential in revolutionising both the mechanics of productivity and the infrastructure of production relations, ensuring that AI's expansive capabilities are harnessed within a framework that upholds transparency, accountability and ethical standards.[6]

Figure 1-4. *Image Generated by the ChatGPT DALL·E 3 Model Based on the Preceding Text*
Source: `https://chat.openai.com/?model=gpt-4`

11

1.2 How Blockchain Works: Hash Functions, Encryption and Digital Signatures

The working mechanism of blockchain technology relies on two core components: hash functions and encryption technologies.

Hash Functions

Hash functions play a central role in blockchain, particularly in the cryptocurrency domain, where cryptographic hash functions possess key characteristics essential for ensuring security and integrity. The following three properties—collision resistance, hiding, and puzzle friendliness—are specifically critical for cryptographic hash functions used in cryptocurrencies.

- **Collision Resistance**: In cryptography, collision resistance is a key attribute of hash functions, requiring that for a given hash function H, it should be computationally infeasible to find two different inputs x and y such that $H(x) = H(y)$. This means, despite the theoretical existence of such input pairs, finding them in reality is extremely difficult due to computational resource limitations. Collision resistance ensures the uniqueness of transactions in cryptocurrency, guaranteeing each transaction generates a unique hash value. Without collision resistance, attackers could create two different transactions with the same hash value, enabling undetected ledger tampering. In blockchain, as each block's hash value is included in the next block, collision resistance is vital for maintaining the integrity of the chain.

- **Hiding**: The hiding feature of hash functions is important for protecting data privacy in cryptography. A hash function with hiding properties means that even if the hash value is known, it is not possible to determine which specific input value produced it. This feature is typically achieved by combining randomness (like random numbers or salt) with the input data, ensuring even slight input variations result in significantly different outputs, making it impossible to deduce or guess the original data without additional information. In blockchain technology, hiding is extremely important as it ensures the privacy of transaction details while allowing network nodes to verify the validity of transactions without revealing actual data. For instance, Bitcoin's hash function uses hiding to prevent unauthorised access to information about transaction amounts and participant identities. This can be likened to the practice of sealing letters with wax in ancient times or using envelopes to conceal the contents of a letter. Just as a sealed letter ensures that only the intended recipient can access the message, the hiding property in hash functions ensures that sensitive transaction details remain private, while still allowing the network to verify the authenticity of the transaction. Additionally, hiding plays a role in creating cryptocurrency addresses and processing smart contracts, further enhancing the security and privacy protection capabilities of the blockchain network.

- **Puzzle Friendliness**: Puzzle friendliness is a unique property of hash functions in the cryptocurrency domain. It implies that for a given output value, finding an input value that maps to this output is very difficult. In other words, there is no effective way to predict which input value will produce a specific hash value, unless all possible inputs are tried. In the mining process of cryptocurrencies like Bitcoin, puzzle friendliness is crucial. Miners must try a vast number of different inputs (including transaction information and a random number) to find a hash value that meets the current difficulty target of the network, typically meaning the hash value must be less than a certain number. This process is computationally intensive, and randomness ensures no shortcuts to complete the task, thus guaranteeing network security and the stable issuance of currency.

These features collectively form the cornerstone of hash functions in cryptocurrency, ensuring the security and functionality of the blockchain network.

Encryption

Asymmetric Encryption: Asymmetric encryption is a key technology in blockchain to ensure the security of transactions. In this system, the public key encrypts information into ciphertext for public transmission, while the private key decrypts the ciphertext back into plaintext, accessible only to the holder of the private key, thus ensuring the confidentiality of the information. In blockchain transactions, participants use their private key to digitally sign transactions. The corresponding public key can be used by others to verify the legitimacy of the signature, but not to forge it, thereby ensuring the authenticity and non-repudiation of the transaction.

Merkle Trees: Merkle trees are structures optimised for validating data. They aggregate transaction data through hash functions, where each leaf node contains the hash value of an individual transaction, and internal nodes contain the hash values of their child nodes. This structure is highly efficient in ensuring data integrity and speeding up information verification, thus working in conjunction with asymmetric encryption to ensure the completeness and validity of data.

Hash Pointers and Data Structures: The hash pointer structure records the hash value of data and pointers to other parts of the data structure. Blockchain uses hash pointers to link each block into a chain, where each block contains the hash value of the previous block, establishing the immutability and historical continuity of the blockchain. This sequential linking maintains a timestamped, orderly record of transactions, providing strong support for the authenticity of data. By linking each block to the hash value of its predecessor, it not only confirms the data's immutability but also establishes a verifiable, sequentially arranged chain of transaction records.

Combining these three elements, blockchain provides a transparent, secure and unalterable environment for transactions, laying the foundation for building trust and value transfer.

Table 1-2 is a comparison table of the cryptographic functions used by Bitcoin (BTC) and Ethereum (ETH).

Table 1-2. Cryptographic Function for BTC and ETH

Feature	Bitcoin (BTC)	Ethereum (ETH)
Hash Function	SHA-256	Keccak-256 (variant of SHA-3)
Signature Algorithm	ECDSA (Elliptic Curve Digital Signature Algorithm)	ECDSA (Elliptic Curve Digital Signature Algorithm)

This table illustrates the differences and similarities in the cryptographic functions employed by both Bitcoin and Ethereum. While both use the ECDSA algorithm for digital signatures, they differ in their choice of hash functions, with Bitcoin using SHA-256 and Ethereum using Keccak-256.

Digital Signatures

Digital signatures play a crucial role in blockchain, ensuring the security and authentication of transactions. The digital signature mechanism includes generating a key pair (public and private keys), the signing process and the verification process. The private key is used to sign messages, while the public key allows anyone to verify the authenticity of the signature. Digital signatures not only ensure that only the signer can generate the signature but also bind the signature to a specific document, ensuring that the signature cannot be used to indicate approval or endorsement of a different document. The design goal of this mechanism is to meet two main properties, very similar to the analogy of handwritten signatures:

1. **Uniqueness**: Only you can generate your signature, but anyone who sees it can verify its validity. This is achieved by using the private key to sign messages, and the private key is confidential and accessible only to the owner of the key.

2. **Binding**: The signature is bound to a specific document, so it cannot be used to indicate agreement or endorsement of a different document. In other words, the signature is a verification of a specific transaction or message and cannot be misused or repurposed for other content.

The digital signature scheme includes the following three algorithms:

- **Key Generation**: This method takes a key size parameter and generates a pair of keys. The private key (secret key) is kept confidential and used to sign messages; the public key (public verification key) is public, and anyone can use it to verify the signature.

- **Signing Method**: This method takes a message and a private key as inputs and outputs the signature of the message under that private key.

- **Verification Method**: This method takes a message, a signature and a public key as inputs. It returns a Boolean value, true if the signature is valid for the message under the given public key and false otherwise.

Additionally, digital signatures must satisfy the following two properties:

- **Valid Signatures Must Verify**: A signature generated by the corresponding private key must return true when verified with the public key.

- **Signatures Are Existentially Unforgeable**: This means that no one can forge someone else's signature. The property of existential unforgeability ensures the security and credibility of transactions in blockchain systems like Bitcoin.

Multi-signature (abbreviated as 'multisig') is an extended application of digital signatures, requiring multiple keys to jointly sign a transaction. In the cryptocurrency domain, such as Bitcoin, multi-signature enhances security by requiring the approval of multiple parties for a transaction to be executed. This is very useful for scenarios requiring high security and joint management, such as partnerships, joint accounts or family trusts. For example, a 2-of-3 multi-signature scheme requires any two of the three participants to provide their signatures to validate and execute the transaction. Such an arrangement provides security as well as flexibility and redundancy, addressing situations like loss of keys or inability of one party to fulfil their duties.

CHAPTER 1   DECRYPTING BLOCKCHAIN TECHNOLOGY

Case Study: Creating a Bitcoin Address Using Python

In this case study, Python libraries like 'bitcoin' can be utilised to handle cryptographic operations and Bitcoin-specific encodings.

1. **Installing Necessary Python Libraries**

    ```
    pip install bitcoin
    ```

2. **Generating a Bitcoin Address**

    - **Generating a Private Key**: Use a cryptographic library in Python to generate a private key.

        ```
        from bitcoin import *
        my_private_key = random_key()
        print("Private Key: %s\n" % my_private_key)
        ```

```
my_private_key = random_key()
print("Private Key: %s\n" % my_private_key)
```
Private Key: 175b01f35f2a8a358b201669f35e7781568b42fc4716126e72dc955b453bba01

Figure 1-5. Private Key

    - **Deriving the Public Key**: Compute the public key from the private key.

        ```
        my_public_key = privtopub(my_private_key)
        print("Public Key: %s\n" % my_public_key)
        ```

```
my_public_key = privtopub(my_private_key)
print("Public Key: %s\n" % my_public_key)
```
Public Key: 04329beef45b0a4b1507b17cb2c65ff21d5e0dc280641f86a5f29d0c3d92260353bc90ec1029bba27b813af2e86bc70c232e1cb7ffdb54102b66406026e4beae56

Figure 1-6. Public Key

- **Creating a Bitcoin Address**: Convert the public key to a standard Bitcoin address using Bitcoin's specific encoding methods.

  ```
  my_address = pubtoaddr(my_public_key)
  print("Bitcoin Address: %s\n" % my_address)
  ```

  ```
  my_address = pubtoaddr(my_public_key)
  print('Bitcoin Address: %s\n' % my_address)
  Bitcoin Address: 1NWtQrmpsNA636KVgzpffqAR9ivVGwvpgj
  ```

Figure 1-7. Bitcoin Address

3. **Creating a Multi-signature Address**

   - **Gathering Multiple Public Keys**: Collect public keys from the involved parties.

   - **Forming a Multi-signature Script**: Use a Bitcoin scripting language to create a script that requires signatures from a specified number of those keys (e.g. 2-of-3, 3-of-5).

   - **Generating the Multi-signature Address**: Encode the multi-signature script into a Bitcoin address.

     ```
     private_key1 = random_key()
     private_key2 = random_key()
     private_key3 = random_key()
     public_key1 = privtopub(private_key1)
     public_key2 = privtopub(private_key2)
     public_key3 = privtopub(private_key3)
     my_mulit_sig = mk_multisig_script(private_key1,
     private_key2, private_key3, 2, 3)
     my_mulit_address = scriptaddr(my_mulit_sig)
     print("My Multisignature Address: %s\n"
     % my_mulit_address)
     ```

```
private_key1 = random_key()
private_key2 = random_key()
private_key3 = random_key()
public_key1 = privtopub(private_key1)
public_key2 = privtopub(private_key2)
public_key3 = privtopub(private_key3)
my_mulit_sig = mk_multisig_script(private_key1, private_key2, private_key3, 2, 3)
my_mulit_address = scriptaddr(my_mulit_sig)
print("My Multisignature Address: %s\n" % my_mulit_address)

My Multisignature Address: 3FMrAHziXgfVWP2ksMgoC353LbhSLGXXxt
```

Figure 1-8. *Multi-signature Address*

4. **Querying Address Transaction History**

    - **Choosing a Blockchain API**: Select an appropriate API service that allows querying Bitcoin's blockchain (e.g. BlockCypher, Blockchain.info).

    - **Fetching Transaction Data**: Use Python requests to call the API with the Bitcoin address and retrieve its transaction history.

    ```
    valid_address = ' 1A1zP1eP5QGefi2DMPTfTL5
    SLmv7DivfNa'
    print(history(valid_address))
    ```

```
valid_address = '1A1zP1eP5QGefi2DMPTfTL5SLmv7DivfNa'
print(history(valid_address))

Fetching more transactions... 4850
Fetching more transactions... 4900
```


```
[{'address': '1A1zP1eP5QGefi2DMPTfTL5SLmv7DivfNa', 'value': 589, 'output': '8628a559115fd410193ff4cd52dc650bd74ee117170d8f77ea8ecbe7b
66ab9fa:2', 'block_height': None}, {'address': '1A1zP1eP5QGefi2DMPTfTL5SLmv7DivfNa', 'value': 589, 'output': '9c96a2e368d9db0c9100268
318b650edc95791486c4684bc3b051309b6a1d44c:0', 'block_height': 818148}, {'address': '1A1zP1eP5QGefi2DMPTfTL5SLmv7DivfNa', 'value': 100
0, 'output': 'b78bb315c05497458abab8d7b2486598e54dcfb244552aba4ce32d13bf132ec5:0', 'block_height': 818143}, {'address': '1A1zP1eP5QGe
fi2DMPTfTL5SLmv7DivfNa', 'value': 546, 'output': '07ea6ebc7d3557181a0dcd0b439b515b685f8c598ba4f180e2be168e06970394:0', 'block_heigh
t': 818099}, {'address': '1A1zP1eP5QGefi2DMPTfTL5SLmv7DivfNa', 'value': 1000, 'output': 'cee2201c88a7356ad13a829a63b5977b9593d00f7fe2
f3a31bcd45aec559b006:0', 'block_height': 817878}, {'address': '1A1zP1eP5QGefi2DMPTfTL5SLmv7DivfNa', 'value': 4632, 'output': '4eb47d0
a736b916086f2b0f32c057c9a0d4e5d44f0ca363122ad993b941764f9:0', 'block_height': 816918}, {'address': '1A1zP1eP5QGefi2DMPTfTL5SLmv7DivfN
a', 'value': 1000, 'output': '8f5c340560307f82b8abfa27b9b241708fc3fe27a972907d67de4e116192bb42:0', 'block_height': 816795}, {'addres
s': '1A1zP1eP5QGefi2DMPTfTL5SLmv7DivfNa', 'value': 546, 'output': '5f90268b1931ecaca1a21ad72613d2c2771d2bb9f34157dba221fc6b4ffb5771:
0', 'block_height': 816783}, {'address': '1A1zP1eP5QGefi2DMPTfTL5SLmv7DivfNa', 'value': 58997, 'output': '1c4924450a0a2c00fd37b2928ba
16e2126ea2d482c5483b2062a91578c92433b:0', 'block_height': 816355}, {'address': '1A1zP1eP5QGefi2DMPTfTL5SLmv7DivfNa', 'value': 1000,
'output': '952c50d2d790e3787fd9abd059ce905ca5b8fe03fcc6a41c61db8abf6d74496a:0', 'block_height': 815770}, {'address': '1A1zP1eP5QGefi2
DMPTfTL5SLmv7DivfNa', 'value': 546, 'output': '7bc45a60eff2886597868f139bce0c91f1cdc83172448b699056a063af4fc3db:0', 'block_height': 8
15168}, {'address': '1A1zP1eP5QGefi2DMPTfTL5SLmv7DivfNa', 'value': 546, 'output': '9cf8a9f24804146f8f032eda77479894e9e0e81e5f8e55c1df
b4e5c7297ba0ca:0', 'block_height': 815168}, {'address': '1A1zP1eP5QGefi2DMPTfTL5SLmv7DivfNa', 'value': 546, 'output': '520f39c2b65e3b
798a7fd458eb1c378f9c1fe4478bc9efe8fd64d34d4e6395c2:0', 'block_height': 815168}, {'address': '1A1zP1eP5QGefi2DMPTfTL5SLmv7DivfNa', 'va
```


Figure 1-9. *Transaction History for the 'Genesis' Bitcoin Address*

The Bitcoin address '1A1zP1eP5QGefi2DMPTfTL5SLmv7DivfNa' is significant in the history of Bitcoin, being recognised as the 'genesis' Bitcoin address. This address is notable for receiving the first-ever Bitcoin transaction. As of the last update, it has a balance of 72.73 BTC, valued at approximately $2,715,604.42. The address first received Bitcoin on 3 January 2009, and the most recent activity was recorded on 23 November 2023. Interestingly, it has never sent any BTC, indicating it has only been used to receive funds.

This address holds a special place in Bitcoin's history and serves as a symbol of the network's beginnings. Analysing such addresses can provide insights into the early usage patterns and distribution of Bitcoin.

This Python code example demonstrates the foundational elements for generating a single-signature Bitcoin address, a multi-signature address, and fetching transaction history. However, this is only a conceptual demonstration and cannot be used for real-world applications. If you need to create a functional Bitcoin address, it is recommended to use a reliable service such as BitAddress (`https://www.bitaddress.org`). It's important to handle private keys securely and to understand the implications of transaction analysis in a public blockchain like Bitcoin.

1.3 Consensus Algorithms

Consensus algorithms are fundamental to the functioning and reliability of blockchain networks. They serve as the mechanism through which multiple nodes in a decentralised network reach a common agreement on a specific value, such as the validity of transaction records. This process is crucial in a blockchain environment, where no central authority exists to dictate or validate the state of the ledger.

CHAPTER 1   DECRYPTING BLOCKCHAIN TECHNOLOGY

In blockchain technology, consensus algorithms enable all participants (or nodes) to agree on the contents of the blockchain in a trustless environment. This agreement is necessary to ensure that each copy of the distributed ledger is consistent and accurate, maintaining the integrity and security of the entire blockchain system.

Consensus mechanisms also play a vital role in resolving potential conflicts in a blockchain network, such as double-spending problems, where a digital token could be spent more than once. They help to synchronise the ledger across different nodes, ensuring that all transactions are recorded in the correct order and that each node has the same version of the truth.

By leveraging consensus algorithms, blockchain networks can operate securely, transparently and efficiently without the need for a central authority. This decentralisation is one of the key attributes that make blockchain technology innovative and valuable for various applications beyond cryptocurrencies, such as supply chain management, digital identity verification and secure voting systems.

The implementation of a consensus algorithm depends on the specific requirements and objectives of a blockchain network, including factors such as transaction speed, security level, energy consumption and the degree of decentralisation desired. The choice of a particular consensus mechanism can significantly impact the performance and characteristics of a blockchain system.

Common consensus algorithms include

1. **Proof of Work (PoW)**
    - **Principle**: PoW requires participants (miners) to prove they have done a certain amount of computational work by solving complex mathematical problems. Bitcoin is the most famous blockchain using PoW.

- **Advantages**: Increases network security and prevents double-spending and other types of attacks.

- **Disadvantages**: High energy consumption, and over time, the tendency for miner centralisation may lead to network centralisation.

2. **Proof of Stake (PoS)**

    - **Principle**: PoS is based on the amount and duration of coin holding to select validators for blocks. Unlike PoW, PoS does not require extensive computational work.

    - **Advantages**: Higher energy efficiency and lower barriers to participation.

    - **Disadvantages**: Might lead to a 'rich get richer' problem as users with more currency are more likely to be chosen as validators.

3. **Delegated Proof of Stake (DPoS)**

    - **Principle**: In DPoS, token holders vote to select a few representatives (validators) to validate blocks. EOS is a notable example that uses the DPoS algorithm.

    - **Advantages**: Faster transaction confirmation and higher energy efficiency compared to PoW and traditional PoS.

    - **Disadvantages**: Potential for power concentration in the network, reducing decentralisation.

4. **Practical Byzantine Fault Tolerance (PBFT)**

    - **Principle**: PBFT aims to tolerate malicious behaviour from a minority of nodes in the network through intensive communication among nodes to reach consensus.

    - **Advantages**: Suitable for many systems requiring high data consistency and reliability.

    - **Disadvantages**: As the network size grows, communication costs significantly increase.

Each algorithm has its specific use cases, advantages and disadvantages. The choice of consensus algorithm depends on the specific needs of the blockchain, such as security, speed, energy efficiency and degree of decentralisation. As blockchain technology continues to evolve, new consensus algorithms may emerge to better meet the needs of different types of networks.

Table 1-3 lists some of the major consensus algorithms along with a representative project for each.

Table 1-3. Consensus Algorithm for Different Blockchains

Consensus Algorithm	Representative Project
Proof of Work (PoW)	Bitcoin
Proof of Stake (PoS)	Ethereum (upcoming Ethereum 2.0)
Delegated Proof of Stake (DPoS)	EOS
Practical Byzantine Fault Tolerance (PBFT)	Hyperledger Fabric

These projects exemplify how the corresponding consensus algorithm is implemented in a real-world blockchain system. We will explore more about the PoW and PoS in the later sections.

1.4 Summary

As this chapter draws to a close, it becomes clear that blockchain technology extends beyond merely serving as a platform for cryptocurrencies; it heralds a new era in digital security and decentralised data management. The transition from the inception of Bitcoin to the development of advanced blockchain applications marks a swift evolution in this technology. Characterised by robust security features, inherent transparency and versatility across various sectors, blockchain emerges as a fundamental technology in the digital age. Future chapters will delve deeper into how blockchain continues to impact industries, redefine privacy and pose challenges to the global economic landscape. The capacity of blockchain to drive substantial innovation is tremendous, and its development is far from complete.

1.5 Notes

1. Nakamoto, S. (2008). Bitcoin: A Peer-to-Peer Electronic Cash System.

2. Wallace, Benjamin (23 November 2011). 'The Rise and Fall of Bitcoin'. Wired. Archived from the original on 31 October 2013. Retrieved 13 October 2012. Wallace, B. (2011). The rise and fall of Bitcoin. Wired, 19(12).

3. Swan, M. (2015). Blockchain: Blueprint for a New Economy. O'Reilly Media, Inc.

4. What Is the Byzantine Generals Problem? | River Learn – Bitcoin Technology. (2023). River. https://river.com/learn/what-is-the-byzantine-generals-problem/ (Accessed: 23 November 2023).

CHAPTER 1 DECRYPTING BLOCKCHAIN TECHNOLOGY

5. Kisters, S. (2022). Blockchain 1.0 vs. 2.0 vs. 3.0 – What's the Difference? OriginStamp. https://originstamp.com/blog/blockchain-1-vs-2-vs-3-whats-the-difference/ (Accessed: 23 November 2023).

6. Banafa, A. (2021). Blockchain and AI: A Perfect Match?. OpenMind. www.bbvaopenmind.com/en/technology/artificial-intelligence/blockchain-and-ai-a-perfect-match/ (Accessed: 23 November 2023).

CHAPTER 2

Bitcoin: The Pioneer of Digital Currency

This chapter traces the origins of Bitcoin, from Satoshi Nakamoto's seminal whitepaper to the cryptocurrency's rapid ascent as a challenger to traditional financial systems. Through an examination of Bitcoin's innovative technological foundations and its impact on the financial landscape, this chapter sets the stage for a comprehensive understanding of why Bitcoin remains the quintessential digital currency.

2.1 The Birth of Bitcoin

The birth of Bitcoin in the aftermath of the 2008 Global Financial Crisis (GFC) represents a fundamental shift in financial technology, introducing a groundbreaking concept that challenged the established monetary systems. The crisis, which began in the United States, quickly spiralled into global turmoil, undermining confidence in the banking system and triggering a liquidity crunch. Financial institutions teetered on the brink of insolvency, leading to government interventions to prevent a complete economic collapse.

As the crisis unfolded, it exposed the inherent weaknesses in the traditional financial system, including a severe credit freeze that slowed economic activities and a general loss of faith in financial institutions and banks. This environment of distrust and the evident limitations of centralised financial authorities laid the groundwork for the inception of Bitcoin.[1]

Satoshi Nakamoto and the Whitepaper

The origin of Bitcoin, a groundbreaking innovation in the world of digital currency, is deeply rooted in a whitepaper titled 'Bitcoin: A Peer-to-Peer Electronic Cash System', screenshot shown in Figure 2-1. Published on 31 October 2008 by an enigmatic figure or group known as Satoshi Nakamoto, this document introduced a novel concept that would go on to revolutionise the financial sector.

Bitcoin: A Peer-to-Peer Electronic Cash System

Satoshi Nakamoto
satoshin@gmx.com
www.bitcoin.org

Abstract. A purely peer-to-peer version of electronic cash would allow online payments to be sent directly from one party to another without going through a financial institution. Digital signatures provide part of the solution, but the main benefits are lost if a trusted third party is still required to prevent double-spending. We propose a solution to the double-spending problem using a peer-to-peer network. The network timestamps transactions by hashing them into an ongoing chain of hash-based proof-of-work, forming a record that cannot be changed without redoing the proof-of-work. The longest chain not only serves as proof of the sequence of events witnessed, but proof that it came from the largest pool of CPU power. As long as a majority of CPU power is controlled by nodes that are not cooperating to attack the network, they'll generate the longest chain and outpace attackers. The network itself requires minimal structure. Messages are broadcast on a best effort basis, and nodes can leave and rejoin the network at will, accepting the longest proof-of-work chain as proof of what happened while they were gone.

Figure 2-1. Bitcoin Whitepaper Abstract Screenshot[2]

The whitepaper presented a meticulously thought-out design for a decentralised digital currency, a concept that was radically different from traditional, centralised financial systems. Nakamoto envisioned a system where the need for financial intermediaries was eliminated, thereby reducing transaction costs and increasing efficiency.

One of the core principles outlined in the whitepaper was the use of a decentralised ledger, known as the blockchain. This technology ensured that all transactions were transparently and immutably recorded, making them tamper-proof and verifiable by anyone. The blockchain was a public ledger, maintained by a network of nodes (computers), each holding a copy of the entire transaction history, thus ensuring no single point of failure.

Nakamoto introduced the concept of miners, network participants who use their computing power to process and verify transactions. Miners compete to solve complex cryptographic puzzles, and the first to solve it gets the right to add a new block of transactions to the blockchain. This process, known as proof of work (PoW), not only secures the network but also introduces new bitcoins into circulation as a reward for the miners.

The whitepaper also addressed the problem of double-spending, where a single digital token could be spent more than once. This issue was resolved through the innovative design of the blockchain, where once a transaction is confirmed, it becomes irreversible and part of an unchangeable record of historical transactions.

Nakamoto's whitepaper was not just a technical document; it was a vision of a new form of money that was completely decentralised, without any central authority, and accessible to anyone with an Internet connection. It represented a paradigm shift in understanding money and financial transactions, laying the groundwork for a new era of digital currencies and the diverse applications of blockchain technology that followed.

CHAPTER 2   BITCOIN: THE PIONEER OF DIGITAL CURRENCY

Bitcoin's introduction was a direct response to the financial crisis, aiming to mitigate the risk of systemic failures and provide complete financial control to individuals. The cryptocurrency implemented innovative cryptographic methodologies, demonstrating strong resistance to fraud and intrusions. This newfound system of accountability and transparency in financial transactions restored public faith in the possibility of a secure and transparent financial system. Moreover, Bitcoin targeted the unbanked population, aiming to create an inclusive financial ecosystem. This approach directly addressed the issues that triggered the GFC, providing a more equitable and accessible financial solution for all, irrespective of their access to traditional banking systems.

In essence, the birth of Bitcoin was not just the emergence of a new digital currency but a philosophical and practical challenge to the established order of financial systems. It represented a move towards a trustless, censorship-resistant financial system, paving the way for a new era of financial independence and security.

The Genesis Block and the First Bitcoin Transaction

Bitcoin's journey began on 3 January 2009 with the creation of the genesis block, also known as block number 0. This block, mined by the enigmatic Satoshi Nakamoto, held a message that critiqued the existing financial system, highlighting the urgency for a decentralised alternative. The text in the coinbase transaction, 'The Times 03/Jan/2009 Chancellor on brink of second bailout for banks', has become a symbol of Bitcoin's purpose: to offer a new monetary paradigm free from traditional banking frailties.

Hal Finney's Legendary Story and Impact on Bitcoin

Hal Finney, recognised as a pivotal figure in the early days of Bitcoin, was not only a renowned cryptographer and software developer but also a significant figure in the cypherpunk movement. His contributions to cryptography were substantial; he was involved in the development of the first anonymous remailer and ran contests to break export-grade encryption used by Netscape, showcasing his commitment to online privacy and security.

Before Bitcoin's inception, Finney had created the first reusable proof-of-work system in 2004, foreshadowing some of the fundamental technologies that would later be integral to Bitcoin. He became one of the first Bitcoin users and, on 12 January 2009, received the first Bitcoin transaction from Satoshi Nakamoto, marking a historic moment in the digital currency's journey.

Finney's life in Temple City, California, where he resided for ten years in the same town as Dorian Satoshi Nakamoto, fuelled speculation about his possible role as Bitcoin's creator, a claim he consistently denied. Despite his battle with amyotrophic lateral sclerosis (ALS), which eventually led to paralysis, Finney's passion for programming and contribution to Bitcoin never waned. Even in his final years, he continued to work on projects like 'bcflick', a software to enhance Bitcoin wallet security.[3]

Tragically, in the last year of his life, Finney and his family became victims of 'swatting' and extortion attempts, where perpetrators demanded a ransom of 1,000 bitcoins. These incidents underscore the sometimes tumultuous and risky landscape that early Bitcoin adopters navigated.

Finney's story is not just one of technological innovation but also of personal resilience and an unwavering belief in the transformative potential of Bitcoin. His early involvement and contributions were crucial in shaping the network's development, and his legacy continues to inspire the cryptocurrency community.[4]

The Legacy of Bitcoin

The creation of Bitcoin sparked a new era of digital currencies and opened the door to a vast array of blockchain applications. It presented a decentralised solution to digital trust, eliminating the need for intermediaries in financial transactions. Over the years, Bitcoin has not only survived but thrived, growing in value and acceptance and paving the way for thousands of other cryptocurrencies.

Bitcoin's origin story remains shrouded in mystery, with the true identity of Satoshi Nakamoto still unknown. This anonymity adds to the enigmatic allure of Bitcoin, a currency that has fundamentally altered our perception of money, value and the way we transact.

Technical Overview of Bitcoin

As Bitcoin ascends in its role as a digital currency pioneer, its underlying technology offers a blend of innovation and practicality. Table 2-1 is a closer look at some key technical aspects of Bitcoin:

Table 2-1. *Properties of Bitcoin*

Smallest Unit – Satosh	Bitcoin is divisible to eight decimal places, with the smallest unit being called a 'Satoshi', named after its mysterious creator. One Satoshi is equivalent to 0.00000001 Bitcoin. This high degree of divisibility makes Bitcoin suitable for micro-transactions, a feature not commonly found in traditional currencies.
Conversion Methodology	Understanding Bitcoin conversion is crucial for transactions. The value of one Bitcoin in terms of traditional currency (like USD, EUR, etc.) is determined by the market demand and supply dynamics on various cryptocurrency exchanges. Due to its volatile nature, the conversion rate can fluctuate significantly in a short period.
Commonly Used Block Explorers	Block explorers are essential tools for navigating the Bitcoin blockchain. Websites like Blockchain.com and BlockCypher provide detailed information about individual blocks, transactions and addresses. They are invaluable for tracking transactions and understanding the blockchain's activity.
Bitcoin Wallets	To use Bitcoin, one needs a digital wallet, which comes in various forms like desktop wallets, mobile wallets, web wallets and hardware wallets. These wallets store the private keys necessary to sign Bitcoin transactions and can range from highly secure cold storage options like hardware wallets to more convenient but less secure hot wallets like mobile and web applications.
Transaction Mechanism	A Bitcoin transaction involves transferring value between wallets. Each wallet has one or more private keys, which are mathematically related to the wallet address. When a transaction is initiated, it is broadcast to the network and, upon validation, included in a block by miners, thereby confirming the transaction.

Understanding these technical aspects provides a foundation for delving deeper into how Bitcoin works, particularly its mining mechanisms, which are central to the creation of new bitcoins and the processing of transactions across the network. Section 2.2 will explore this in detail, shedding light on the process that keeps the Bitcoin network secure and functional.

2.2 How Bitcoin Works: Mining Mechanisms

Understanding Bitcoin Mining

Bitcoin mining is indeed the backbone of the Bitcoin network, serving as the mechanism through which new bitcoins are introduced and transactions are added to the blockchain. This process is decentralised, unlike traditional currency issuance by central banks. Miners use powerful computers to solve complex mathematical problems, and the first to solve a block's problem earns the right to add it to the blockchain and receives a reward in bitcoins.

The concept of Bitcoin halving is critical to understanding Bitcoin's supply mechanics. Halving is a scheduled event that occurs approximately every four years, or after every 210,000 blocks are mined. During each halving, the reward for mining a new block is cut in half. This reduction in block rewards effectively slows down the rate of new Bitcoin creation, making the asset more scarce over time.

Historically, Bitcoin halving events have had significant implications for the Bitcoin ecosystem, impacting miner incentives and the market supply of Bitcoin and often correlating with substantial price movements.

Table 2-2 summarises the past Bitcoin halving events, including the dates, block rewards and the estimated number of bitcoins produced daily.

Table 2-2. *Past Bitcoin Halving*

Halving Event	Date	Block Reward (BTC)	Bitcoins Produced Daily
1st Halving (2012)	28 November 2012	25.000	3600.0
2nd Halving (2016)	9 July 2016	12.500	1800.0
3rd Halving (2020)	11 May 2020	6.250	900.0
4th Halving (2024)	20 April 2024	3.125	450.0

The 'Bitcoins Produced Daily' column is calculated based on the block reward and the average number of blocks mined per day. The Bitcoin network typically targets 6 blocks per hour, which equates to 144 blocks per day. The daily production of bitcoins is therefore the block reward multiplied by 144.

The Process of Mining

1. **Transaction Validation**: Miners collect transactions from the network's mempool (a collection of all unconfirmed transactions) and validate them. This includes checking for double-spending and ensuring the transaction has not already been included in the blockchain.

2. **Block Creation**: Once transactions are validated, they are bundled into a block. Each block contains a reference to the previous block's hash, creating a chain of blocks – hence the term 'blockchain'.

CHAPTER 2 BITCOIN: THE PIONEER OF DIGITAL CURRENCY

3. **Solving the Proof of Work (PoW)**: To add a block to the blockchain, miners must solve a PoW problem. This involves finding a hash that is below a certain target. The process requires massive computational effort, making it difficult and time-consuming.

4. **Block Reward and Transaction Fees**: The first miner to solve the PoW problem broadcasts the new block to the network. If other miners confirm that the block is valid, it is added to the blockchain. The successful miner is rewarded with newly created bitcoins (block reward) and the transaction fees paid by users. This reward serves as an incentive for miners to contribute their computational power to the network.

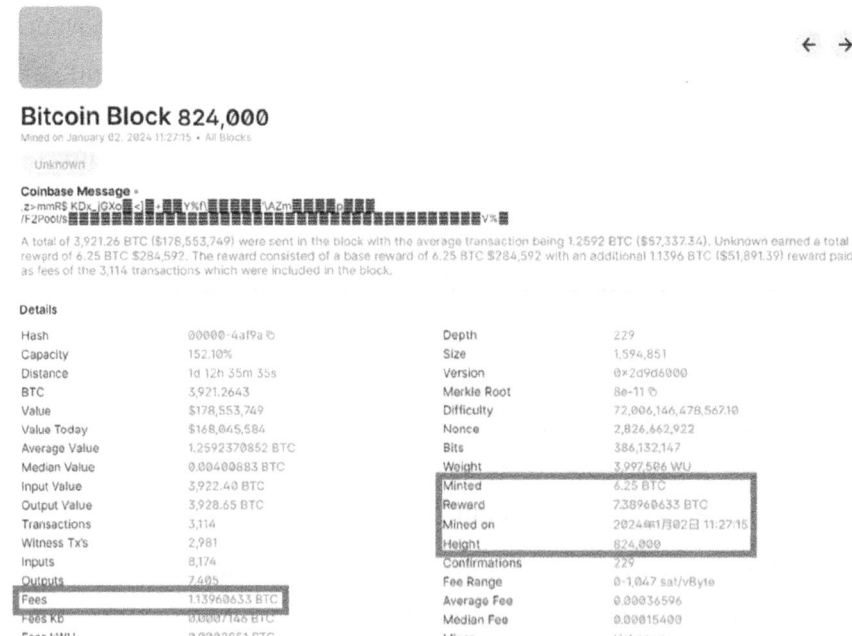

Figure 2-2. Screenshot of Bitcoin Block 824,000
Source: www.blockchain.com/explorer/blocks/btc/824000
(Accessed: 4 January 2024)

Figure 2-2 shows information for Bitcoin block 824,000. Here are the key details:

- **Minted**: 6.25 BTC. This is the block reward that the miner received for successfully mining the block. It reflects the halving event that occurred in May 2020, which reduced the block reward from 12.5 to 6.25 BTC.

- **Fees**: 1.13960633 BTC. This amount was collected by the miner as transaction fees. Miners receive transaction fees from the Bitcoin users who send transactions, and these fees incentivise miners to include transactions in the next block. The higher the fee attached to a transaction, the more likely it is to be included in the next block.

- **Block Height**: 824,000. This is the position of the block in the blockchain. Each block is sequentially numbered, and the height indicates the length of the blockchain. A higher block number means a longer chain, reflecting more cumulative proof of work and security.

- **Mined on**: 11:27:15 2 January 2024. This is the timestamp for when the block was successfully mined and added to the blockchain.

The Coinbase Message, which is typically used by miners to include extra nonces or voting tags, in this block contains what appears to be random characters, possibly a result of the software or the pool that mined this block encoding their message in this way.

The value of transactions in this block totalled 3,921.2643 BTC, worth $178,553,749 at the time the block was mined. This high value reflects the cumulative value of all transactions included in the block.

Additionally, the block contains 3,114 transactions and has a size of 1,594,851 bytes, indicating the amount of data stored in the block. It also has a weight of 3,997,506 WU (weight units), which is a measure of the block's 'size' in terms of block capacity in the context of the block size limit.

Finally, it's worth noting that the block's difficulty is listed, a metric that shows how hard it was to find a hash below a given target. The higher the difficulty, the more computational power and time it takes on average to mine a new block. Bitcoin mining difficulty is a measure of how hard it is to find a hash below the target value. The Bitcoin network adjusts this difficulty approximately every two weeks to ensure that a new block is added approximately every ten minutes. This adjustment is crucial to maintaining the blockchain's steady and predictable creation rate. The difficulty is calculated as follows:

$$New\ difficulty = Old\ difficulty \times \frac{2016\ blocks}{time\ taken\ to\ mine\ last\ 2016\ blocks}$$

Evolution of Mining Hardware

Over the years, Bitcoin mining has evolved from CPUs to GPUs and finally to specialised hardware known as ASICs (Application-Specific Integrated Circuits), shown in Figure 2-3. ASICs are designed specifically for Bitcoin mining and are much more efficient than general-purpose hardware.

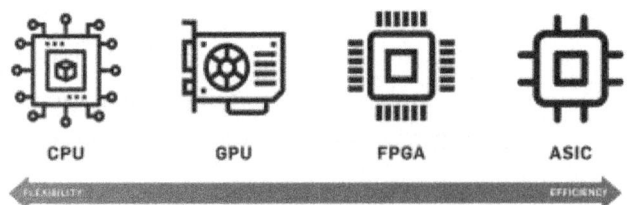

Figure 2-3. *Screenshot of Bitcoin Block 824,000*
Source: `www.ecmwf.int/sites/default/files/elibrary/2020/19380-ecmwf-scalability-programme-progress-and-plans.pdf` *(Accessed: 4 January 2024)*

Mining Pools

Mining pools have become a cornerstone of the Bitcoin mining landscape. They provide individual miners with the opportunity to combine their computational resources, thereby increasing the likelihood of successfully mining blocks and receiving Bitcoin rewards. This collective effort not only stabilises revenue for participants but also democratises access to mining, which might otherwise be prohibitive due to the escalating costs of mining hardware and the electricity required for such operations.

The rise in the complexity of mining puzzles, directly tied to the number of miners and the overall hash rate of the network, has necessitated the pooling of resources. Without such collaboration, small-scale miners face significant financial risk due to the high variance and unpredictability of mining solo. By joining forces in mining pools, these individuals can attain a more steady and predictable flow of income, reflecting a proportionate share of the collective mining output relative to their individual contributions.

Additionally, mining pools facilitate network upgrades. Central pool managers, who construct blocks and manage the pool's operations, can implement software upgrades, thereby streamlining the process for all miners within the pool. When the mining pool's software is updated, it effectively updates the software for all members, simplifying the transition and encouraging more consistent adoption across the network.

CHAPTER 2   BITCOIN: THE PIONEER OF DIGITAL CURRENCY

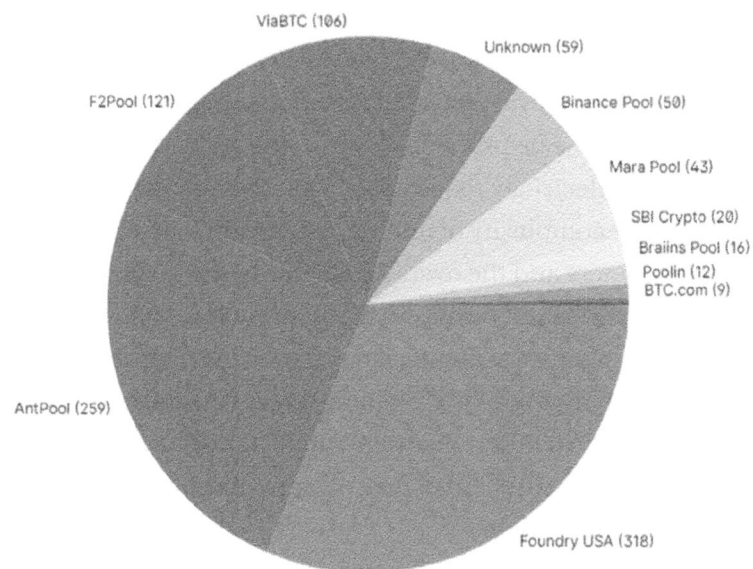

Figure 2-4. *Hash Rate Distribution*
Source: www.blockchain.com/explorer/charts/pools *(3 January 2024)*

Figure 2-4 illustrates the distribution of hash rate among the largest Bitcoin mining pools over a selected period. Each slice represents a mining pool and its contribution to the total hash rate, measured in blocks mined. Foundry USA has the largest share with 318 blocks, followed by AntPool with 259 blocks and F2Pool with 121 blocks.

CHAPTER 2   BITCOIN: THE PIONEER OF DIGITAL CURRENCY

Figure 2-5. *Example of Bitcoin Mining Pool in China*

Figure 2-5 shows my precious Bitcoin mining pool in China. Such facilities are structured to maintain critical conditions for efficient mining. Key aspects include a reliable and robust Internet connection to ensure continuous communication with the Bitcoin network, stable electrical voltage to keep the mining rigs running optimally and controlled temperatures to prevent overheating, which is especially important given the heat generated by the intensive computational processes. Dry conditions are also necessary to protect the sensitive electronic equipment from moisture-related damage. Due to the significant noise produced by the cooling fans required to maintain such an environment, these operations are typically situated in secluded areas. It's important to note in May 2021, China's State Council announced measures to crack down on Bitcoin mining and trading, leading to the closure of mining activities across several provinces. This was part of a broader effort to mitigate financial risks and control speculative trading of cryptocurrencies. The measures resulted in a significant migration of mining operations out of China.

However, the concept of mining pools is not without its drawbacks. One significant concern is the centralisation they introduce to the Bitcoin network. While Bitcoin's design is inherently decentralised, large mining pools amass considerable influence, potentially wielding significant power over the network's operations. Although miners can theoretically migrate to different pools if a particular pool gains excessive power, the reality of such shifts in allegiance is not well documented. Another downside to the prominence of mining pools is the reduced number of full node operators. Historically, miners maintained fully validating nodes, each independently storing and confirming the entire blockchain. Now, the trend has shifted towards offloading these responsibilities to the pool managers, resulting in fewer nodes that fully validate and store the blockchain. This consolidation of responsibility could pose risks to the network's resilience and the full verification process that underpins Bitcoin's trust model.

In essence, while mining pools have made Bitcoin mining more accessible and reliable for individual miners, they introduce a layer of centralisation that could, in theory, conflict with the cryptocurrency's foundational ethos of decentralisation. The balance between making Bitcoin mining feasible for individuals and maintaining the decentralised nature of the network remains a delicate and ongoing consideration within the Bitcoin community.

2.3 The Challenges of Bitcoin: Security Concerns, Wallet Storage and the Issue of Scaling

51% Attacks: A Theoretical Threat to Bitcoin's Integrity

The concept of a 51% attack in the context of Bitcoin and cryptocurrency networks is a significant concern, though it remains largely theoretical for more established networks like Bitcoin. This type of attack occurs when a single entity or group gains control of more than 50% of a network's mining power. With such control, they could potentially double-spend coins, prevent the confirmation of certain transactions and monopolise the creation of new blocks.

In the Bitcoin network, executing a 51% attack is extremely challenging, primarily due to the network's vast and distributed mining power. The substantial computational resources and the associated financial cost required to gain such control make this type of attack impractical and unfeasible. Moreover, succeeding in a 51% attack would likely lead to a loss of trust in the network and a consequent drop in Bitcoin's value, ultimately harming the attacker's interests.

However, other cryptocurrencies, particularly newer or less established ones, have been vulnerable to this type of attack. For instance, Bitcoin Gold (BTG), a hard fork of Bitcoin, experienced a 51% attack. This attack led to significant double-spending of approximately $70,000 worth of BTG. In January 2020, the BTG blockchain was hit by two deep reorganisations of over ten blocks, resulting in two separate incidents of 51% attacks within six hours. In these attacks, blocks were removed and new ones were added to facilitate double-spending of thousands of BTG, highlighting the vulnerability of smaller networks to such threats.[5]

These incidents underscore the importance of robust and decentralised mining networks for maintaining the security and integrity of blockchain systems. While Bitcoin itself has remained secure from such attacks, the Bitcoin Gold incidents serve as a reminder of the potential risks associated with blockchain and cryptocurrency networks.

Block Size Debate and Bitcoin Forks: The Scaling Challenge

The Bitcoin 'Blocksize War' from 2015 to 2017 was a pivotal period debating the blockchain's block size, crucial for transaction capacity and scalability. Originally capped at 1 MB by Satoshi Nakamoto, the block size limited the network's throughput. The community was divided into 'small blockers', prioritising decentralisation and the ability for individuals to run nodes, and 'big blockers', pushing for larger blocks to reduce costs and enhance Bitcoin as a payment system.[6]

The debate saw several solutions: Bitcoin XT proposed progressive block size increases, while SegWit, a compatible restructuring of block data, offered more transactions within the original limit and enabled the Lightning Network for off-chain transactions, promoting scalability. Although forks like Bitcoin XT didn't prevail, they led to the creation of Bitcoin Cash (BCH) and Bitcoin SV (BSV), which adopted larger blocks. SegWit and the Lightning Network's successful implementation were milestones in Bitcoin's evolution, balancing scalability with the ideals of the original block size debate.

Diverse Wallet Types

Bitcoin wallets are diverse, each tailored with distinct features and potential risks. Explore their nuances in Table 2-3.[7]

CHAPTER 2   BITCOIN: THE PIONEER OF DIGITAL CURRENCY

Table 2-3. Diverse Wallet Types with Their Challenges

	Software (Hot) Wallets	Paper Wallets	Web Wallets	Brain Wallets	Hardware (Cold) Wallets
Functionality	Installed on personal computers, they offer control and access to private keys.	Physical documents containing private and public keys. They offer a high level of security by being completely offline.	Operated by third parties, they provide easy access and convenience for transactions.	Seed phrases memorised or written down by the user, with no physical or digital trace.	Similar to a USB, they store private keys offline and are accessible only through physical contact.
Challenges	Vulnerable to malware and hacking. Loss of data due to hardware failure can result in permanent loss of Bitcoins.	Risk of physical damage or loss. Transferring Bitcoin back online can expose the wallet to online vulnerabilities.	Dependence on the security measures of the third party. Risk of hacking and theft.	Risk of forgetting the phrase or incapacity of the user, leading to permanent loss of access to the Bitcoins.	Risks include loss of the device, forgetting the PIN or damage to the hardware.

45

CHAPTER 2   BITCOIN: THE PIONEER OF DIGITAL CURRENCY

The evolution of Bitcoin involves navigating through various security and scalability challenges. The diversity in wallet types offers users a range of choices for storing their Bitcoins, each with its unique set of challenges. Meanwhile, the block size debate and potential security threats like 51% attacks highlight the ongoing need for development and adaptation in the Bitcoin ecosystem. These factors play a crucial role in shaping the future trajectory of Bitcoin as it continues to mature and evolve.

2.4 Gold Jewellery: Ordinals (Inscriptions)

The introduction of the Ordinals Protocol to the Bitcoin blockchain, which allows for the creation of 'Inscriptions' directly on Bitcoin, can be likened to the relationship between gold and gold jewellery. In this analogy, Bitcoin is akin to gold – a fundamental, valuable asset with a primary purpose as a store of value, akin to digital gold. The Inscriptions, enabled by the Ordinals Protocol, are comparable to gold jewellery – they are unique, ornamental expressions derived from the base material but adding a new dimension of cultural and artistic value.

These Inscriptions, essentially data like images, videos or text attached to individual satoshis (the smallest unit of Bitcoin), represent a new layer of utility and expression within the Bitcoin ecosystem. Unlike traditional NFTs on other blockchains like Ethereum, Inscriptions are entirely native to Bitcoin, operating seamlessly within its existing framework without necessitating additional layers or protocol changes. This integration is made possible by the SegWit and Taproot updates to the Bitcoin protocol in 2017 and 2021, respectively, which expanded Bitcoin's capacity to store arbitrary data directly on the blockchain.[8]

This development introduces a novel concept – each satoshi, through ordinal theory, is assigned a unique number based on the order it was mined. This mirrors how each piece of gold jewellery is distinct, carrying its own design and craftsmanship, despite being made from the same base material. The Inscriptions, like intricate designs on gold jewellery, add a layer of cultural, artistic and memetic value to the otherwise uniform satoshis, enhancing their significance in the digital realm. Some enthusiasts view these developments as a positive expansion of the blockchain's uses, adding memetic and cultural value. This innovation revitalises the ecosystem by introducing new functionalities and applications, such as digital art creation and the possibility of building on-chain applications and an Internet built on Bitcoin.[9]

In addition to art and NFTs, the Bitcoin blockchain, through the Ordinals Protocol, also supports the BRC-20 token standard. This standard is an experimental fungible token standard for the Bitcoin blockchain, created by an anonymous on-chain analyst named 'domo' in March 2023. Inspired by Ethereum's ERC20, BRC-20 tokens enable developers to create and transfer fungible tokens using the Ordinals Protocol. The first token contract deployed under this standard was for the 'ordi' token, which mirrored the Bitcoin maximum supply with a limit of 21M tokens in total supply, shown in Figure 2-6. This development underlines the evolving nature of the Bitcoin ecosystem and the expanding range of its applications.[10, 11]

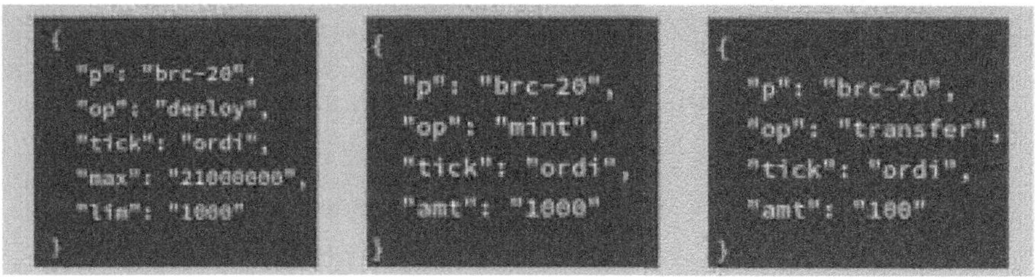

Figure 2-6. *Deploy, Mint and Transfer of 'ordi'*
Source: *https://domo-2.gitbook.io/brc-20-experiment/*
(2 January 2024)

However, these innovations have not come without debate. The Bitcoin community is currently engaged in a significant discourse regarding the balance between preserving the original intent and design of the Bitcoin network and embracing innovation.[12] This debate centres on several key points:

1. **Network Integrity and Purpose**: Critics argue that these new features, particularly Inscriptions, deviate from Bitcoin's original purpose as a decentralised digital currency. They express concerns that these additions might lead to network congestion, higher transaction fees and challenges to Bitcoin's core value proposition as a digital gold.

2. **Decentralisation and Security**: There are also concerns about the impact of these new developments on Bitcoin's decentralisation and security. Some worry that the additional data load from Inscriptions might centralise network validation in the hands of those with more substantial computing resources, thus potentially compromising the network's security.

3. **Economic Implications**: From an economic standpoint, the concept of a 'fair launch' is pivotal. In the context of Bitcoin and the Ordinals Protocol, a fair launch refers to the equitable distribution and accessibility of new tokens or assets. The Ordinals inherently support a fair launch mechanism, allowing users to directly participate in asset circulation by sending transactions with specific parameters to the blockchain. This democratises the asset issuance process, contrasting with traditional

finance systems where asset distribution can be heavily skewed towards early adopters or those with insider access.

4. **Cultural and Memetic Value**: On the other side of the debate, proponents of the Ordinals Protocol and Inscriptions argue that these innovations have infused Bitcoin with new cultural and memetic value. They see these developments as a natural evolution of the blockchain technology, bringing fresh vitality and interest to the Bitcoin ecosystem.

5. **Impact on Bitcoin's Image and Usage**: There's also a discussion on how these changes might affect Bitcoin's image as a serious financial asset. While some view these developments as beneficial, diversifying Bitcoin's use cases, others worry that the association with digital art and NFTs might detract from its gravitas as a store of value.

In conclusion, the introduction of the Ordinals Protocol, Inscriptions and BRC-20 tokens on the Bitcoin blockchain marks a significant milestone in the evolution of Bitcoin. However, it has sparked a complex debate within the community, reflecting broader discussions about innovation, decentralisation and the future direction of Bitcoin. This debate underscores the dynamic nature of blockchain technology and the diverse perspectives within the cryptocurrency community.

2.5 Summary

This chapter has charted the transformative journey of Bitcoin from a conceptual anomaly to a cornerstone of digital finance. Its inception marked a pivotal shift towards decentralised financial solutions, offering a stark alternative to conventional financial systems. Bitcoin's resilience and evolution underscore its potential to redefine financial interactions on a global scale. The subsequent chapters will delve deeper into the ramifications of Bitcoin's technology on traditional financial paradigms and explore the broader implications of digital currencies in reshaping economic transactions.

2.6 Notes

1. Holman, T. (2023). Why did Satoshi Nakamoto invent Bitcoin after the 2008 crisis?, CryptoNewsZ. www.cryptonewsz.com/why-did-satoshi-nakamoto-invent-bitcoin-after-the-2008-crisis/ (Accessed: 30 November 2023).

2. Nakamoto, S. (2008). Bitcoin: A peer-to-peer electronic cash system. Satoshi Nakamoto.

3. Finney, H. (2013). Bitcoin and me (Hal Finney). https://bitcointalk.org/index.php?topic=155054.0 (Accessed: 30 November 2023).

4. Hal Finney (computer scientist) (2024). Wikipedia. https://en.wikipedia.org/wiki/Hal_Finney_(computer_scientist)#:~:text=Harold%20Thomas%20Finney%20II%20,1%5D%E3%80%91 (Accessed: 25 April 2024).

CHAPTER 2   BITCOIN: THE PIONEER OF DIGITAL CURRENCY

5. Martin, J. (2020). Bitcoin Gold Blockchain Hit by 51% Attack Leading to $70k Double Spend, Cointelegraph. https://cointelegraph.com/news/bitcoin-gold-blockchain-hit-by-51-attack-leading-to-70k-double-spend (Accessed: 4 January 2024).

6. Musshoff, T. (2021). The Bitcoin Block Size Wars Explained, Bitrawr. www.bitrawr.com/bitcoin-block-size-debate-explained (Accessed: 4 January 2024).

7. Coincover (2023). What Are the Different Types of Bitcoin Wallets?, Coincover (Digital Assets Services Limited). www.coincover.com/blog/what-are-the-different-types-of-bitcoin-wallets (Accessed: 4 January 2024).

8. Bitcoin Ordinals Inscriptions: gamma.io. https://gamma.io/learn/ordinals/inscriptions (Accessed: 4 January 2024).

9. What Are Ordinals? A Guide to NFT Inscriptions on Bitcoin. www.xverse.app/blog/what-are-ordinals-a-guide-to-nft-inscriptions-on-bitcoin (Accessed: 4 January 2024).

10. Bitcoin NFTs – How the Ordinals Protocol Works, Crypto.com. https://crypto.com/university/bitcoin-nfts-ordinals-protocol (Accessed: 4 January 2024).

11. Bitcoin NFTs? Ordinals Inscriptions Explained (Finding, Buying, & More). https://nftnow.com/guides/bitcoin-nfts-ordinals-inscriptions-explained-finding-buying-more/ (Accessed: 4 January 2024).

12. Dashjr, L. (2023). Miners on ocean are making far more profit than those on other pools. Shareholders should start asking their mining enterprises why they're choosing less profitable pools that also harm bitcoin, Twitter. https://twitter.com/LukeDashjr/status/1732392718431645696?s=20 (Accessed: 4 January 2024).

PART II

Ethereum: The Cradle of Smart Contracts

CHAPTER 3

The Rise of Ethereum

The origins and development of Ethereum, a platform created by Vitalik Buterin to extend the capabilities of blockchain technology, can be traced to his vision of creating a more versatile system. Ethereum introduced the Ethereum Virtual Machine (EVM), a core innovation that enables the execution of smart contracts and decentralized applications, significantly enhancing blockchain technology beyond its initial applications, as seen with Bitcoin. He sought to create a more general-purpose and powerful system, comparing Bitcoin to a pocket calculator and Ethereum to a smartphone, which could perform a variety of tasks, including those a calculator does.[1]

Buterin started his journey in the crypto world as a writer for *Bitcoin Weekly* and later co-founded *Bitcoin Magazine*. He was initially sceptical about Bitcoin, but his views changed, leading him to conceive Ethereum. In 2013, at the age of 19, he published a whitepaper proposing Ethereum, and the project was launched in 2015.[2]

Ethereum's distinct features, particularly the EVM and smart contracts, are pivotal to its functionality and innovation. This chapter expands on these aspects to provide a deeper understanding of Ethereum's capabilities and how it stands out from centralised computing systems like AWS.

3.1 Ethereum Virtual Machine

The EVM is a core component of Ethereum's architecture, serving as a runtime environment for smart contracts. It's a powerful, stack-based, Turing-complete virtual machine that executes smart contracts in an isolated environment, ensuring security and stability (see Table 3-1). Features of EVM:

- **Turing Completeness**: EVM can perform any logical step of a computational function, a capability not present in many blockchain platforms.

- **Isolation**: Smart contracts in the EVM run in an isolated environment, ensuring that they operate without affecting other processes on the blockchain.

- **Deterministic Execution**: Every EVM node executes smart contracts identically, leading to consistent results across the network.

- **Security**: Designed to avoid common vulnerabilities and attacks, offering a secure environment for executing decentralised applications.

Table 3-1. Comparison with Ethereum and Centralised Systems (e.g. AWS)

Feature	Ethereum Virtual Machine (EVM)	AWS (Centralised System)
Control	Decentralised, no single entity controls the network	Centralised, controlled by Amazon
Uptime	High availability, designed to avoid downtime	Generally high but susceptible to outages
Data Integrity	Immutable ledger, ensuring data integrity	Data can be altered or deleted by service provider
Accessibility	Open to anyone, globally	Access controlled by Amazon, region-specific services
Security	Distributed ledger reduces risk of attacks	Centralised servers can be more vulnerable to attacks

Turing Completeness of Ethereum

Ethereum's Turing-complete language allows it to function as a general-purpose computer. This means it can execute a wide range of computational tasks, from simple to complex algorithms, making it versatile for various applications. Implications of Turing Completeness:

- **Versatility**: Ethereum can theoretically execute any algorithm, allowing it to support diverse applications beyond simple transactions.

- **Complex Smart Contracts**: Enables the creation of complex smart contracts that can perform various functions, from automated token distribution to operating decentralised autonomous organisations (DAOs).

- **Decentralised Applications (DApps)**: Facilitates the development of DApps with complex logic and interactions, not limited to financial transactions.

Ethereum As a Decentralised Computing Infrastructure

Ethereum is often viewed as a deterministic state machine, with a globally accessible state and a virtual machine that applies changes to this state. Key aspects:

- **Open Source**: Ethereum's codebase is open for anyone to review, contribute to and build upon.

- **Decentralised Execution**: Operates on a blockchain network, ensuring decentralised execution and consensus.

- **Global Accessibility**: Its infrastructure is globally accessible without any geographical restrictions.

- **Smart Contract Execution**: Uses ether (ETH) to meter and constrain the execution resource costs, ensuring efficient use of the network's resources.

The Development Journey of Ethereum

The evolution of Ethereum is a testament to its adaptability and the community's commitment to innovation. From its initial launch to the pioneering shift with The Merge, Ethereum has continually faced and overcome technical challenges (see Table 3-2).

Table 3-2. The Journey of Ethereum

Early Days and Challenges (2015–2016)	• **Initial Launch**: Ethereum was launched in 2015 as a revolutionary blockchain platform enabling smart contracts and decentralised applications (DApps). In terms of funding and support, Ethereum conducted the first successful Initial Coin Offering (ICO), raising $18 million to grow the platform. This was a landmark event in the crypto world, showing the potential of ICOs as a mechanism for funding blockchain projects. • **DAO Incident and Fork**: In 2016, the Ethereum network faced a significant challenge with the DAO hack. This led to a controversial hard fork, resulting in Ethereum (ETH) and Ethereum Classic (ETC).[3]
Key Upgrades and Innovations (2016–2022)	• **Constantinople and St. Petersburg**: These were part of Ethereum's multi-staged upgrade process, focusing on improving efficiency, speed and scalability. • **Istanbul**: Introduced in 2019, this upgrade brought several improvements, including enhanced security and interoperability with privacy coin Zcash.

(continued)

CHAPTER 3   THE RISE OF ETHEREUM

Table 3-2. (*continued*)

| The Merge: A Landmark Upgrade (15 September, 2022) | <ul><li>**Integration of Mainnet with Beacon Chain**: The Merge involved combining Ethereum's original execution layer (mainnet) with the Beacon Chain, marking a transition from proof-of-work (PoW) to proof-of-stake (PoS) consensus mechanism.</li><li>**Energy Efficiency**: This shift significantly reduced Ethereum's energy consumption, estimated to decrease by around 99.95%, aligning with global sustainability efforts.</li><li>**Maintaining Historical Data**: Despite the fundamental change in consensus mechanism, The Merge preserved the entire transactional history of Ethereum, ensuring continuity and integrity of data.</li><li>**Minimal Impact on Users**: For ETH holders and users, The Merge did not necessitate any action; their assets remained accessible and unchanged, with wallets functioning as before.</li><li>**Node and Developer Adjustments**: Post-Merge, node operators and DApp developers had to adapt to new requirements, such as running clients for both the execution and consensus layers of Ethereum.</li><li>**Setting Stage for Future Upgrades**: The Merge laid the groundwork for subsequent scalability enhancements, including sharding and Layer 2 solutions, which aim to further improve Ethereum's transaction capacity and efficiency.</li><li>**Clarifying Misconceptions**: It addressed common misconceptions, clarifying that The Merge did not intend to reduce gas fees or significantly increase transaction speed and that running a node does not require staking 32 ETH.</li><li>**Terminology Changes**: Post Merge, the terms 'Eth1' and 'Eth2' were updated for clarity: 'Eth1' is now known as the 'execution layer', and 'Eth2' as the 'consensus layer', simplifying the Ethereum ecosystem's terminology.</li></ul> |

(*continued*)

Table 3-2. (*continued*)

The Road Ahead: Future Upgrades (2022–)	• **Sharding**: Post Merge, the focus is on implementing sharding to further enhance scalability. Sharding will break the Ethereum blockchain into smaller pieces, or 'shards', to distribute the load. • **Scalability Target**: Vitalik Buterin has set an ambitious target for Ethereum to process 100,000 transactions per second, a significant leap from its current capability. • **Layer 2 Solutions**: Alongside sharding, Layer 2 solutions like rollups are being integrated to improve transaction throughput and reduce fees.

The Ethereum Cancun-Deneb upgrade, commonly referred to as Dencun, which went live in March 2024, marks a significant advancement in Ethereum's scalability efforts, particularly impacting Layer 2 solutions. This upgrade introduced Proto-Danksharding with EIP-4844, aiming to enhance the efficiency and reduce the costs of transactions on Layer 2 networks like rollups.[4]

Proto-Danksharding achieves this by introducing a new structure called 'data blobs', which are temporary storage spaces allowing Layer 2 networks to store transaction data more economically. These blobs are designed to improve data availability and reduce storage costs, thereby lowering the fees associated with Layer 2 transactions. This setup is crucial for supporting higher transaction throughput and reducing costs, making Ethereum more scalable and capable of handling more extensive and complex operations on its network.

Additionally, the upgrade fosters improved interoperability between the main Ethereum blockchain and Layer 2 solutions, streamlining transactions and enhancing security protocols. These enhancements are designed to ensure that Layer 2 solutions can operate more efficiently while maintaining the robust security of the Ethereum mainnet.[5]

This strategic upgrade is a part of Ethereum's broader road map towards significantly increasing its scalability, aiming to support a larger user base and more complex applications with lower transaction costs.[6]

The future direction, focusing on sharding, Layer 2 solutions and a significant scalability target, positions Ethereum as a leading blockchain platform ready to handle a wide range of real-world applications. This ongoing journey ensures that Ethereum remains at the forefront of blockchain technology, offering a more sustainable, efficient and versatile platform.

3.2 Getting Started with Smart Contracts

A smart contract is a self-executing contract with the terms of the agreement directly written into lines of code. They are deployed on the blockchain and run exactly as programmed without any possibility of downtime, fraud, censorship or third-party interference. Smart contracts allow the performance of credible transactions without third parties. These transactions are trackable and irreversible.

The following provides the general architecture of smart contracts:

1. **Structure and Components**

    - **Contract Declaration**: Begins with **contract ContractName { }**. This is akin to declaring a class in object-oriented programming.

    - **State Variables**: These are variables stored on the contract permanently. They represent the contract's state (e.g. **uint public count;** to store a numeric value).

    - **Constructor**: A special function called at the time of contract deployment to initialise the contract's state (e.g. **constructor() public { count = 0; }**).

- **Functions**: Functions allow the smart contract to interact with other contracts and perform actions. They can change the state or return some data (e.g. **function incrementCounter() public { count += 1; }**).
- **Function Modifiers**: Used to change the behaviour of a function (e.g. visibility like **public** or **private** or custom modifiers for access control).
- **Events**: Events allow logging to the Ethereum blockchain. Clients (like web3.js) can listen for these events (e.g. **event ValueChanged(uint newValue);**).

2. **Programming Language**
   - **Solidity**: The primary language for writing Ethereum smart contracts. It's a contract-oriented, high-level language influenced by C++, Python and JavaScript.

3. **Execution Environment**
   - Executed on the Ethereum Virtual Machine (EVM) – an isolated runtime environment.

4. **Deployment and Interaction**
   - **Deployment**: After writing a smart contract, it's compiled and deployed to the Ethereum blockchain, where it gets a unique address.
   - **Interaction**: Once deployed, it can be interacted with through Ethereum transactions or from a web interface using a library like web3.js.

CHAPTER 3   THE RISE OF ETHEREUM

In Solidity, the main programming language used for Ethereum smart contracts, state variables can be declared with different visibility specifiers: public, private, internal and external. These specifiers affect how these variables can be accessed and manipulated within and outside of the contract. Here's a brief overview of each:

- **Public**
    - Public state variables are automatically accessible externally and internally in the smart contract. Solidity automatically creates a getter function for public variables.
    - These can be read from any contract and externally via transactions.
- **Private**
    - Private state variables are only accessible within the contract they are defined in and not in derived contracts.
    - No contracts outside the one where the private variable is declared can read or modify these, making them suitable for sensitive data that should not be exposed.
- **Internal**
    - Internal state variables are accessible within the contract they are defined in and by other contracts that inherit from it.
    - They cannot be accessed externally, which means that no external calls can view or modify these variables, only transactions or calls within the contract or its derivatives.

- **External**

  - External is not used for state variables but for functions. It specifies that the function can only be called from outside the contract and not internally, except when using this.functionName().

Key differences:

- **Accessibility**: Public variables are the most accessible, followed by internal and then private. External is not applicable to state variables.

- **Use Cases**

  - Use public for variables that need to be readily readable from outside the contract without a custom getter function.

  - Use private for sensitive data that should only be manipulated by the contract's functions.

  - Use internal for variables that should be accessible to derived contracts but not outside the smart contract framework.

Each specifier plays a crucial role in defining the security and functionality of a smart contract by controlling access to its data, ensuring that each variable is exposed only as necessary to support the contract's operations and security requirements.

Listing 3-1 provides the basic contract **SimpleStorage** that allows storing and retrieving a uint (unsigned integer). The **set** function updates **storedData**, and **get** returns its current value.

Listing 3-1. Simple Smart Contract Example – 1

```solidity
pragma solidity ^0.5.0;
contract SimpleStorage {
    uint storedData;

    function set(uint x) public {
        storedData = x;
    }
    function get() public view returns (uint) {
        return storedData;
    }
}
```

Smart contracts are the cornerstone of Ethereum's functionality, enabling automated, transparent and secure transactions on the blockchain. Understanding their architecture and learning the basics of Solidity is the first step towards building decentralised applications and systems on the Ethereum platform. The provided example demonstrates a fundamental smart contract, forming a basis for more advanced and complex contracts.

3.3 Introduction to Remix – Ethereum IDE

Remix, accessible via https://remix.ethereum.org/, is a powerful, open source web and desktop application that is widely used for Ethereum smart contract development. It's an integrated development environment (IDE) designed specifically for writing, testing, debugging and deploying smart contracts written in Solidity, the primary programming language for Ethereum.

CHAPTER 3   THE RISE OF ETHEREUM

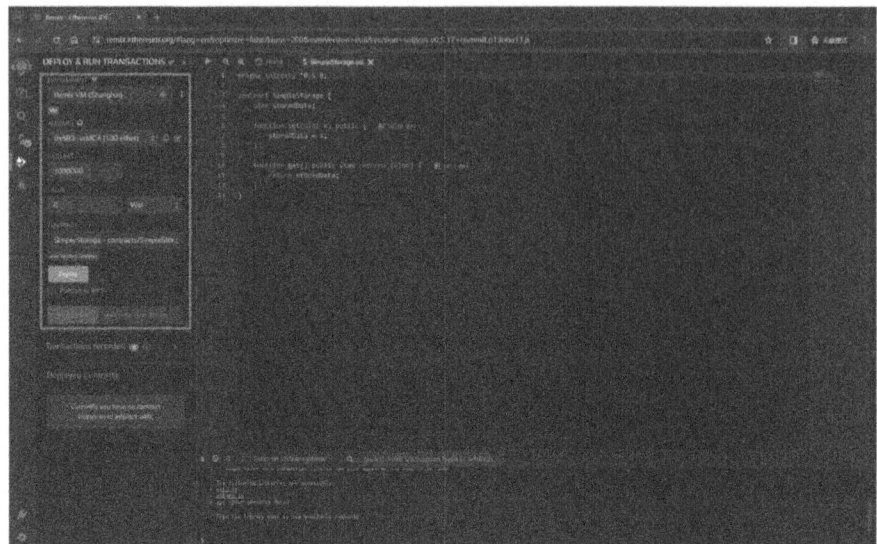

Figure 3-1. *Remix Ethereum IDE*

Key features of Remix include

1. **Accessible and User-Friendly Interface**

   - **Web Based**: No need to install any software; it's accessible directly through the browser.

   - **Desktop Version**: For offline development, a desktop version is also available.

2. **Smart Contract Development**

   - **Solidity Editor**: Provides an advanced code editor for writing Solidity contracts with features like syntax highlighting and error checking.

   - **Compilation**: Remix compiles smart contracts and provides detailed information about warnings and errors.

3. **Testing and Debugging**

    - **Built-in Testing Environment**: Allows for easy testing of smart contracts within the IDE.

    - **Debugging Tools**: Offers step-by-step debugging to analyse and optimise code.

4. **Deployment and Interaction**

    - **Deploy on Various Networks**: Enables deploying contracts on Ethereum test networks (like Ropsten, Kovan, Rinkeby) or the Ethereum mainnet.

    - **Interaction Interface**: Once deployed, Remix provides an interface to interact with the contract functions.

5. **Plug-ins and Extensibility**

    - **Extensive Plug-in Support**: Offers a range of plug-ins for additional functionalities like static analysis, gas estimation and more.

    - **Custom Plug-ins**: Developers can create and integrate their own plug-ins for personalised needs.

Using Remix for Smart Contract Development

Remix is an essential tool for Ethereum developers, offering a comprehensive suite of functionalities for smart contract development. Its ease of use, combined with powerful features like built-in testing and debugging tools, makes it an ideal platform for both beginners and

CHAPTER 3   THE RISE OF ETHEREUM

experienced developers in the Ethereum ecosystem. Whether you're writing your first smart contract or deploying a complex DApp, Remix provides the tools you need to succeed in the Ethereum development space. The following shows the step-by-step process from Listing 3-1:

1. **Writing the Contract**: Start by writing your Solidity smart contract in the Remix editor.

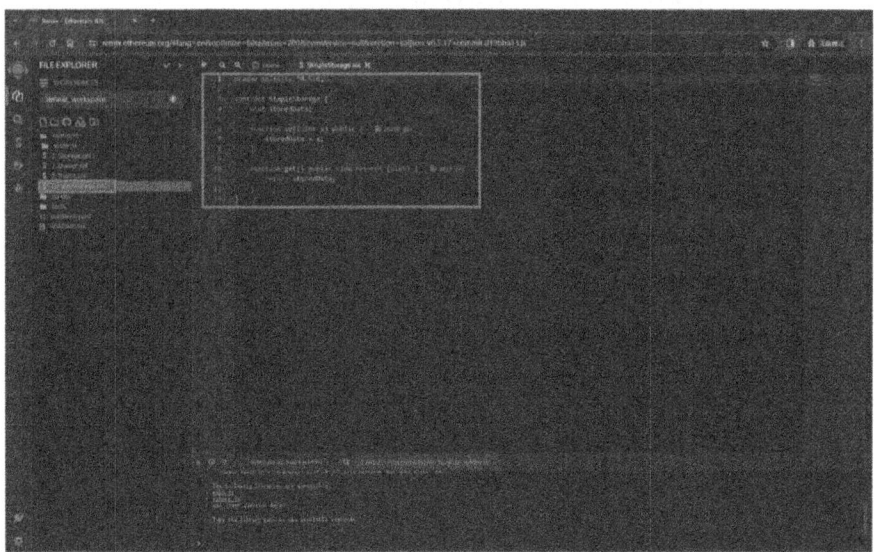

Figure 3-2.   Writing the Contract for 'SimpleStorage.sol'

CHAPTER 3   THE RISE OF ETHEREUM

2. **Compilation**: Use the built-in compiler to compile your contract and check for any errors or warnings.

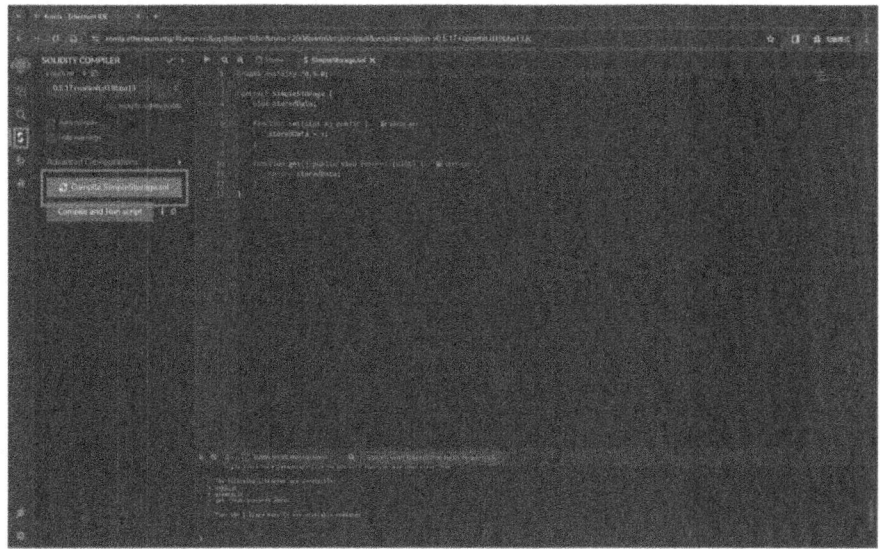

Figure 3-3. *Compile 'SimpleStorage.sol'*

CHAPTER 3   THE RISE OF ETHEREUM

3. **Testing**: Write and execute tests for your contract using the Remix testing environment.

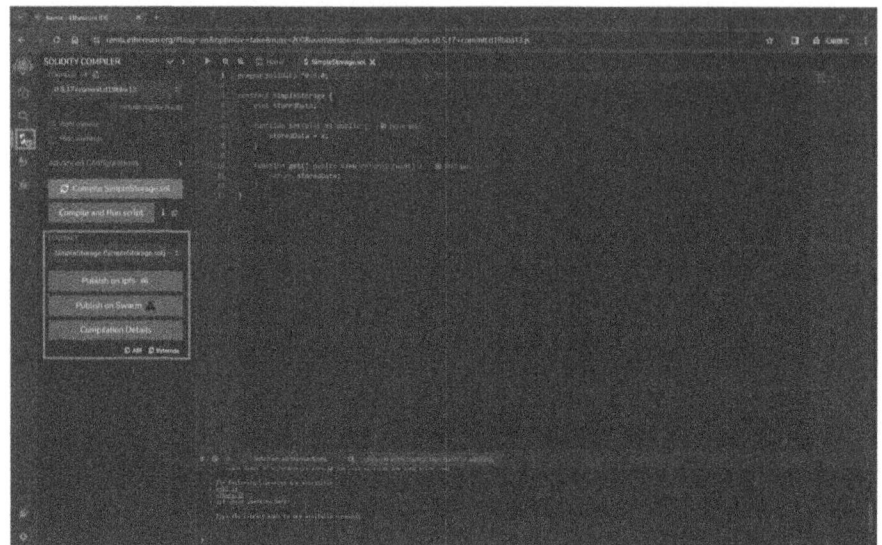

Figure 3-4.   Test 'SimpleStorage.sol'

CHAPTER 3   THE RISE OF ETHEREUM

4. **Debugging**: Utilise the debugger to step through your code and optimise it.

5. **Deployment**: Deploy your contract to a test network or the Ethereum mainnet directly from Remix.

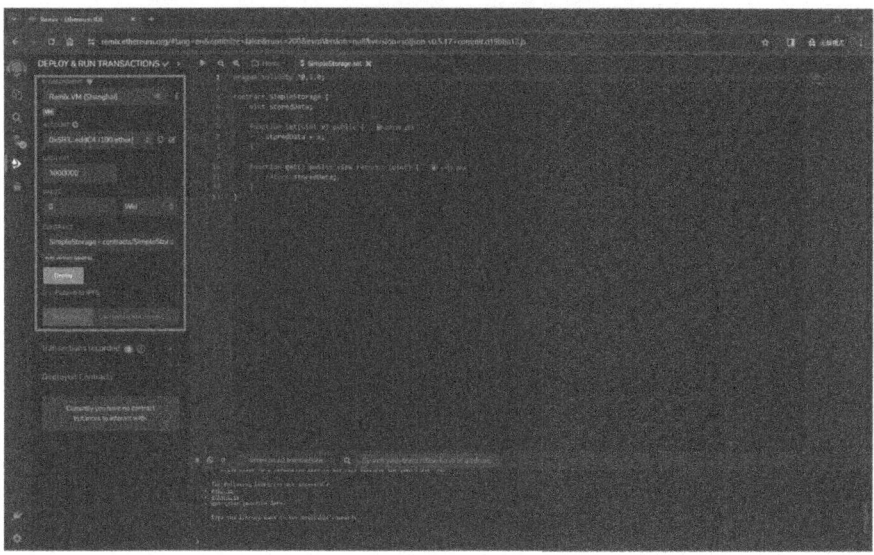

Figure 3-5. Deploy 'SimpleStorage.sol'

CHAPTER 3   THE RISE OF ETHEREUM

6. **Interaction**: After deployment, interact with your contract functions using the Remix interface.

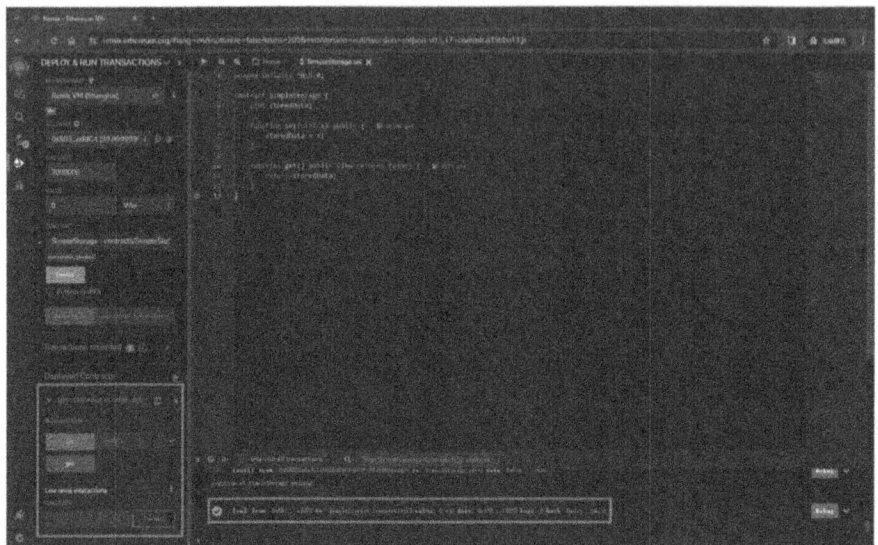

Figure 3-6. *Interaction 'SimpleStorage.sol'*

CHAPTER 3 THE RISE OF ETHEREUM

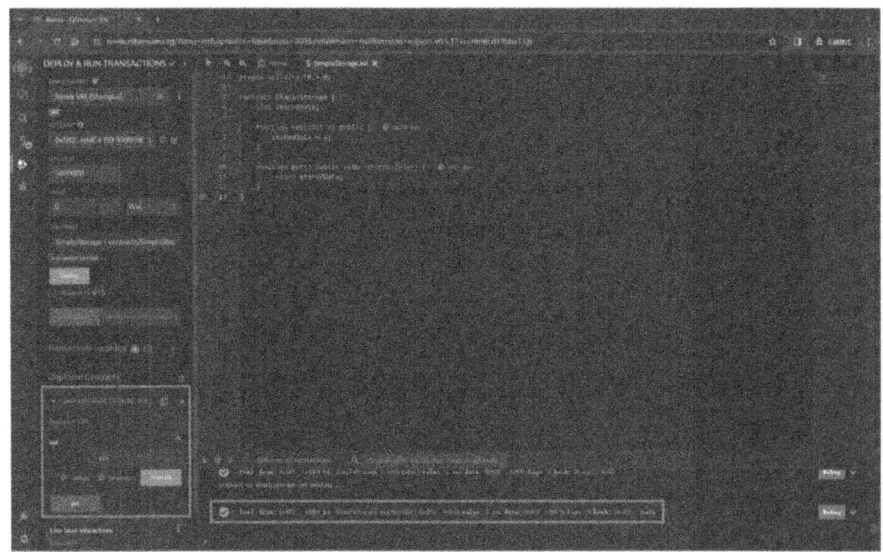

Figure 3-7. *Interaction 'SimpleStorage.sol' – transact*

Figure 3-8. *Interaction 'SimpleStorage.sol' – get*

Now that you have a foundational understanding of how Remix can streamline your Ethereum development process, let's apply this knowledge. In the following sections, we will explore practical examples of smart contracts. These examples will demonstrate how to effectively utilise Remix's powerful features for writing, testing and deploying smart contracts, providing you with hands-on experience in crafting efficient and secure blockchain applications.

3.4 Simple Smart Contract Examples

The smart contract in Listing 3-2 defines a straightforward contract named MyContract. It primarily consists of a public string variable named value, initially set to 'MyValue'. This variable's public status allows external entities to read its value, thanks to an automatically generated getter function by Solidity. Additionally, the contract includes a function set, which enables the modification of value.

Listing 3-2. Smart Contract Example – 2

```
pragma solidity ^0.5.1;
contract MyContract{
    string public value = "MyValue";
    function set(string memory _value) public {
        value = _value;
    }
}
```

When invoked, this function accepts a new string value as an argument and assigns it to value, thereby updating its content. This simple structure of the contract suggests its utility in basic data storage and retrieval operations, demonstrating a fundamental example of state management and interaction within a smart contract on the Ethereum blockchain.

The smart contract then establishes a contract named **MyContract** with a variety of state variables, each showcasing different data types and characteristics in Solidity (Listing 3-3).

Listing 3-3. Smart Contract Example – 3

```
pragma solidity ^0.5.1;

contract MyContract{
    string public constant stringvalue = "MyString";
    bool public myBool = true;
    int public myInt = -1;
    uint public myUint = 1;
    uint8 public myUnit8 = 8;
    uint256 public myUnit256 = 9999;
}
```

Here's a consolidated explanation:

1. **String Variable**: The contract declares a constant public string variable named **stringvalue** with an initial value of 'MyString'. Being constant, its value is fixed and cannot be changed after the contract is deployed.

2. **Boolean Variable**: It includes a public boolean variable **myBool**, initially set to true. This variable, like the string, can be read externally and is mutable, meaning its value can be changed.

3. **Integer Variables**: The contract features two integer variables: **myInt**, an integer with a value of –1, demonstrating the capability to handle negative numbers, and **myUint**, an unsigned integer (cannot

be negative) set to 1. The distinction between int and uint is important in Solidity for representing different types of numeric data.

4. **Specific Integer Types**: Additionally, there are more specific types of unsigned integers declared: **myUint8** and **myUint256**, initialised with values 8 and 9999, respectively. These types specify the size of the integer in bits, with **uint8** being an 8-bit unsigned integer and **uint256** being a 256-bit unsigned integer, which is the default size for **uint**.

This smart contract serves as an example of how different types of variables can be declared and initialised in Solidity. It demonstrates the use of constant values, mutable state variables and the distinction between signed and unsigned integers, as well as integers of specific bit sizes. Such contracts are fundamental in understanding data storage and manipulation in the context of Ethereum smart contracts.

Listing 3-4 provides a more advanced example than the previous ones. It introduces an enumeration and state management, along with function definitions for state manipulation and query.

Listing 3-4. Smart Contract Example – 4

```
pragma solidity ^0.5.1;

contract MyContract{
    enum State { Waiting, Ready, Active }
    State public state;

    constructor() public{
        state = State.Waiting;
    }
```

CHAPTER 3   THE RISE OF ETHEREUM

```
    function activate() public{
        state = State.Active;
    }
    function isActive() public view returns(bool) {
        return state == State.Active;
    }
}
```

Here's a comprehensive explanation:

- **Enumeration Declaration**: The contract starts with the declaration of an enumeration State, which includes three possible states: Waiting, Ready and Active. Enumerations are user-defined types in Solidity that allow for the creation of a set of named constants, improving code readability and maintainability.

- **State Variable**: It then declares a public state variable of type State. The visibility of this variable as public means that Solidity will automatically create a getter for it, allowing external contracts or interfaces to check the current state of the contract.

- **Constructor**: The contract includes a constructor, which is a special function that is executed once when the contract is deployed. In this constructor, the state variable is initialised to State.Waiting. This sets the initial state of the contract to Waiting when it is deployed on the Ethereum blockchain.

- **Function to Change State**: There is a function activate that, when called, changes the contract's state to Active. This demonstrates how contract states can be manipulated through functions.

- **State Query Function**: Finally, the contract has a function isActive that returns a boolean indicating whether the contract's current state is Active. This function is a view function, meaning it does not modify the state of the contract but merely reads and returns information.

Overall, this contract exemplifies the use of enums to manage and query contract states in Solidity, showcasing a common pattern in Ethereum smart contracts where the state of a contract changes based on interactions with functions defined within it. This pattern is crucial in many decentralised applications, where the state of the contract often determines the logic that should be executed.

Listing 3-5 includes a combination of state management, access control and structured data handling. It provides a practical example of how smart contracts on the Ethereum blockchain can use access control mechanisms to restrict certain actions to specific users.

Listing 3-5. Smart Contract Example – 5

```
pragma solidity ^0.5.1;

contract AddPerson{

    uint256 public peopleCount = 0;
    mapping(uint => Person) public people;

    address owner;

    modifier onlyOwner() {
        require(msg.sender == owner);
        _;
    }

    struct Person{
        uint _id;
        string _firstName;
```

```
        string _lastName;
    }
    constructor() public {
        owner = msg.sender;
    }
    function addPerson(string memory _firstName, string memory
    _lastName) public onlyOwner{
        incrementCount();
        people[peopleCount] = Person(peopleCount, _firstName,
        _lastName);
    }
    function incrementCount() internal {
        peopleCount += 1;
    }
}
```

Let's break down its key components, especially focusing on the **onlyOwner** modifier:

1. **State Variables and Structure**

    - The contract initialises a public state variable **peopleCount** to 0, which tracks the number of people added.

    - It employs a mapping **people** to associate an unsigned integer (uint) with a **Person** structure, facilitating the storage and retrieval of person data.

    - The **Person** structure is defined with properties **_id**, **_firstName** and **_lastName**, allowing grouping of related information about a person.

2. **Ownership and Access Control (onlyOwner Modifier)**
   - A significant feature of this contract is the **onlyOwner** modifier. It's designed to restrict certain functionalities to the owner of the contract.
   - The contract declares an **address** variable named **owner**. In Ethereum, addresses are used to identify accounts, which can be external users or other contracts.
   - The **onlyOwner** modifier uses the **require** statement to ensure that the **msg.sender** (the address calling the function) is equal to **owner**. This guarantees that only the user who deployed the contract (the owner) can call functions that are protected by this modifier.
   - The _; in the modifier represents the placeholder for the function body that the modifier is applied to.

3. **Contract Constructor**
   - In the contract's constructor, **owner** is set to **msg.sender**, meaning the address deploying the contract is recorded as the owner.

4. **Function to Add Person (addPerson)**
   - The **addPerson** function is used to add new people with their first and last names to the contract. This function is governed by the **onlyOwner** modifier, meaning only the owner of the contract can add new people.
   - The function increments **peopleCount** and adds a new **Person** to the **people** mapping.

5. **Internal Function to Increment Count**

    - There's also an internal function **incrementCount** which simply increases the **peopleCount** by one. Being internal, this function can only be called from within the contract.

The **onlyOwner** modifier is a common pattern in smart contracts for ensuring that sensitive functions can only be executed by the contract's owner, adding a layer of security and control.

Listing 3-6 is a more complex example than Listing 3-5 that illustrates the use of a time-based modifier, a mapping and a structure. It is designed to manage a list of people with a constraint on when certain operations can be performed.

Listing 3-6. Smart Contract Example – 6

```
pragma solidity ^0.5.1;

contract AddPerson{

    uint256 public peopleCount = 0;
    mapping(uint => Person) public people;

    uint256 openingTime = 1704067200;

    modifier onlyWhileOpen() {
        require(block.timestamp >= openingTime);
        _;
    }

    struct Person{
        uint _id;
        string _firstName;
        string _lastName;
    }
```

```
    function addPerson(string memory _firstName, string memory
    _lastName) public onlyWhileOpen{
        incrementCount();
        people[peopleCount] = Person(peopleCount, _firstName,
        _lastName);
    }
    function incrementCount() internal {
        peopleCount += 1;
    }
}
```

This contract is an example of how smart contracts can integrate time-based logic and manage a collection of structured data. The use of the **openingTime** variable along with the **onlyWhileOpen** modifier showcases a common pattern where certain functionalities of a contract are restricted until a predefined condition, like a specific time or date, is met. This pattern is useful in scenarios like timed events, restricted access periods or phased contract functionalities.

Here's the main differences between Listings 3-5 and 3-6:

Time-Based Modifier (openingTime)

- The contract includes a state variable **uint256 openingTime = 1704067200;**. This value represents a specific point in time as a Unix timestamp. The specific value **1704067200** corresponds to seconds since 1 January, 2024.

- A modifier **onlyWhileOpen** is defined using this timestamp. It uses the **require** statement to ensure that the current block's timestamp (**block.timestamp**, which gives the current time in Unix timestamp format) is greater than or equal to **openingTime**. This means that the functions using this modifier can only be executed after the time specified by **openingTime**.

3.5 ERC Standards: ERC20, ERC721, ERC1155

In this section, we will focus exclusively on the types of smart contracts in the realm of Ethereum blockchain, particularly delving into token standards. We reserve a more in-depth discussion of the legal attributes of tokens for Part 3, 'Decentralised Finance (DeFi) and Applications'. Here, our attention is on the technical token standards.

A Brief Overview of ERC Standards

Tokens on the blockchain represent various entities like money, time, services or even virtual items. By tokenising these entities, smart contracts can interact, exchange or modify them. Understanding tokens requires distinguishing between token contracts and the actual tokens. Token contracts are Ethereum smart contracts that map addresses to balances, allowing for the addition and subtraction of these balances.

ERC, which stands for Ethereum Request for Comment, is a protocol or standard that Ethereum developers agree to follow while creating smart contracts. These standards ensure interoperability and reusability in smart contract coding.[7]

ERC20 Standard

Introduced in 2015 and adopted in 2017, the ERC20 standard is used for creating fungible tokens, meaning each token is identical and interchangeable with another. It's widely used for various purposes like stablecoins, ICOs, crowdfunding and other related activities. ERC20 tokens, such as Tether (USDT), Chainlink (LINK) and Basic Attention Token (BAT), have set functionalities allowing them to interact with each other and compatible services like cryptocurrency wallets.

Here is an example of an ERC20 token contract:

```
// contracts/HGToken.sol
// SPDX-License-Identifier: MIT
pragma solidity ^0.8.0;

import "@openzeppelin/contracts/token/ERC20/ERC20.sol";

contract HGToken is ERC20 {
    constructor(uint256 initialSupply) ERC20("HGToken",
    "HGT") {
        _mint(msg.sender, initialSupply);
    }
}
```

Let's break down its components:

1. **SPDX License Identifier and Solidity Version**

    ```
    // SPDX-License-Identifier: MIT
    pragma solidity ^0.8.0;
    ```

    These lines specify the license (MIT in this case) and the Solidity compiler version (^0.8.0), indicating the contract is compatible with Solidity version 0.8.0 or any minor version above it.

2. **Import Statement**

    ```
    import "@openzeppelin/contracts/token/ERC20/ERC20.sol";
    ```

    This line imports the ERC20 token standard implementation from the OpenZeppelin library. OpenZeppelin is a widely used and trusted library in the Ethereum developer community that provides secure, standardised and audited smart contract

CHAPTER 3   THE RISE OF ETHEREUM

implementations. The **ERC20.sol** contract from OpenZeppelin includes the basic functionalities of an ERC20 token, such as transferring tokens, getting account balances, the total supply of tokens and allowances (how many tokens one account allows another to spend on its behalf).

3. **Contract Declaration**

    `contract HGToken is ERC20 {`

    Here, a new smart contract named **HGToken** is declared, which extends the ERC20 token implementation from OpenZeppelin. This means **HGToken** inherits all functionalities of a standard ERC20 token.

4. **Constructor**

    `constructor(uint256 initialSupply) ERC20("HGToken", "HGT") { _mint(msg.sender, initialSupply); }`

    The constructor is executed once when the contract is deployed. It takes an initial supply of tokens as a parameter. The **ERC20("HGToken", "HGT")** part is calling the constructor of the imported ERC20 contract, setting the name of the token to 'HGToken' and its symbol to 'HGT'. The **_mint** function is then called to create the initial supply of tokens and assign them to the address deploying the contract (**msg.sender**).

In summary, this contract is a basic ERC20 token with an initial supply set at deployment. It uses OpenZeppelin's secure and standard implementation of the ERC20 protocol, ensuring compliance with the token standard and reducing the risk of vulnerabilities in the token's code.

85

CHAPTER 3   THE RISE OF ETHEREUM

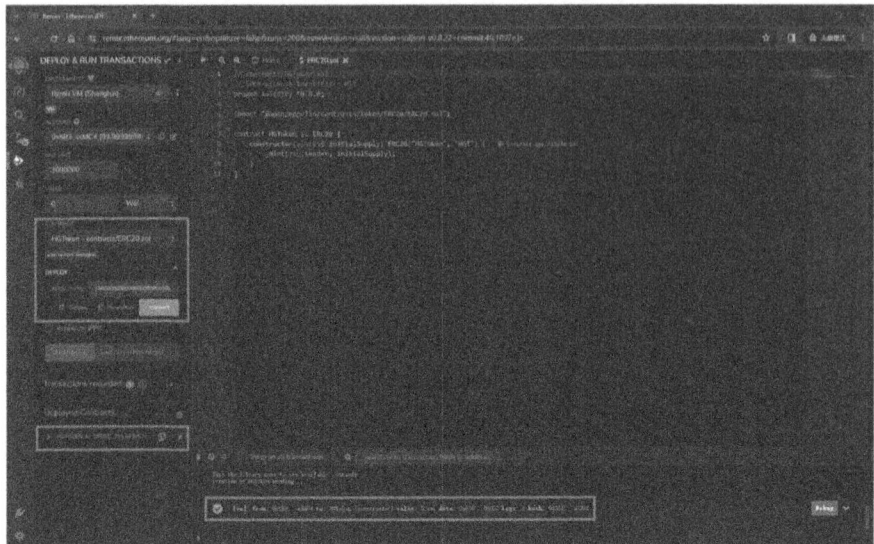

Figure 3-9. *Deploy 'ERC20.sol'*

Figure 3-9 shows the deployment of an ERC20 token smart contract. Several elements are highlighted, particularly within a red box. Let's break down the elements inside the red box and the process of deploying this smart contract:

1. **HGToken - contracts/ERC20.sol**: This indicates the smart contract **HGToken** is ready to be deployed. The contract is likely located in a file named **ERC20.sol** within a folder or path called **contracts**. This contract is an ERC20 token, which is a standard for creating fungible tokens on the Ethereum blockchain.

2. **DEPLOY**: This section is where you input the initial parameters required by the smart contract's constructor function before deploying it to the blockchain.

86

3. **INITIALSUPPLY**: This input field is for the **initialSupply** parameter of the HGToken contract's constructor. This value determines the total supply of tokens that will be minted upon deployment.

4. **1,000,000,000,000,000,000,000,000**: The very large number entered in the **INITIALSUPPLY** field is due to the fact that ERC20 tokens use a unit called 'wei' for the smallest sub-unit of the token, similar to how the smallest unit of Ether is also called wei. Since the ERC20 standard allows for up to 18 decimal places, if you want to issue 1 million tokens (1,000,000), you would need to add 18 zeros to the end of that number to account for the decimals. Hence, **1,000,000** becomes **1,000,000** followed by 18 zeros, making it **1,000,000,000,000,000,000,000,000** to represent 1 million tokens with 18 decimal places.

5. **Deploy Button (Transact)**: This button initiates the deployment process. Once you click it, Remix will send a transaction to the blockchain to create the contract with the specified initial supply.

6. **Console Output**: At the bottom, there's a console output indicating that the deployment transaction is pending. It shows the account from which the contract is being deployed (**0x583...edc4**), the value being sent with the transaction (0 ETH in this case, indicated by **value: 0x0**), the gas limit and the transaction hash (**0x38...0394**), which is a unique identifier for this transaction on the blockchain.

CHAPTER 3   THE RISE OF ETHEREUM

If the deployment is successful, the **HGToken** contract will be created on the blockchain with an initial supply of 1 million tokens (accounting for the 18 decimal places), and the account that deployed the contract will initially hold all these tokens. The tokens can then be distributed or used according to the contract's logic and the intentions of the deploying entity.

Figure 3-10. *Deployed Contracts – ERC20*

Figure 3-10 shows the interface of an ERC20 token contract after it has been deployed. This interface is generated by Remix to interact with the deployed smart contract's functions and queries. Let's explain the elements within the red box and distinguish between the orange and blue text. Here are the contract functions and queries:

1. **approve:** This is a function that allows the owner of the tokens to approve another address to spend a specific amount of tokens on their behalf.

2. **transfer:** This function is used to send a certain amount of tokens from the total supply to another address.

CHAPTER 3   THE RISE OF ETHEREUM

3. **transferFrom**: This function allows a third party to transfer tokens from one address to another, but only if they have been given an allowance by the token owner using the **approve** function.
4. **allowance**: This query returns the remaining number of tokens that a spender is allowed to withdraw from an owner's account.
5. **balanceOf**: This query returns the token balance of a specific account address.
6. **decimals**: This shows the number of decimal places the token can be divided into, which affects the token's divisibility. In ERC20 tokens, this is often set to 18, allowing for fractional tokens similar to how Ether is divisible.
7. **name**: This returns the name of the token, which in this case is 'HGToken'.
8. **symbol**: This returns the token's symbol, 'HGT' in this case, which is like a ticker symbol for the token.
9. **totalSupply**: This query returns the total number of tokens in circulation for this contract.

The orange text represents the names of functions and queries that are part of the ERC20 token's interface. They are the operations that you can perform on the contract, such as transferring tokens (**transfer**), checking an account's balance (**balanceOf**) or checking the total supply (**totalSupply**).

The blue text signifies the parameters needed for a function or the return type of a query. For example, the **transfer** function requires the address to transfer to and the value to transfer. The **decimals** query has a blue 'uint8: 18' beside it, indicating that it returns an unsigned integer of 8 bits and that the value is 18.

The orange identifiers are the names of the operations you can invoke on the contract. The blue text provides additional context for those operations, either specifying what inputs are required for functions or what outputs are returned by queries. Hence, the **low-level interactions** allows for direct interaction with the contract by sending raw data encoded as hexadecimal CALLDATA. This is typically used by developers who need to construct and send complex calls that may not be covered by the preceding simplified interface. And the **CALLDATA** field is where raw transaction data would be entered if you were to make a low-level call to the contract.

In summary, after deploying an ERC20 token contract, Remix provides a user interface to interact with the contract's functions. The orange text identifies the operations available, while the blue text details the parameters for functions or the returned data for queries. Low-level interactions are for advanced operations beyond the scope of the standard interface.

ERC721 Standard

In contrast, ERC721, proposed in 2017 and accepted in 2018, focuses on non-fungible tokens (NFTs). These tokens are unique and cannot be interchanged. ERC721 tokens represent distinct items like digital artwork, collectibles or real estate property. They play a crucial role in creating a market for unique digital assets, as evidenced by the sale of a $69 million digital artwork by Beeple.[8]

Here is an example of an ERC721 token contract:

```
// contracts/HGNFT.sol
// SPDX-License-Identifier: MIT
pragma solidity ^0.8.0;

import "@openzeppelin/contracts/token/ERC721/extensions/ERC721URIStorage.sol";
import "@openzeppelin/contracts/utils/Counters.sol";
```

```solidity
contract HGNFT is ERC721URIStorage {
    using Counters for Counters.Counter;
    Counters.Counter private _tokenIds;

    constructor() ERC721("HGNFT", "HGN") {}

    function awardItem(address player, string memory tokenURI)
        public
        returns (uint256)
    {
        uint256 newItemId = _tokenIds.current();
        _mint(player, newItemId);
        _setTokenURI(newItemId, tokenURI);

        _tokenIds.increment();
        return newItemId;
    }
}
```

Here's a breakdown of its components:

1. **SPDX-License-Identifier and Solidity Version**

    ```
    // SPDX-License-Identifier: MIT pragma
    solidity ^0.8.0;
    ```

    This specifies the contract's license and the Solidity compiler version, indicating that the contract is to be compiled with Solidity version 0.8.0 or newer.

2. **Import Statements**

    ```
    import "@openzeppelin/contracts/token/ERC721/extensions/ERC721URIStorage.sol";
    import "@openzeppelin/contracts/utils/Counters.sol";
    ```

- **ERC721URIStorage** is an extension of OpenZeppelin's ERC721 standard. It adds functionality to set and manage a token URI (Uniform Resource Identifier), which typically points to a JSON file that conforms to the 'ERC721 Metadata JSON Schema.'
- **Counters** is a utility library from OpenZeppelin that provides a counter variable type, which is used to safely increment and decrement numerical values.

3. **Contract Declaration and Inheritance**

   contract HGNFT is ERC721URIStorage {

   This declares the contract **HGNFT**, which inherits from **ERC721URIStorage**, meaning it will have all the standard functionality of an ERC721 token plus the additional URI storage features.

4. **Using Statements and State Variables**

   using Counters for Counters.Counter;
   Counters.Counter private _tokenIds;

   - The **using** statement allows the contract to use the functions defined in the **Counters** library for **Counter** types.
   - **_tokenIds** is a private state variable that keeps track of the current token ID using the **Counter** utility.

5. **Constructor**

   solidityCopy code
   constructor() ERC721("HGNFT", "HGN") {}

The constructor initialises the contract by calling the ERC721 constructor with the name of the token ('HGNFT') and its symbol ('HGN').

6. **awardItem Function**

    ```
    function awardItem(address player, string memory tokenURI)
        public
        returns (uint256)
    {
        uint256 newItemId = _tokenIds.current();
        _mint(player, newItemId);
        _setTokenURI(newItemId, tokenURI);

        _tokenIds.increment();
        return newItemId;
    }
    ```

- **awardItem** is a public function that can be called to mint a new NFT and assign it to the **player** address.

- It first gets the current token ID value, mints a new token with this ID to the **player** and sets the token's URI.

- Afterwards, it increments the **_tokenIds** counter to ensure that the next token has a unique ID.

- The function returns the new item ID, which can be used to reference the newly minted token.

In essence, this contract provides a simple yet functional example of an NFT contract that can be used to create unique digital assets, where each token can be associated with a distinct URI pointing to metadata that describes the token's properties. The contract uses the OpenZeppelin library to ensure secure and standardised functionality.

CHAPTER 3   THE RISE OF ETHEREUM

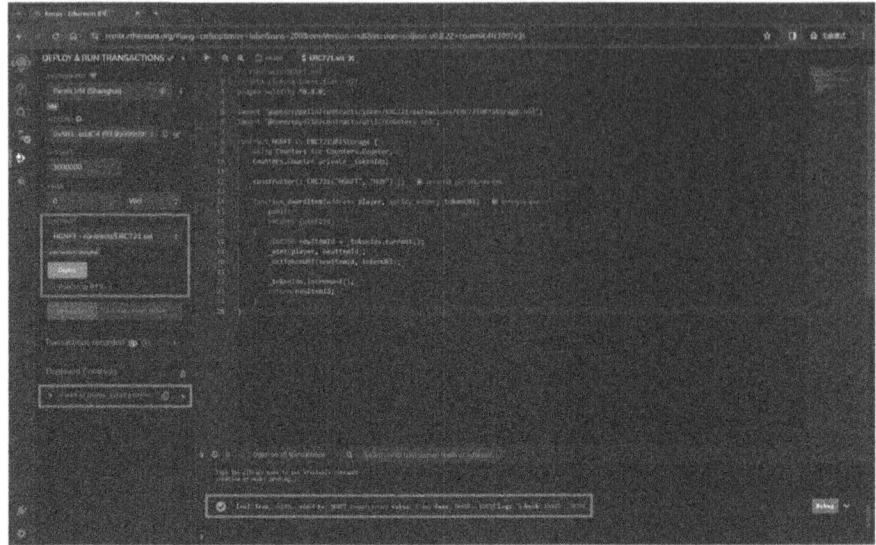

Figure 3-11. *Deploy 'ERC721.sol'*

Figure 3-11 shows the process of deploying an ERC721 smart contract, specifically a non-fungible token (NFT) contract named **HGNFT**. Here's a breakdown of the elements within the red box:

1. **HGNFT - contracts/ERC721.sol**: This indicates that the **HGNFT** contract is selected and ready to be deployed. The contract is located within the **contracts** folder and in a file named **ERC721.sol**. This file conventionally contains the code for the NFT.

2. **Deploy**: The 'Deploy' button, when clicked, will send the smart contract to the blockchain. It uses the account and gas limit specified in the environment settings. Once deployed, the contract will become a part of the blockchain and will be able to interact with other contracts and addresses.

CHAPTER 3 THE RISE OF ETHEREUM

In the console at the bottom, you can see the transaction details for the deployment. It shows the account that is deploying the contract, the gas limit and the value being sent along with the deployment (which is 0 in this case, as deploying contracts typically does not require sending Ether unless the constructor function specifies otherwise). The transaction hash (a unique identifier for the transaction on the blockchain) is also visible.

Once the contract is deployed, it will appear under 'Deployed Contracts', and you'll be able to interact with it using the functions defined in the contract, like **awardItem**, which is used to mint new NFTs in Figure 3-12.

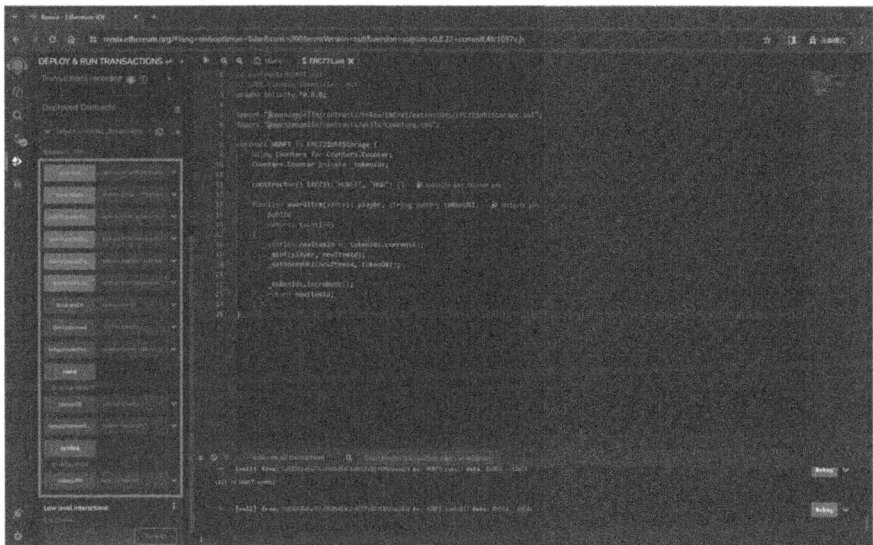

Figure 3-12. *Deployed Contracts – ERC721*

After deploying an ERC721 smart contract, which is typically used to create non-fungible tokens (NFTs), the interface generated by Remix highlights the functions and queries available for interaction with the **HGNFT** contract. Below is a detailed explanation of the key elements highlighted in the interface:

95

1. **approve**: This function allows a token owner to approve another account to transfer the specified amount of the owner's tokens to a third party.

2. **awardItem**: This custom function in the HGNFT contract allows the contract owner (or the function caller) to mint a new NFT and assign it to a player's address. The **tokenURI** parameter typically references a JSON file hosted on IPFS.

Once your digital assets (e.g. images for NFTs) are generated, the next crucial step is uploading them to IPFS (InterPlanetary File System). IPFS is a decentralised storage solution that preserves the permanence and integrity of your files by distributing them across multiple nodes globally. This step is essential in the NFT creation process, as it provides a unique, immutable URI that is embedded in the NFT's metadata, ensuring that the digital asset cannot be altered or removed. You can choose to either set up your own IPFS node for full control (Option 1) or use a third-party service like Pinata for ease of use (Option 2), depending on your technical preferences and needs.

Option 1: Setting Up Your Own IPFS Node

Setting up your own IPFS node involves installing IPFS on your machine, initialising your IPFS repository and starting the IPFS daemon to connect your node to the IPFS network. This method gives you full control over your content's hosting but comes with increased complexity and responsibility.

CHAPTER 3   THE RISE OF ETHEREUM

You'll need to manage your node's availability and connectivity to ensure your assets remain accessible. This approach might involve:

- Downloading and installing IPFS
- Initialising your IPFS node with `ipfs init`
- Starting the IPFS daemon using `ipfs daemon`
- Adding your files to IPFS using `ipfs add -r /path/to/your/folder`

While running your own node offers a high degree of control and direct engagement with the IPFS network, it requires a good understanding of IPFS and might not be the most straightforward option for beginners or those looking for quick and easy solutions.

Option 2: Using Third-Party Services like Pinata

For many users, especially those new to IPFS or seeking convenience, third-party services like Pinata offer an easier way to upload and manage content on IPFS. Pinata simplifies the process by providing a user-friendly interface and additional features like pinning services to ensure your content remains readily available on the IPFS network.

To use Pinata for uploading your NFT assets:

- Create an Account: Sign up on Pinata.cloud and log in to your account.
- Upload Content: Navigate to the 'Upload' section and choose to upload a folder. Pinata will automatically pin your uploaded content, ensuring its availability on the IPFS network.

- Retrieve IPFS Hashes: Once uploaded, Pinata will provide an IPFS hash (CID) for your folder and each contained file. These hashes serve as permanent, immutable links to your assets, which you'll include in your NFTs' metadata.

Instead of providing a step-by-step explanation, please refer to Section 7.3 in Chapter 7, which covers the detailed process of managing metadata, including handling multiple images and JSON files for NFTs. Chapter 7 offers more comprehensive guidance on utilising Pinata and other methods for uploading digital assets and managing them on IPFS.

Option 1 vs. Option 2

While setting up your own IPFS node gives you full control and a hands-on experience, it comes with a steeper learning curve and ongoing management responsibilities. In contrast, third-party services like Pinata offer a more straightforward, user-friendly solution, making it ideal for creators who want to streamline their NFT creation process. Regardless of the method you choose, the key goal is to securely upload your digital assets to IPFS, enabling their transformation into NFTs.

For instance, if you have a JSON file hosted on IPFS with the URI (e.g. ipfs://Qm...), you would use this URI as the **tokenURI** parameter when calling the **awardItem** function.

CHAPTER 3   THE RISE OF ETHEREUM

3. **safeTransferFrom:** There are two versions of this function. They allow for the safe transfer of tokens from one address to another, ensuring that the receiving address is capable of handling ERC721 tokens (to prevent accidental loss).

4. **setApprovalForAll**: This function allows the owner of tokens to grant permission to another address to transfer all of the owner's tokens on their behalf.

5. **transferFrom**: This function is used to transfer a token from one address to another. The caller must be authorised to move the token, either by being the owner, approved or an authorised operator.

6. **balanceOf**: This query returns the number of tokens owned by a given address.

7. **getApproved**: This returns the approved address for a single token.

8. **isApprovedForAll**: This checks if an operator is approved to transfer all tokens owned by a given address.

9. **name**: This returns the name of the token collection, which is **HGNFT** in this case.

10. **ownerOf**: This query returns the owner of a specific token ID.

11. **supportsInterface**: Contracts in Ethereum can announce which functions they support by returning true for a given interface ID. This is a technical function used by other contracts to determine what functionalities are supported by this contract.

99

12. **symbol**: This query returns the token symbol, which is **HGN**.

13. **tokenURI**: For a given token ID, this returns the URI of the associated resource, which is typically a link to a JSON file containing metadata.

In the case of **awardItem**, the function is meant to 'award' an NFT to a player, where the **player** is the address of the recipient, and the **tokenURI** is the link to the NFT's metadata. The metadata file could look something like this:

```
{
    "name": "Hui Gong Digital Artwork",
    "description": "A unique piece of digital art",
    "image": "ipfs://QmXxXxXxXxXxXxXxXxXxXxXxXxXxXxX",
    "attributes": [
        {
            "trait_type": "Rarity",
            "value": "Rare"
        },
        {
            "trait_type": "Artist",
            "value": "Hui Gong"
        }
    ]
}
```

This file would be uploaded to IPFS, and the resulting IPFS URI would be used as the **tokenURI** parameter when minting the NFT.

It's worth noting that the detailed mechanics of how NFTs function, including how they're integrated within the broader ecosystem of DeFi and applications such as digital art platforms, will be explored in Part 3, 'Decentralised Finance (DeFi) and Applications', specifically in Chapter 7, 'Non-fungible Tokens (NFTs) and Digital Art'.

ERC1155 Standard

The ERC1155 standard, introduced in 2018, bridges the gap between ERC20 and ERC721 by allowing a single contract to represent multiple fungibles, semi-fungible and non-fungible tokens. It brings in the concept of batch transfers and secure token transfers, reducing transaction costs and network congestion. This standard is particularly beneficial in gaming and digital collectibles, where a variety of token types coexist.

Here is an example ERC1155 multi-token standard contract:

```solidity
// contracts/HGCollections.sol
// SPDX-License-Identifier: MIT
pragma solidity ^0.8.0;

import "@openzeppelin/contracts/token/ERC1155/ERC1155.sol";

contract HGCollections is ERC1155 {
    uint256 public constant HGT = 0;
    uint256 public constant HGNFT = 1;

    constructor() ERC1155("https://huigong.info/api/item/{id}.json") {
        _mint(msg.sender, HGT, 10**18, "");
        _mint(msg.sender, HGNFT, 1, "");
    }
}
```

Here is an explanation of the code:

1. **SPDX-License-Identifier and Solidity Version**

   ```solidity
   // SPDX-License-Identifier: MIT
   pragma solidity ^0.8.0;
   ```

CHAPTER 3 THE RISE OF ETHEREUM

This specifies that the contract is licensed under the MIT License and is written to be compiled with Solidity version 0.8.0.

2. **Import Statement**

   ```
   import "@openzeppelin/contracts/token/ERC1155/ERC1155.sol";
   ```

   This imports the ERC1155 contract from the OpenZeppelin Contracts library, which is a collection of reusable and secure smart contract components.

3. **Contract Declaration**

   ```
   contract HGCollections is ERC1155 {
   ```

   HGCollections is declared as a contract extending the OpenZeppelin **ERC1155** contract, which means it inherits all the standard methods and properties of an ERC1155 token contract.

4. **Constants for Token Types**

   ```
   uint256 public constant HGT = 0; uint256 public constant HGNFT = 1;
   ```

   Two constants, **HGT** and **HGNFT**, are declared to represent different token types within this ERC1155 contract. **HGT** represents a fungible token type with the ID **0**, and **HGNFT** represents a non-fungible token type with the ID **1**.

CHAPTER 3 THE RISE OF ETHEREUM

5. **Constructor and Token Metadata**

   constructor() ERC1155("https://huigong.info/api/item/{id}.json") {

   The constructor initialises the contract with a URI for token metadata. This URI contains a placeholder **{id}** which can be replaced by the token's ID to retrieve metadata for each specific token type.

6. **Minting Tokens**

   _mint(msg.sender, HGT, 10**18, "");
   _mint(msg.sender, HGNFT, 1, "");

   Within the constructor, there are two **_mint** calls:

   - The first call mints **10**18** (1 followed by 18 zeros, mimicking the smallest denomination of Ether, wei) units of the fungible token **HGT** and assigns them to the contract deployer (**msg.sender**).

   - The second call mints **1** unit of the non-fungible token **HGNFT**, also assigning it to the contract deployer. This reflects the typical property of NFTs being unique or at least not having a large supply.

The empty string *""* passed as the last parameter to **_mint** could be replaced with data if needed for more complex minting logic or to trigger events.

This contract showcases the flexibility of the ERC1155 standard, where a single contract can manage a variety of token types and quantities. The ERC1155 standard is especially popular in scenarios like gaming where a user might have multiple items (fungible tokens for consumables and non-fungible tokens for unique items) that need to be managed in a unified way.

CHAPTER 3   THE RISE OF ETHEREUM

Figure 3-13 shows after deploying an ERC1155 smart contract named **HGCollections**. Similar to the previously discussed ERC721 contract, deploying this ERC1155 contract is as straightforward as clicking the 'Deploy' button in Remix. Once deployed, the contract's functions and features become available for interaction.

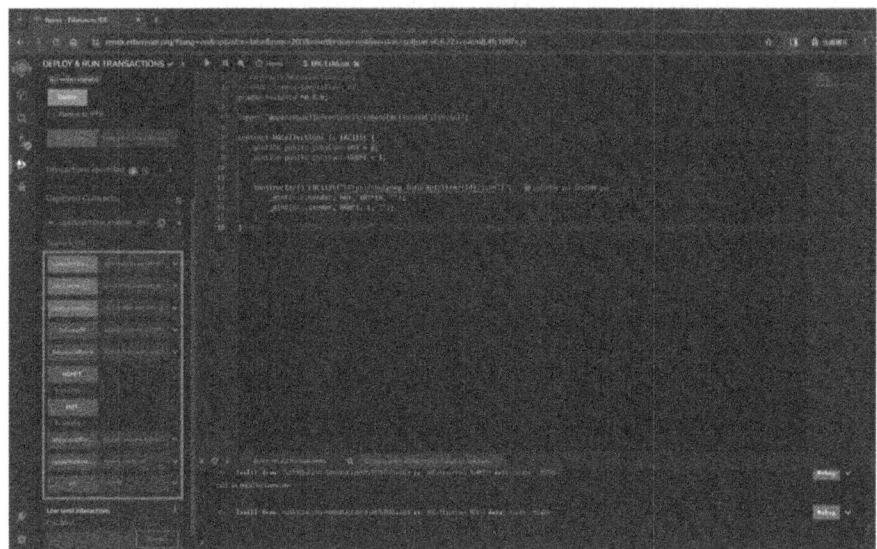

Figure 3-13. *Deployed Contracts – ERC1155*

Here are the details of each function and feature outlined in the red box within the deployed **HGCollections** smart contract:

1. **safeBatchTransferFrom**: Allows an address to transfer multiple types of tokens to another address in a single transaction. It's a batch operation for transferring various token IDs and amounts, ensuring that each transfer is safe and that the recipient can handle the tokens.

2. **safeTransferFrom**: Enables the safe transfer of a specific amount of a token (identified by ID) from one address to another. This function ensures that the receiving address has the necessary logic to handle ERC1155 tokens.

3. **setApprovalForAll**: Grants or revokes permission for another address (an operator) to manage all the current address's tokens. This is similar to a power of attorney for all tokens in this contract.

4. **balanceOf**: Provides the balance of a specific token ID for a single account, telling you how many tokens of a particular ID the account holds.

5. **balanceOfBatch**: An extension of **balanceOf**, which allows querying balances for multiple accounts and token IDs simultaneously, making it useful for fetching balances in bulk.

6. **HGNFT**: Represents a non-fungible token type within this contract, with an ID of **1**. It indicates that this specific token type is unique and non-interchangeable.

7. **HGT**: Stands for a fungible token type within this contract, with an ID of **0**. This token type is interchangeable, and each unit is indistinguishable from another.

8. **isApprovedForAll**: Checks if an operator is approved to manage all of an owner's tokens, which can include both fungible and non-fungible tokens.

9. **supportsInterface**: Determines if the contract implements a certain interface, according to the ERC165 standard. This helps other contracts or services to understand what functionalities the contract supports.

10. **uri**: Retrieves the URI for a token's metadata based on its ID. For ERC1155 contracts, the metadata URI often points to a JSON file with details about the token.

11. **Low-Level Interactions**: This part of the interface allows for direct interaction with the contract by sending raw data encoded as hexadecimal CALLDATA. It's meant for advanced users who need to send custom transactions not covered by the standard interface.

After deploying the contract, the **HGCollections** contract is ready to manage an assortment of both fungible and non-fungible tokens using the unified ERC1155 standard. The initial minting creates a large supply of the fungible token (**HGT**) and a single instance of the non-fungible token (**HGNFT**), both assigned to the deployer's address. The contract's URI structure (`'https://huigong.info/api/item/{id}.json'`) indicates where metadata for each token ID can be found, allowing external entities to retrieve detailed information about each token managed by the contract.

Comparing the Standards

The evolution of these ERC token standards reflects Ethereum's response to the rapidly changing blockchain landscape. Each standard serves specific use cases and requirements, making them integral to Ethereum's functionality and versatility in the digital ecosystem:

CHAPTER 3   THE RISE OF ETHEREUM

- ERC20 focuses on fungible tokens, suitable for straightforward token transfers.

- ERC721 is for unique, non-fungible tokens, each representing something distinct.

- ERC1155 offers flexibility, combining features of both ERC20 and ERC721, and supports semi-fungible tokens.

3.6 Summary

This chapter delved into the rise of Ethereum, born out of Vitalik Buterin's vision to create a platform surpassing Bitcoin's capabilities. Ethereum's strength lies in its Ethereum Virtual Machine (EVM) and the smart contracts it powers. These technologies enable Ethereum to operate as a decentralised computing platform, allowing for a wide range of applications beyond basic transactions. The chapter also explored significant developments, such as Ethereum's shift to a proof-of-stake consensus model with 'The Merge', which enhanced both its efficiency and environmental sustainability.

Through the ERC standards (ERC20, ERC721, and ERC1155), Ethereum has shown adaptability to various tokenisation needs, ranging from fungible to non-fungible assets. Ethereum's robust community and continuous upgrades ensure that it remains a leading blockchain platform, capable of supporting diverse real-world applications, from decentralised finance (DeFi) to NFTs. This chapter emphasises Ethereum's critical role in the blockchain ecosystem, positioning it as a foundation for the next wave of decentralised applications and technologies.

3.7 Notes

1. Zirojevic, A. (2022). Here's how Vitalik Buterin came up with the idea of creating ethereum, Finbold. https://finbold.com/heres-how-vitalik-buterin-came-up-with-the-idea-of-creating-ethereum/ (Accessed: 16 December 2023).

2. NodeFlair (2021). How Vitalik Buterin co-founded Ethereum at the age of 19 as a developer, NodeFlair. https://nodeflair.com/blog/vitalik-buterin-co-founded-ethereum-at-the-age-of-19-heres-what-he-did-as-a-developer (Accessed: 16 December 2023).

3. Thompsett, L. (2023). Vitalik Buterin: co-founder of Ethereum, crypto visionary. FinTech Magazine. https://fintechmagazine.com/articles/founding-ethereum-vitalik-buterin (Accessed: 16 December 2023).

4. Cancun-Deneb (Dencun) FAQ | Ethereum.org (2024). ethereum.org. https://ethereum.org/en/roadmap/dencun/ (Accessed: 9 April 2024).

5. Daye, W. (2024). What to Expect From Ethereum's Cancun-Deneb Upgrade. CoinDesk. www.coindesk.com/tech/2024/02/28/what-to-expect-from-ethereums-cancun-deneb-upgrade/ (Accessed: 9 April 2024).

CHAPTER 3   THE RISE OF ETHEREUM

6. A complete guide to the Ethereum Dencun upgrade (2024). Chain. www.chain.com/blog/a-complete-guide-to-the-ethereum-dencun-upgrade (Accessed: 9 April 2024).

7. Tokens - OpenZeppelin Docs (n.d.). https://docs.openzeppelin.com/contracts/4.x/tokens (Accessed: 16 December 2023).

8. Art and NFTs: Beeple reflects one year after historic $69 million digital art sale (11 March 2022). NBC News. www.nbcnews.com/tech/tech-news/art-nfts-beeple-reflects-one-year-historic-69-million-digital-art-sale-rcna18989 (Accessed: 16 December 2023).

CHAPTER 4

The Pillars of Web3: Ethereum's Wallet, Faucet and Layer 2 Solutions

4.1 The Gateway to Web3: Crypto Wallets

Blockchain wallets are not just digital equivalents of physical wallets; they are more akin to personal bankers, integrated seamlessly into the fabric of the Web3 experience. These wallets are the essential interface for interacting with the decentralised web, allowing users to manage their digital identities and assets. The type of Ethereum wallets is the same as the Bitcoin's, which we have introduced in Section 2.3.

Within these wallet types, security practices are paramount. Private keys are the literal keys to one's digital vault and must be guarded with utmost diligence. Wallet backups through seed phrases and secure storage options are critical. Against hacking and theft, measures like two-factor authentication (2FA), multi-signature requirements and avoiding phishing attacks are necessary defences.

CHAPTER 4   THE PILLARS OF WEB3: ETHEREUM'S WALLET, FAUCET AND LAYER 2 SOLUTIONS

Ethereum hosts two distinct account types:

- **Externally Owned Accounts (EOAs)**: Controlled by private keys and capable of initiating transactions

- **Contract Accounts**: Governed by their contract code and can execute complex functions when transactions are received

Table 4-1. Accounts: EOA vs. Contract Account[1]

Feature	EOA	Contract Account
Control	By a private key	By contract code
Transactions	Can initiate transactions	Can only respond to received transactions
Creation	Created by users	Created when a contract is deployed
Use Case	Holding, sending/receiving ETH and other crypto-assets, interacting with DApps	Smart contract operations
Example	Coinbase Wallet, MetaMask	Coinbase.com

Coinbase operates both as a crypto brokerage and a wallet provider, offering distinct services tailored to the nature of the account – whether it's an Externally Owned Account (EOA) or a Contract Account. This differentiation underpins their provision of both custodial and non-custodial wallet solutions to meet diverse user needs.[2]

CHAPTER 4   THE PILLARS OF WEB3: ETHEREUM'S WALLET, FAUCET AND LAYER 2 SOLUTIONS

Figure 4-1. *Coinbase.com (Left) Logo vs. Coinbase Wallet (Right) Logo (Source:* `https://help.coinbase.com/en/wallet/getting-started/what-s-the-difference-between-coinbase-com-and-wallet`*)*

Coinbase.com As a Crypto Brokerage (Contract Account): Utilising Coinbase.com for buying or selling cryptocurrency engages the platform's role as a Contract Account. In this capacity, all transactions are managed through the platform's smart contracts, not directly by users. This arrangement is typical of custodial wallets, where Coinbase retains control over the private keys, securing the assets purchased on their exchange. Users must complete a Know Your Customer (KYC) process, enhancing security and compliance. This setup exemplifies the custodial aspect, where a third party manages the security and access to funds.

Coinbase Wallet (EOA): In contrast, the Coinbase Wallet operates as a non-custodial solution, typifying an EOA. It allows users to retain direct control over their cryptocurrencies by storing the private keys on their own devices. This setup demands that users maintain their 12-word recovery phrase securely since the loss of this phrase means irreversible loss of access to their funds. The direct control afforded by EOAs enables real-time interactions with the blockchain and decentralised applications (DApps), such as engaging in decentralised exchange (DEX) trading, lending and liquidity pools.

113

Coinbase also offers a hybrid solution in the form of a DApp wallet, blending both custodial and non-custodial features. In this hybrid model, Coinbase manages one part of your private key, while the other resides securely on your device, providing a balance between ease of use and control over assets.

The clear distinction between EOAs and Contract Accounts is pivotal. EOAs offer full user control and necessitate private key management for all operations, emphasising user responsibility for security. Conversely, Contract Accounts operate under automated governance by contractual rules, where users do not handle private keys directly. This distinction is critical in highlighting the diverse array of services Coinbase offers, catering to both novice users seeking simplicity and security and experienced users demanding greater control over their digital assets.

Setting Up and Using a Wallet: The MetaMask Example

Transitioning from discussing the intricacies of Coinbase's wallet services, we now focus on setting up and using a purely EOA-based wallet, such as MetaMask. MetaMask is widely recognised for its role in the Web3 infrastructure, offering a user-friendly interface for interacting with the Ethereum blockchain and beyond. Here's how to get started with MetaMask:

1. **Download and Install**: Visit the official MetaMask website (`https://metamask.io/`) or your device's app store to download and install the MetaMask extension for your browser or the mobile app for your phone.

CHAPTER 4   THE PILLARS OF WEB3: ETHEREUM'S WALLET, FAUCET AND LAYER 2 SOLUTIONS

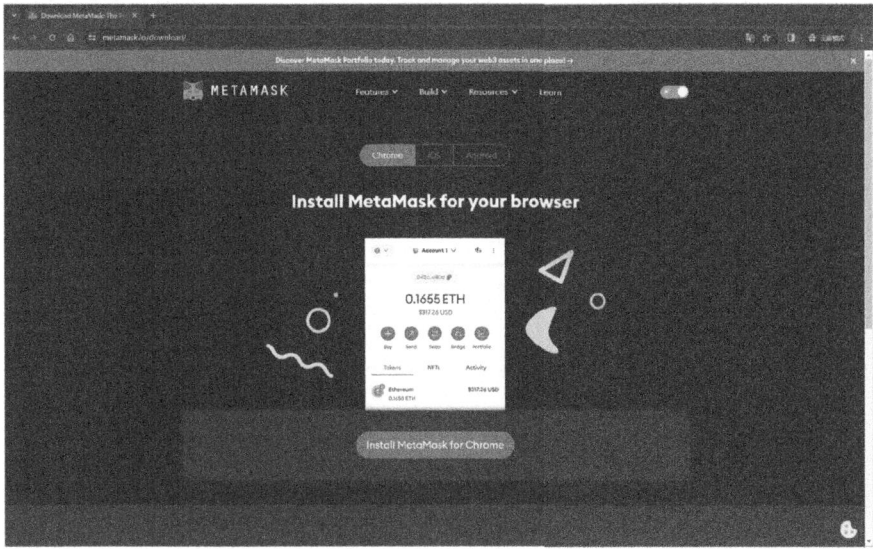

Figure 4-2. *MetaMask Download Page*

Figure 4-2 shows the download page for MetaMask. This page is the hub for downloading the MetaMask extension, ensuring that you get the legitimate version of the wallet.

Select the Chrome Version: On the download page, you will find options for different platforms – Chrome, iOS and Android. Since we're focusing on using MetaMask with Chrome, click the 'Install MetaMask for Chrome' button. There's no functional difference between the versions; they all provide the same features and security across different devices.

Once you click the Chrome version button, you'll be redirected to the Chrome Web Store. From there, you can add the MetaMask extension to your browser by clicking the 'Add to Chrome' button. A pop-up window will appear, asking for permissions that the MetaMask extension requires to operate. Review the permissions, and if you agree, proceed by clicking 'Add Extension'. This will initiate the download and installation process.

2. **Create a Wallet**: Follow the prompts to create a new wallet. During this process, you will create a password that encrypts your wallet, ensuring that only you have access to it.

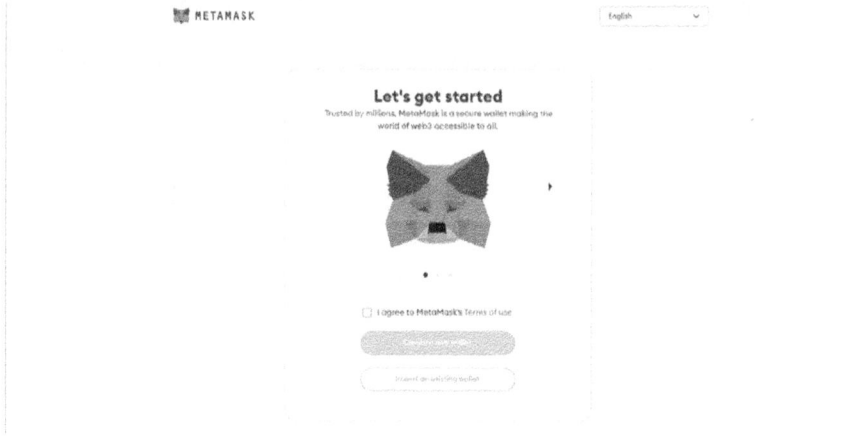

Figure 4-3. MetaMask Download Landing Page

The first step in using MetaMask is creating a new wallet. This process starts with setting a strong password, which is your first line of defence. It's essential to choose a password that is both secure and memorable, as this password will encrypt your wallet data and ensure that only you can access your funds and manage your assets.

CHAPTER 4   THE PILLARS OF WEB3: ETHEREUM'S WALLET, FAUCET AND LAYER 2 SOLUTIONS

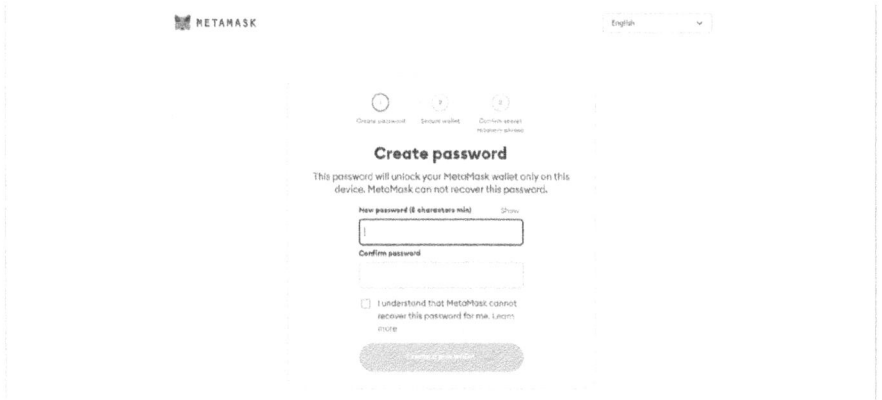

Figure 4-4. *Setting a Password in MetaMask*

MetaMask emphasises the importance of this password, reminding users that the password cannot be recovered by MetaMask itself. This design is a fundamental aspect of self-custody, placing the responsibility of wallet security in the hands of the user.

3. **Backup**: Securely back up the 12-word recovery phrase provided during the setup process. This seed phrase, which can be extended up to 24 words for enhanced security against brute-force attacks, is crucial as it's the only way to restore your wallet if you forget your password or if your device is lost or damaged. In practice, the mnemonic phrase should never be shared or exposed to others, as it grants complete access to your wallet. For added security, it's possible to generate a mnemonic phrase using tools like the one available at Ian Coleman's BIP39 Tool[3] and then use this same phrase to recover your wallets in applications like MetaMask.

CHAPTER 4   THE PILLARS OF WEB3: ETHEREUM'S WALLET, FAUCET AND LAYER 2 SOLUTIONS

This flexibility ensures that you can manage your security across different platforms while maintaining control over your digital assets.

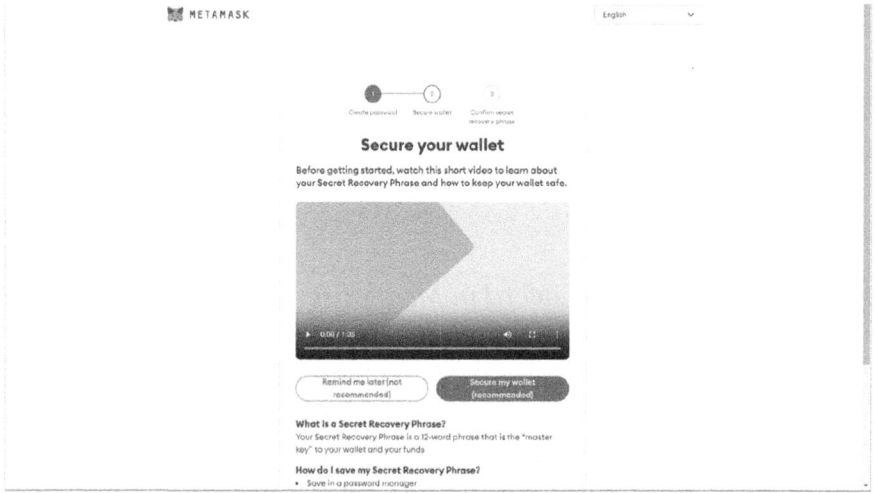

Figure 4-5. Securing Your MetaMask Wallet

Following the password creation, MetaMask prompts you to secure your wallet with a secret recovery phrase. This phrase acts as a master key to your wallet, allowing you to regain access to your funds on any device. This crucial step is safeguarded with tips and best practices to ensure your phrase remains confidential and secure.

CHAPTER 4   THE PILLARS OF WEB3: ETHEREUM'S WALLET, FAUCET AND LAYER 2 SOLUTIONS

Figure 4-6. *Write Down Your Secret Recovery Phrase*

Figure 4-7. *Confirm Secret Recovery Phrase*

MetaMask will ask you to write down and confirm your secret recovery phrase to ensure that you've recorded it accurately. This process reinforces the importance of the recovery phrase and helps prevent any mistakes in recording the phrase, which could be disastrous if you ever need to restore your wallet.

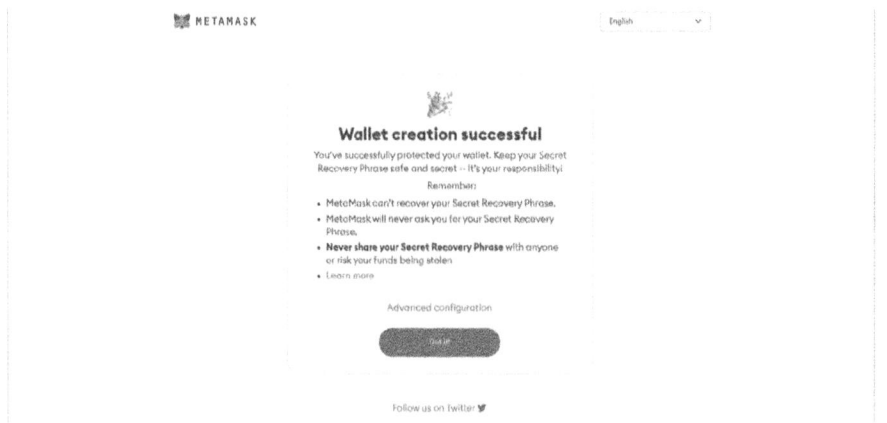

Figure 4-8. *Successful Wallet Creation*

Upon successful verification of your secret recovery phrase, MetaMask confirms that your wallet has been created and secured. A final reminder underscores the gravity of keeping your recovery phrase private, as MetaMask cannot help you recover it if lost. You're now ready to venture into the world of Web3 with your MetaMask wallet as your gateway.

4. **Fund Your Wallet and Interact with DApps**: After funding your MetaMask wallet, you'll arrive at a pivotal moment where your journey within the

CHAPTER 4   THE PILLARS OF WEB3: ETHEREUM'S WALLET, FAUCET AND LAYER 2 SOLUTIONS

Web3 realm truly begins. This interface, as shown in the image, is your command centre for managing and using Ethereum and other ERC20 tokens, as well as interacting with decentralised applications (DApps).

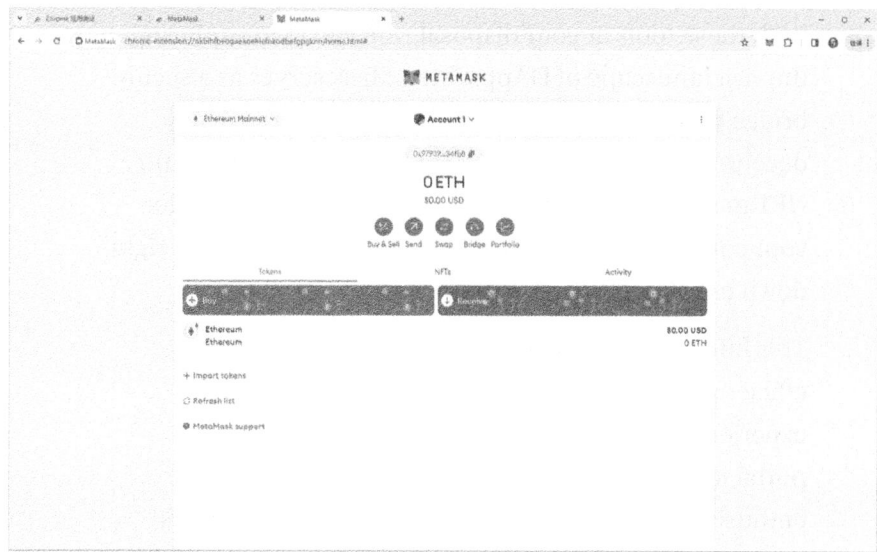

Figure 4-9. *Navigating Your MetaMask Wallet Interface*

The MetaMask wallet provides various functionalities directly accessible from this screen:

- **Buy & Sell**: Facilitates the purchase and sale of Ethereum, sometimes through integrated third-party services

- **Send**: Allows you to send Ethereum or tokens to other addresses on the blockchain

- **Swap**: MetaMask's built-in feature to swap one token for another directly within the wallet

- **Bridge**: A function to move assets between different networks, such as from a Layer 2 solution back to the Ethereum mainnet

- **Portfolio**: Keeps track of your cryptocurrency holdings and their current market value

With these tools at your disposal, you can start exploring the vast landscape of DApps. MetaMask serves as a secure bridge between your assets and applications such as decentralised exchanges (DEXs), lending platforms and NFT marketplaces. Each transaction you make is under your complete control, from the decision to initiate it right down to setting the transaction fee.

This interface is a testament to the simplicity and efficiency that MetaMask brings to the Web3 user experience, providing a streamlined and intuitive portal for both newcomers and seasoned blockchain enthusiasts. Whether you're engaged in complex DeFi protocols or simply managing your digital asset portfolio, MetaMask equips you with the tools you need, all accessible from this centralised dashboard.

CHAPTER 4   THE PILLARS OF WEB3: ETHEREUM'S WALLET, FAUCET AND LAYER 2 SOLUTIONS

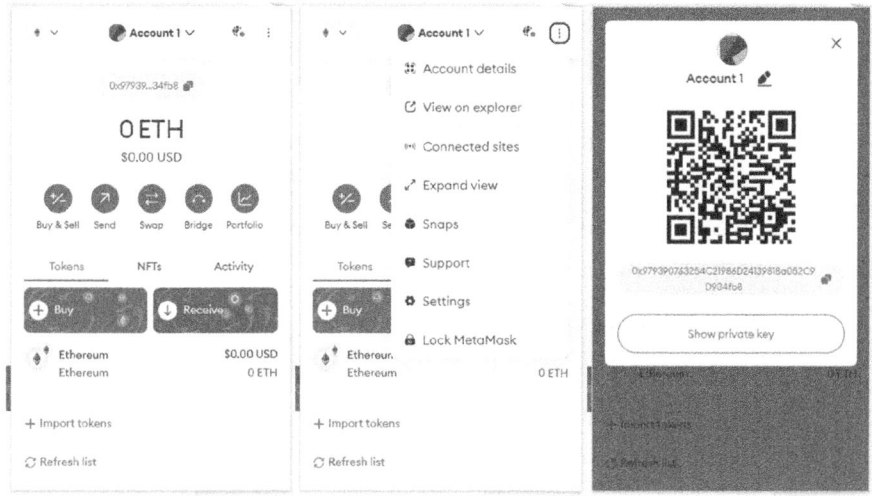

Figure 4-10. Your MetaMask Externally Owned Account Wallet Address

When you open the MetaMask extension from your browser's toolbar, you are presented with a clean and intuitive interface, designed to make your journey into Web3 as seamless as possible.

Clicking the three dots in the upper-right corner reveals a drop-down menu packed with options. From here, you can delve into 'Account details', 'View on explorer' to see your transactions on the blockchain, manage 'Connected sites' and access other settings. This menu is the control centre for customising and securing your MetaMask experience.

This view provides a snapshot of your wallet, displaying your Ethereum balance and offering quick access to essential functions. It is here where you can find your unique Ethereum address, represented both in the traditional hexadecimal format (0x979390763254C21986D24139818a052C9D934fb8) and as a QR code for easy sharing and transactions. Your public address is like a mailbox for your digital assets; anyone can send Ethereum or tokens to this address, but only you can access and manage them with your private key.

A warning screen within the MetaMask extension cautions users about the importance of keeping their private key secure. It explains that the private key provides full access to the wallet and funds and should never be shared with anyone. Phishing attacks often target unsuspecting users to steal this sensitive information.

After acknowledging the security warning and entering your password, you can choose to reveal your private key. This key is the encrypted version of your wallet's seed phrase and grants complete control over your funds. It is imperative to keep this key private and secure at all times. This is just an example to show you that the private key is 2e9d5342cb7237aa66499e5923fe7d93b59488 59e22548ba33238af855ee7d05, **but in actual use, you must never share your private key**.

CHAPTER 4   THE PILLARS OF WEB3: ETHEREUM'S WALLET, FAUCET AND LAYER 2 SOLUTIONS

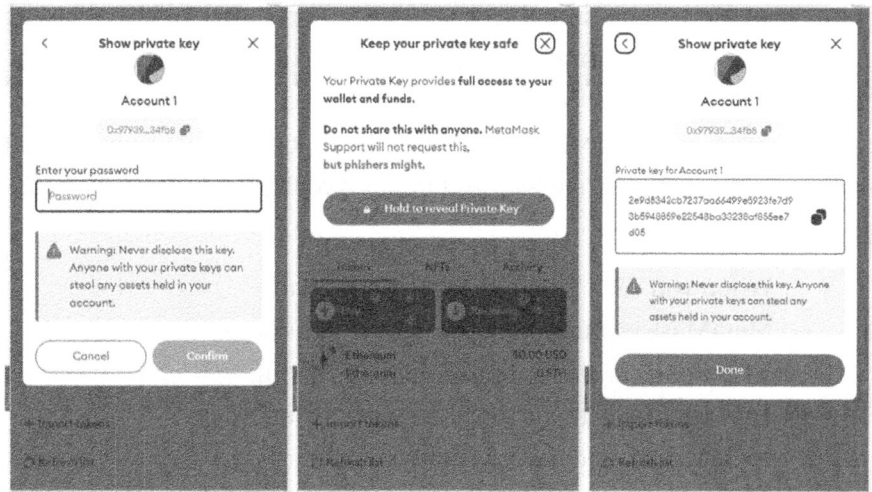

Figure 4-11. Your Private Key

The 12-word recovery phrase and the private key serve two critical but distinct roles in wallet security and access:

- **12-Word Recovery Phrase**: Also known as a seed phrase, this is a human-readable format of your wallet's master key. It is generated when you first create your wallet and can be used to restore access to your wallet on any device. This phrase is crucial for backup and recovery purposes.

- **Private Key**: This is a cryptographic key that allows you to sign transactions and proves ownership of your wallet and its contents. It is mathematically related to your public address and is generated from your seed phrase. Unlike the seed phrase, which can regenerate an entire wallet, each private key corresponds to a specific address within your wallet.

CHAPTER 4   THE PILLARS OF WEB3: ETHEREUM'S WALLET, FAUCET AND LAYER 2 SOLUTIONS

Both the seed phrase and the private key are essential for maintaining control over your wallet, but they should never be revealed to anyone else. Sharing these could result in the loss of your digital assets. MetaMask provides a user-centric design that emphasises security, ensuring users are aware of the importance of these credentials and the risks associated with mishandling them.

When you click 'View on explorer' in your MetaMask wallet, you're directed to Etherscan, where you can see an array of details about your wallet's activity, including your balance, transactions and any associated gas fees.

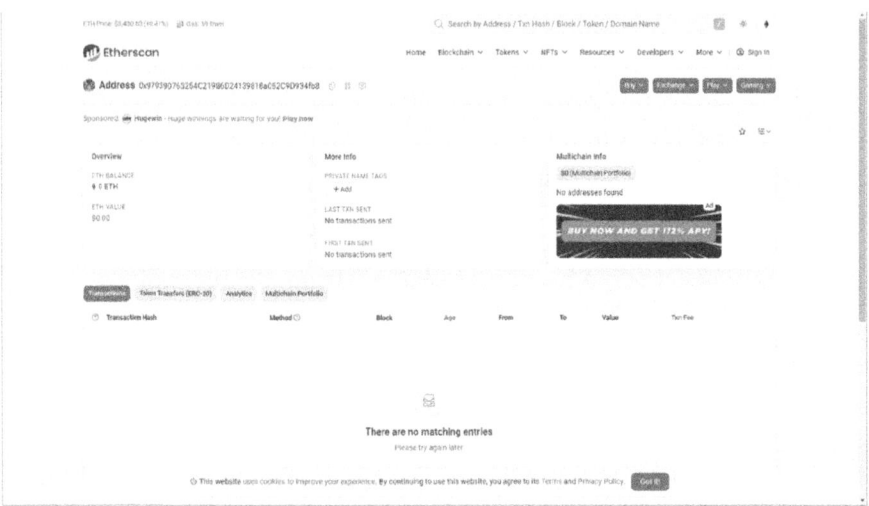

Figure 4-12. Screenshot of Etherscan

CHAPTER 4   THE PILLARS OF WEB3: ETHEREUM'S WALLET, FAUCET AND LAYER 2 SOLUTIONS

Ethereum Explorer: Etherscan

Etherscan is essentially a search engine and analytics platform for the Ethereum blockchain. It allows you to view public data like transactions, smart contracts and addresses on the Ethereum network.

Etherscan works by retrieving real-time data from the Ethereum blockchain, maintaining an organised record of this data and presenting it to users in an easily navigable interface. It doesn't store your private keys or allow you to trade; instead, it serves as a comprehensive database of on-chain activities, smart contracts and transactions.

The platform is widely used for various purposes, such as tracking wallet activities, examining transaction and block details, reading and interacting with smart contracts, checking real-time gas prices to estimate transaction fees and much more. For developers, it offers API access to its blockchain explorer data, which can be particularly helpful for creating decentralised applications.

You don't need an account to use Etherscan, but having one can grant you additional functionalities like setting up alerts for transactions to your addresses. Importantly, Etherscan is a tool that can help ensure transparency and security in your blockchain interactions by allowing you to monitor wallet authorisations and revoke them if necessary, helping to prevent unauthorised access to your assets.

4.2 Dripping Resources for Blockchain Newcomers: Faucets

In the burgeoning world of blockchain, a 'faucet' serves as a pivotal starting point for those new to the space. A faucet is a system that dispenses small, free amounts of cryptocurrency, acting as a vital resource for users to experience cryptocurrency transactions firsthand without the need for an initial investment. This not only provides a practical learning experience but also supports the wider ecosystem by fostering a deeper understanding of transaction processes within the blockchain network.

The operation of a faucet is underpinned by a simple mechanism: it is typically funded by donations or advertisements and programmed to release small quantities of cryptocurrency at specified intervals or for completing certain tasks. This tool is particularly crucial in test networks like Ethereum's Goerli or Sepolia, where developers and users can simulate transactions, test applications and ensure the integrity of their projects in a risk-free environment.

Faucets play a role beyond the mere distribution of tokens; they are also an introduction to the concept of airdrops. An airdrop involves the distribution of tokens, usually for free, to the digital wallets of the active members of the blockchain community to encourage engagement or disperse rewards. Both faucets and airdrops are central to the infrastructure that supports the growth and accessibility of blockchain technology, functioning as a foundational pathway for new entrants into the space.

The smart contract example for an Ethereum faucet is designed to dispense a specified amount of ETH when requested by a user. The contract includes features such as

- An ownership designation that can be transferred
- A set amount of ETH to dispense per request
- A donation function to receive funds
- Tracking of addresses that have requested ETH
- A time lock to limit requests to once per day

Here is an example of a simple Solidity smart contract for an Ethereum faucet based on the common features described in online resources.

Smart Contract Example – Faucet

```solidity
pragma solidity ^0.8.3;

contract ETHFaucet {
    address public owner;
    uint public dispenseAmount = 1 ether;
    mapping(address => uint) public lastAccessTime;

    constructor() payable {
        owner = msg.sender;
    }

    modifier onlyOwner {
        require(msg.sender == owner, "Only the owner can call
        this function.");
        _;
    }

    function requestEth() public {
        require(address(this).balance >= dispenseAmount,
        "Insufficient funds in faucet.");
        require(lastAccessTime[msg.sender] + 1 days < block.
        timestamp, "Wait 24h");

        payable(msg.sender).transfer(dispenseAmount);
        lastAccessTime[msg.sender] = block.timestamp;
    }

    function donateToFaucet() public payable {}

    function setDispenseAmount(uint newAmount) public
    onlyOwner {
        dispenseAmount = newAmount;
    }
}
```

This contract allows users to request a fixed amount of ETH once every 24 hours and allows for donations to the faucet. The owner can set the dispense amount. Keep in mind that for a real implementation, additional security checks and optimisations would be necessary. This code is for educational purposes and should be thoroughly audited before use on the mainnet.

To illustrate the process of using the faucet, let's take the Ethereum test network, Sepolia, as an example. To receive test ETH (SepoliaETH), one would need to do the following:

1. To get started with Ethereum's Sepolia test network using MetaMask, open the MetaMask extension in your browser. At the top of the MetaMask interface where the network is displayed, click to open the network selection drop-down menu. If the test networks are not visible, toggle the 'Show test networks' option on. From the list of available networks, select 'Sepolia'. MetaMask will then switch to the Sepolia test network, and your account will be connected to it.

    You can now interact with the Sepolia network, which mirrors the Ethereum mainnet environment, allowing you to test transactions and smart contract interactions without using real ETH. Remember to ensure that the wallet address displayed in MetaMask is correct and that you have access to the private keys or seed phrase for that wallet.

CHAPTER 4   THE PILLARS OF WEB3: ETHEREUM'S WALLET, FAUCET AND LAYER 2 SOLUTIONS

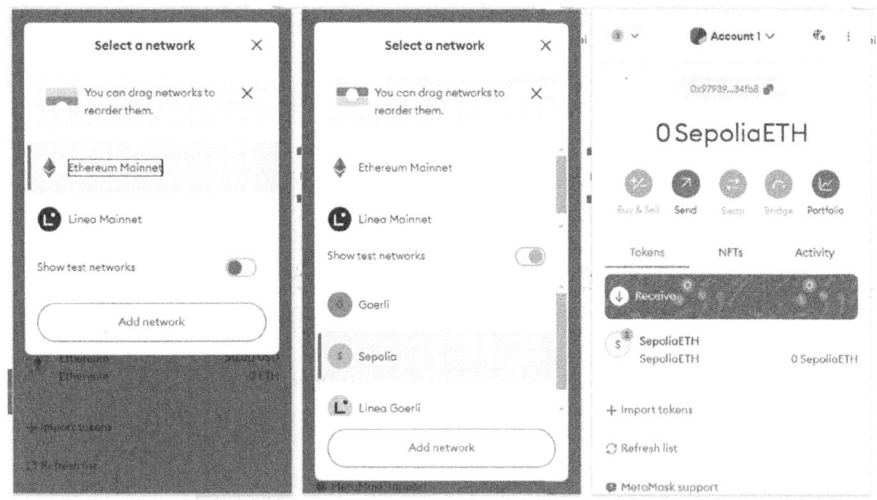

Figure 4-13. *Sepolia Network*

2. Visit a reputable Sepolia faucet website, like the one provided by Alchemy (www.alchemy.com/faucets/ethereum-sepolia). On this platform, you can request free Sepolia ETH to be used for testing purposes.

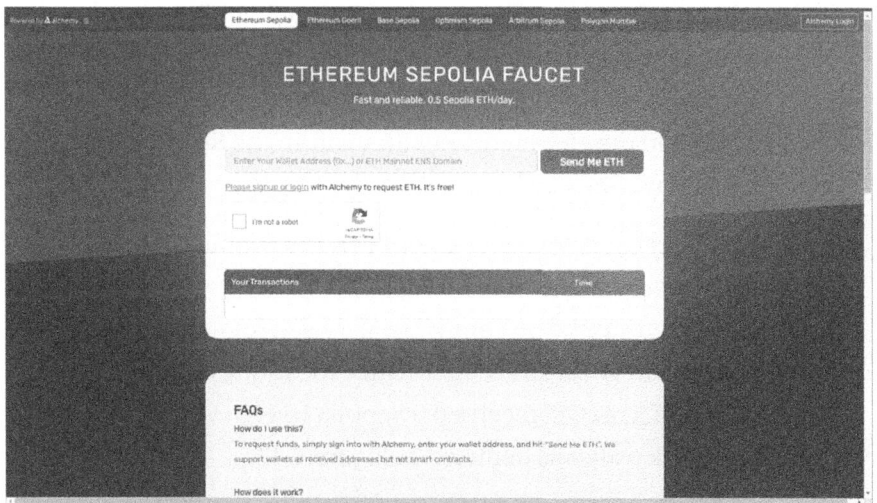

Figure 4-14. *Alchemy Sepolia Faucet*
(Source: www.alchemy.com/faucets/ethereum-sepolia*)*

These websites usually require you to

- Sign in or create an account with the faucet provider.
- Enter your Sepolia wallet address in the designated field.
- Complete any necessary security checks, such as CAPTCHAs, to confirm that you're not a bot.
- Click the 'Send Me ETH' or equivalent button to receive the test ETH in your wallet.

When using the Sepolia faucet, you can request up to 0.5 Sepolia ETH per day. This limitation ensures fair distribution among users and simulates a real-world environment where transactional limits are often in place. This daily allowance of test ETH allows developers and testers to conduct numerous transactions and test various blockchain operations without the fear of running out of funds too quickly. It's an ideal setup for continuous development and testing on the Sepolia testnet. Remember, the provided test ETH has no real-world value and is meant solely for testing and development activities within the Sepolia testnet environment.

3. After entering your wallet address on the Sepolia Faucet website and completing any required verification steps, you simply need to wait for approximately 10–15 seconds. Once the request is processed, you will receive 0.5 Sepolia ETH in your MetaMask wallet as depicted in Figure 4-15.

CHAPTER 4   THE PILLARS OF WEB3: ETHEREUM'S WALLET, FAUCET AND LAYER 2 SOLUTIONS

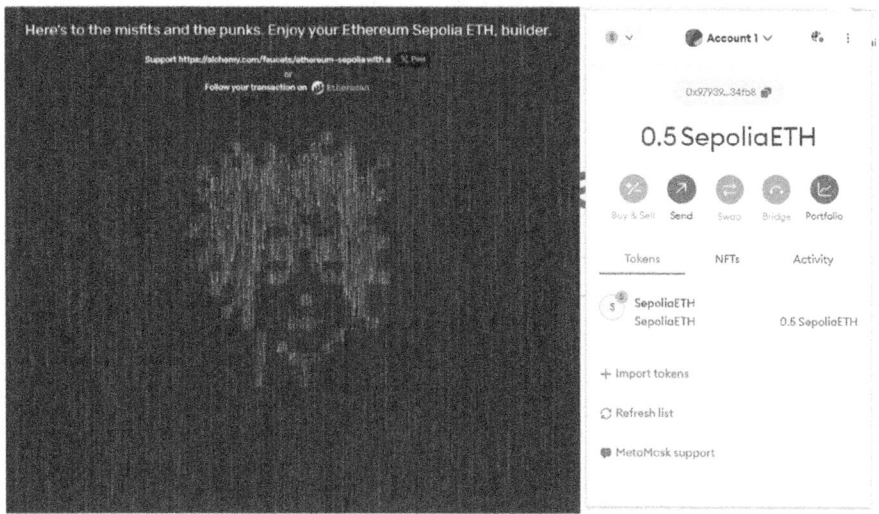

Figure 4-15.   *Updated Balance on the MetaMask Wallet – Sepolia*

This transaction, although not on the Ethereum mainnet, can be verified on the Sepolia Testnet version of Etherscan. Just look for the Sepolia Testnet indicator in the top corner of the Etherscan page. This allows you to follow the transaction and confirm that the test ETH has been credited to your account.

Figure 4-16. *Sepolia Testnet Etherscan (Source:* `https://sepolia.etherscan.io/`*)*

This process allows newcomers to not only acquire test assets without cost but also to engage with the blockchain environment directly, fostering a practical understanding of its operations and the potential applications within.

4.3 Expanding Horizons with Layer 2 Solutions

Layer 2 solutions on the Ethereum network are essential because they address the blockchain trilemma of decentralisation, scalability and security. The blockchain trilemma posits that it is challenging to achieve all three properties simultaneously; typically, a blockchain can only excel at two out of the three. Ethereum, like other Layer 1 blockchains, is decentralised and secure but has struggled with scalability, especially as the network has grown and the demand for block space has increased. This results in high transaction fees and slower processing times during periods of congestion.

CHAPTER 4   THE PILLARS OF WEB3: ETHEREUM'S WALLET, FAUCET AND LAYER 2 SOLUTIONS

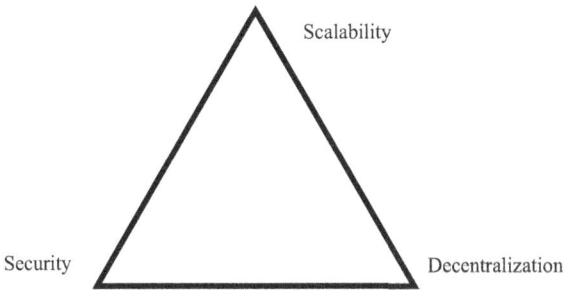

Figure 4-17. *Blockchain Trilemma*

Layer 2 solutions, such as Rollups, aim to alleviate these issues by handling transactions off the main chain, thus increasing throughput and reducing costs without compromising on the network's decentralisation or security. Rollups work by grouping or 'rolling up' multiple transactions into a single one and then submitting this to the main Ethereum chain. This process helps in relieving congestion on the network and makes transactions faster and less expensive.

There are two main types of Rollups: Optimistic Rollups and ZK-Rollups. Optimistic Rollups assume transactions are valid by default and only run computations in the event of a challenge, whereas ZK-Rollups use zero-knowledge proofs to verify transactions' validity without revealing their contents. Both have their own set of advantages and trade-offs. ZK-Rollups, for instance, offer faster transaction speeds and lower fees but require a more complex setup that can lead to centralisation. Optimistic Rollups, on the other hand, are easier to implement but have a challenge period that can delay withdrawals.

Here's a summary of their differences based on several key factors:

1. **Security**: Optimistic Rollups depend on fraud proofs and economic incentives to ensure transaction validity, requiring only one honest node to challenge fraud. However, this means that security relies on the presence of honest actors. ZK-Rollups,

on the other hand, use cryptographic proofs (zero-knowledge proofs) to validate transactions, offering mathematical security guarantees without relying on human validators.

2. **Cost**: Optimistic Rollups typically have lower computation costs since they don't require specialised hardware for fraud proofs. However, they do post all transaction data on the Ethereum main chain, which could increase costs. ZK-Rollups can reduce costs with efficient data compression techniques, but they have higher hardware requirements for generating cryptographic proofs, which can make them more expensive for users.

3. **Transaction Finality**: In Optimistic Rollups, there's a challenge period which can delay transaction finality. ZK-Rollups offer immediate withdrawals due to the validity proofs, which confirm the authenticity of transactions without delay.

4. **EVM Compatibility**: Optimistic Rollups are compatible with the Ethereum Virtual Machine (EVM), making it easier for developers to transition existing Ethereum-based applications. ZK-Rollups are not fully EVM compatible, which can present higher barriers for developers.

As for specific project examples, Optimistic Rollups such as Arbitrum and Optimism have been utilised by Ethereum-based decentralised exchanges like Uniswap and SushiSwap. ZK-Rollups, such as those used by Polygon ID for private on-chain verification, offer high security and privacy standards, which are crucial for identity verification protocols.

Table 4-2 shows a comparison of projects using these technologies.

Table 4-2. Optimistic Rollups vs. ZK-Rollups

Feature	Optimistic Rollups Example	ZK-Rollups Example
EVM Compatibility	Arbitrum, Optimism	Polygon zkEVM, Scroll zkEVM
Transaction Costs	Lower due to minimal data on-chain	Potentially higher due to proof generation
Security	Based on economic incentives and fraud proofs	Based on cryptographic proofs
Use Cases	DeFi applications, decentralised exchanges	Identity verification, private crypto trading

These examples highlight how the choice between Optimistic and ZK-Rollups may depend on the specific needs and priorities of a project, such as cost considerations, security requirements and the desired level of EVM compatibility.[4]

The development and implementation of Layer 2 solutions are crucial for the future of Ethereum as they offer a path towards higher scalability, which is necessary for wider adoption and the overall growth of the network. With the advent of Ethereum 2.0 and sharding, the efficiency and transaction throughput are expected to further increase, reinforcing the network's position in the blockchain ecosystem.[5, 6]

4.4 Summary

This chapter explored the foundational components of Web3, focusing on Ethereum's wallets, faucets, and Layer 2 solutions. It began by highlighting the critical role of blockchain wallets, not just as digital storage solutions, but as personal gateways into the decentralized web. The distinction between Externally Owned Accounts (EOAs) and Contract Accounts was emphasized, with examples such as Coinbase Wallet and MetaMask illustrating how users manage digital assets and identities securely.

The chapter then transitioned to the concept of faucets, tools that distribute small amounts of cryptocurrency, primarily in test networks like Goerli and Sepolia. These faucets allow users, especially newcomers, to engage with blockchain technology without financial risk, helping them understand transaction processes in a practical, hands-on way.

Finally, the discussion covered Layer 2 solutions and their significance in overcoming Ethereum's scalability challenges. Technologies such as Optimistic Rollups and ZK-Rollups were analyzed, showcasing their respective advantages and trade-offs in terms of security, cost, and transaction finality. These solutions are vital for addressing the blockchain trilemma and ensuring that Ethereum can scale while maintaining decentralization and security.

Through this exploration, the chapter underscored the ongoing evolution of Ethereum and its ecosystem, positioning it as a leader in Web3's infrastructure development.

4.5 Notes

1. Chittoda, J. (2019). Mastering Blockchain Programming with Solidity. Packt Publishing. p. 29–30.

2. What's the difference between Coinbase.com and Coinbase Wallet? | Coinbase Help (2022). https://help.coinbase.com/en/wallet/getting-started/what-s-the-difference-between-coinbase-com-and-wallet (Accessed: 9 April 2024).

3. Coleman, I. (2019). BIP39 - Mnemonic Code. https://iancoleman.io/bip39/ (Accessed: 9 April 2024).

4. Synfutures Academy. (2021). Optimistic Rollups vs. ZK Rollups: What's the Difference? SynFutures Academy | Blockchain, Crypto, DeFi & Crypto Derivatives. https://academy.synfutures.com/optimistic-vs-zk-rollups/ (Accessed: 9 April 2024).

5. Layer 2 | Ethereum.org (n.d.). ethereum.org. https://ethereum.org/en/layer-2/ (Accessed: 9 April 2024).

6. Deutscheda (30 March 2024). How Layer 2 Solutions Are Helping Ethereum Scale – Deutsche Digital Assets. Deutsche Digital Assets. https://deutschedigitalassets.com/insights/news/ethereum-layer-2-solutions/ (Accessed: 9 April 2024).

PART III

Decentralised Finance (DeFi) and Applications

CHAPTER 5

The Rise of Decentralised Finance (DeFi)

5.1 Core Concepts and Applications of DeFi

Decentralised finance (DeFi) encompasses a broad range of financial services on blockchain technology that operates independently of traditional financial intermediaries like banks, brokerages or exchanges. Utilising smart contracts on blockchains such as Ethereum, DeFi applications offer a platform for lending, borrowing, trading, investment and risk management without the need for a centralised authority.

DeFi revolutionises financial transactions by leveraging blockchain technology, initially popularised by Bitcoin. Unlike traditional financial systems that rely on centralised entities like banks and credit card companies, DeFi operates on a distributed ledger, allowing for a decentralised and transparent transaction process. This model eliminates the need for intermediaries, granting users more control over their funds and enabling faster, more sophisticated financial operations.

CHAPTER 5   THE RISE OF DECENTRALISED FINANCE (DEFI)

The emergence of Bitcoin showcased the potential for digital assets to facilitate direct transactions without middlemen, contrasting sharply with conventional digital payment systems such as Visa and PayPal. In traditional settings, financial institutions act as gatekeepers, controlling and recording transactions on their private ledgers. DeFi, however, cuts these intermediaries out, ensuring that transactions like purchasing a coffee or engaging in complex financial activities such as loans, insurance and derivatives are executed directly between the parties involved.

Initially referred to as 'open finance', DeFi has expanded the blockchain's utility beyond mere value transfer to encompass a wide array of financial applications. This shift towards a more open, inclusive and efficient financial ecosystem challenges the centralised control model, advocating for a system where transactions and financial services are governed by protocols and smart contracts on the blockchain. This not only enhances transparency and security but also opens up financial services to a broader segment of the global population, promoting financial inclusion.

Core Concepts of DeFi

- **Smart Contracts and Blockchain**: The foundation of DeFi is smart contracts, self-executing contracts with the terms of the agreement between buyer and seller directly written into lines of code. These contracts run on blockchain technology, ensuring transparency, immutability and decentralisation.

- **Permissionless**: DeFi platforms are typically permissionless, meaning anyone with an Internet connection can access them without any approval from a governing body. This characteristic fosters financial inclusion and equality.

- **Interoperability and Composability:** Often referred to as 'money Legos', DeFi protocols are designed to be interoperable and composable, allowing for the creation of complex financial services by combining different DeFi products seamlessly.

- **Decentralisation:** The degree of decentralisation varies across DeFi platforms, determined by factors like governance models, the autonomy of smart contracts and the distribution of token ownership. True decentralisation removes the need for trust in a central authority, replacing it with trust in code.

- **Intrinsic Characteristics:** The shift from centralised (TradFi) to decentralised systems introduces a new financial paradigm that is permissionless, inclusive and often referred to as 'trustless' due to its reliance on transparent and immutable blockchain technology.

- **Functional Differences:** Unlike traditional finance, which relies on centralised entities and double-entry bookkeeping, DeFi utilises blockchain technology for an economy-wide, triple-entry accounting system that enhances transparency and efficiency.

- **Operational Differences:** DeFi operations are more transparent and non-custodial, enabling users to have full control over their assets without the need for intermediaries. This contrasts with the opaque and custodial nature of traditional financial services.

- **Regulatory Landscape:** The regulatory framework for DeFi is evolving. While DeFi operates under the premise of being governed by code, existing laws and regulations still apply, highlighting the need for a balance between innovation and consumer protection.

CHAPTER 5   THE RISE OF DECENTRALISED FINANCE (DEFI)

DeFi vs. TradFi (Traditional Finance)

DeFi represents a transformative shift from traditional finance (TradFi) towards a more open, efficient and inclusive financial system leveraging blockchain technology. Unlike TradFi's centralised and permissioned frameworks, DeFi offers a permissionless and transparent environment, eliminating intermediaries and reducing transaction times. It introduces innovative financial services through smart contracts, ensuring immediate settlement and promoting a trustless ecosystem where transactions are irreversible and publicly verifiable. While TradFi benefits from established regulatory practices and user familiarity, DeFi challenges these norms by offering non-custodial asset control and fostering rapid technological innovation. This evolution underscores a pivotal movement towards democratising finance, though it also emphasises the need for users to navigate emerging risks and regulatory landscapes independently.[1]

Table 5-1. The Comparison of TradFi and DeFi Across Various Dimensions[2]

Aspect	Traditional Finance (TradFi)	Decentralised Finance (DeFi)
Access	Permissioned models with exclusive, controlled access	Permissionless models offering inclusivity and immutability
Data Integrity	Segmented, reliant on intermediaries	Composable, interoperable 'money Legos'
Interoperability	Limited due to centralised control	High, facilitated by blockchain technology
Settlement	Can take days (T+day(s)) due to intermediaries	Immediate settlement through smart contracts

(continued)

Table 5-1. (*continued*)

Aspect	Traditional Finance (TradFi)	Decentralised Finance (DeFi)
Value Representation	Uses data to record nominal value, often linked to real-world assets	Considers data as value itself, with blockchain verifying transactions
Accounting	Double-entry system requiring manual reconciliation	Triple-entry system with blockchain as an immutable record
Trust	Centralised institutions as trusted intermediaries	Trustless system where code enforces rules
Data Availability	Transaction history is private and controlled	Transaction history is publicly accessible and transparent
Innovation	Incremental and sustaining, with slower adaptation to new technologies	Radical and disruptive, quickly adapting and innovating
User Experience	Established and user-friendly, but innovation-limited	Nascent and often requires technical knowledge, but highly innovative
Risk Management	Managed through regulations and established practices	Individual responsibility to understand and manage risks
Transaction Reversibility	Reversible with the possibility to amend permissions	Mostly irreversible, with transactions being append-only
Custody	Custodial, with intermediaries controlling assets	Mostly non-custodial, granting users control over their assets
Regulatory Compliance	Heavily regulated with clear guidelines	Emerging regulatory landscape, with code and law defining operations
Transparency	Operationally opaque, disclosing limited information to authorities	Fully transparent with all operations verifiable on the blockchain

CHAPTER 5   THE RISE OF DECENTRALISED FINANCE (DEFI)

The DeFi landscape is rich with applications that are reshaping the financial sector. These platforms harness the power of blockchain to offer services ranging from exchanges and lending to stablecoins and insurance, each with the goal of decentralising and democratising finance.[3, 4, 5] Table 5-2 exemplifies the breadth of DeFi's reach, highlighting key players and innovations that exemplify this new era of financial independence and interoperability.

Table 5-2. *DeFi Applications*

DeFi Application Category	Examples/Platforms
Decentralised Exchanges (DEXs)	Uniswap, 1inch, SushiSwap, Balancer, dYdX, PancakeSwap
Lending Platforms	Aave, Compound, Dharma
Stablecoins	Dai, Gemini Dollar
Insurance	Etherisc, Nexus Mutual
Prediction Markets/Oracles	Chainlink, Band Protocol, Pyth

Decentralised Exchanges (DEXs)

Decentralised exchanges (DEXs) have become an integral part of the cryptocurrency landscape, providing an alternative to traditional, centralised exchanges by facilitating peer-to-peer cryptocurrency trading directly between users. DEXs utilise smart contracts on blockchain platforms like Ethereum to execute trades without the need for intermediaries, preserving the user's control and ownership of their private keys throughout the transaction process.

The concept of DEXs is built on the ethos of 'disintermediation', aiming to remove middlemen from financial transactions. This approach has led to a surge in popularity for DEXs due to their numerous benefits, including the availability of a broader range of tokens, enhanced user anonymity, reduced counterparty risk and increased security, as users maintain custody of their funds. These benefits come from the fact that DEXs allow users to trade directly from their wallets without relinquishing control of their assets to the exchange.

There are various models of DEXs, each addressing different aspects of decentralised trading:

- **Automated Market Makers (AMMs)**: This model removes the traditional order book and uses liquidity pools and smart contracts to set the price of assets. AMMs have gained popularity due to their ability to provide liquidity and allow for earning interest through liquidity mining.

- **On-Chain Order Books**: In this model, all orders, as well as their modifications and cancellations, are recorded on the blockchain. While this method offers high transparency, it can be less practical due to associated fees and potential delays due to blockchain processing times.

- **Off-Chain Order Books**: These DEXs store orders off the blockchain and only use the blockchain for transaction settlement. This approach can offer a balance between decentralised trading and the faster execution typically found on centralised exchanges.

- **DEX Aggregators**: These protocols source liquidity from multiple DEXs to find the most efficient trading routes, potentially offering better prices and lower slippage for users.

Despite their advantages, DEXs also come with challenges, such as potentially higher fees during network congestion, lower trading volumes and liquidity compared to centralised exchanges, and they can be less user-friendly for those new to the cryptocurrency space. Furthermore, the decentralised nature of DEXs means that users must be diligent in safeguarding their private keys, as lost keys equate to irretrievable funds.

The landscape of DEXs is continually evolving, with new innovations seeking to blend different models for improved efficiency and user experience. As the DeFi sector grows, DEXs are expected to see continued innovation and increased usage, aligning with the broader ethos of blockchain and cryptocurrency which emphasises self-sovereignty and trustless transactions.[6, 7]

Lending Platforms

In the DeFi ecosystem, loans are predominantly overcollateralised, meaning borrowers must provide collateral exceeding the value of the loan they're taking out. This concept may seem counterintuitive at first glance – why borrow if you must lock up more valuable assets as collateral? The answer lies in the incentives for both borrowers and lenders within the DeFi space. Lenders participate primarily for compensation, often in the form of interest or governance tokens which can be sold on the market, leading to potential profit. Borrowers, on the other hand, may use these loans for leverage, to maintain exposure to their collateral assets which they speculate will appreciate in value, or for capital efficiency, using otherwise unproductive assets as collateral.

Collateralisation is a crucial mechanism for mitigating financial risk in DeFi. Since blockchain and smart contracts don't rely on traditional credit scores to assess borrower risk, the overcollateralisation acts as a buffer against default. If a borrower fails to repay, the collateral is liquidated

CHAPTER 5   THE RISE OF DECENTRALISED FINANCE (DEFI)

to cover the lender's losses, which contrasts with the traditional finance (TradFi) system that uses a mix of credit scores, regulatory mechanisms and legal enforcement to manage default risks.

Flash loans represent a novel DeFi borrowing mechanism where loans are issued and repaid within the same transaction block. They're uncollateralised, as they rely on the unique principle that if the loan cannot be repaid by the transaction's end, it's as if the loan never happened due to the atomic nature of blockchain transactions. This mechanism allows for sophisticated financial operations like arbitrage, collateral swaps and self-liquidating loans, providing a powerful tool for DeFi users who can leverage these features without the same kind of capital requirements as collateralised loans.

Real-world examples in DeFi lending platforms include Aave's introduction of flash loans, which have opened up new strategies for traders and arbitrageurs, and MakerDAO's collateralised debt positions (CDPs), allowing users to mint DAI against their ETH collateral. These innovative mechanisms have propelled DeFi's growth by expanding the scope of financial operations beyond the reach of traditional banking systems.

Stablecoins

Stablecoins, essential to the DeFi ecosystem, are designed to maintain a stable value against a target price, typically a widely recognised asset like the US dollar. These digital currencies achieve price stability through various mechanisms and can be issued in both centralised and decentralised formats.

Stablecoins are broadly categorised based on two primary criteria:

1. Degree of (De)centralisation

    - **Custodian or Centralised Stablecoins**: These are issued and managed by centralised entities and are often backed by reserves of fiat currencies or other assets.

    - **Non-custodian or Decentralised Stablecoins**: These operate on blockchain technology without a central managing authority and use on-chain collateral or algorithms to maintain their value.

2. Mechanism for Maintaining Their Peg

    - **Reserve-Backed**: These stablecoins maintain a reserve of assets (such as fiat money, commodities or sometimes other cryptocurrencies) to back the value of the stablecoin.

    - **Collateral-Backed**: Similar to reserve-backed, but specifically use cryptocurrency as collateral, which can be more volatile.

    - **Algorithmic**: These do not have a reserve but instead use a set of algorithms to manage the supply of the stablecoin to maintain its peg.

    - **Mixed-Approach**: These stablecoins utilise a combination of the preceding methods to maintain price stability.

Each type comes with its own set of trade-offs concerning capital efficiency, decentralisation and price stability. For example, reserve-backed stablecoins are often seen as more stable and capital efficient but may lack in decentralisation. Collateral-backed stablecoins are decentralised and transparent but may be less capital efficient. Algorithmic stablecoins offer decentralisation and capital efficiency but can sometimes be less stable in maintaining their peg.

The choice of stablecoin depends on user preferences for decentralisation, trust in the issuer and the intended use case within the DeFi ecosystem.

Insurance

In the decentralised context of DeFi, insurance is interpreted in at least two distinct ways. One broader interpretation encompasses coverage against all possible events, whether they occur on-chain or off-chain, online or offline. This wide-ranging approach is facilitated by decentralised prediction markets, which allow the creation and trading of shares for various potential outcomes of future events. Such markets employ decentralised protocols with a game-theoretic foundation to ensure the integrity of event reporting and prevent manipulation by any single participant. These mechanisms are particularly suitable for insuring against diverse scenarios, from adverse weather to the bankruptcy of a centralised partner, although they require sufficient liquidity to be effective.

On the other hand, a narrower interpretation of decentralised insurance is focused specifically on the DeFi space, providing coverage against failures or risks associated with DeFi protocols. This includes protection against technical risks like smart contract failures, liquidity or financial risks that may emerge during extreme market conditions and admin key risks where the protocol may not be fully decentralised.

For example, Nexus Mutual is a DeFi insurance protocol that offers coverage against technical risks and bugs in other smart contracts on the Ethereum blockchain. It allows users to purchase insurance for a specific period and amount, with an independent claims assessment process determining the validity of claims in the event of a smart contract malfunction.[8]

Similarly, Opyn provides insurance for not just smart contract failures but also liquidity, financial and admin key risks. It uses options to hedge against these unexpected events. For instance, through Opyn, users can buy a put option on stablecoin deposits on platforms like Compound, ensuring that they can sell their stablecoin holdings at a predetermined rate in the event of a protocol failure or security breach.[9]

These insurance protocols contribute to the risk management ecosystem in DeFi by offering innovative solutions that align with the principles of decentralisation. They provide users with mechanisms to protect their investments against a variety of risks inherent in this emerging financial technology space.

Prediction Markets/Oracles

Prediction markets and oracles play a crucial role in the decentralised finance (DeFi) ecosystem by enabling innovative financial instruments and mechanisms for information aggregation and dissemination.

Here's an in-depth look at their functionality, significance and some leading platforms in this space:

1. Prediction Markets

    - **Functionality**: Prediction markets in DeFi enable participants to buy and sell contracts based on the outcomes of future events, similar to betting or futures markets but with a broader scope, including non-financial outcomes like election results or weather forecasts. These markets leverage blockchain technology and smart contracts to create decentralised platforms where no central authority is required to match buyers and sellers. Platforms like Augur and TotemFi are prominent examples, utilising Ethereum's ERC20 protocol for creating user-generated markets and offering low fees and innovative reward mechanisms.

- **Advantages over Centralised Markets**: DeFi prediction markets offer significant benefits over their centralised counterparts, including global accessibility, reduced need for intermediaries, lower fees, enhanced privacy and the ability to participate using digital assets. These markets also tend to have more liquidity and can innovate more rapidly thanks to blockchain technology and smart contracts.

2. Oracles

- **The Oracle Problem**: Smart contracts, while autonomous, cannot access off-chain data independently, creating the 'oracle problem'. Oracles solve this by acting as data feeds between the blockchain and the external world, enabling smart contracts to execute based on real-world events. However, designing secure, reliable and decentralised oracles is challenging, with issues around data accuracy, manipulation and centralisation risks.

- **Oracle Designs**: Oracles vary from centralised (single data source) to decentralised (multiple data sources achieving consensus). Each design has its trade-offs regarding speed, security and reliability. Centralised oracles are quicker but pose a single point of failure, while decentralised oracles offer higher security and resistance to manipulation at the cost of speed and efficiency. Innovative platforms like Chainlink and Tellor represent advancements in oracle technology, offering solutions to securely and accurately provide off-chain data to on-chain smart contracts.

- **Significance**: Oracles are vital for the functionality of numerous DeFi applications, including prediction markets, lending platforms and insurance contracts, by ensuring that these applications can interact with real-world data in a trustless manner. The development and integration of reliable oracles are critical for the DeFi ecosystem's growth and stability.

In summary, prediction markets and oracles are foundational components of the DeFi space, offering mechanisms for decentralised betting on future events and securely bridging the gap between blockchain applications and external data. Their continued evolution and adoption are crucial for the DeFi sector's aim to create an open, transparent and accessible financial system.

5.2 Analysis of Mainstream DeFi Protocols

The DeFi (decentralised finance) ecosystem is comprised of various protocols, each contributing unique features, mechanisms and impacts to the broader financial landscape. Among the most influential in this space are Uniswap, Aave and MakerDAO. They each play pivotal roles in liquidity provision, lending and stablecoin issuance. Here's an in-depth look at each protocol along with an evaluation of their performance and impact based on Total Value Locked (TVL), user adoption and their transformative potential on the financial landscape.

Uniswap

Uniswap's evolution has been characterised by continuous innovation and adaptation to meet the ever-changing needs of the DeFi ecosystem. This journey reflects a series of significant upgrades from its initial version to the latest, illustrating the protocol's commitment to improving liquidity, trading efficiency and user experience.

Table 5-3. Uniswap's Evolution[10, 11]

V0 and V1	Uniswap's journey began with the creation of a prototype in 2017, leading to the official launch of Uniswap V1 in November 2018. V1 introduced the Automated Market Maker (AMM) mechanism to the Ethereum blockchain, allowing permissionless token trading without the need for a traditional order book. This version used a constant product model for pricing, laying the foundation for future iterations of Uniswap.
V2	Launched in May 2020, Uniswap V2 introduced significant enhancements, such as enabling ERC20 to ERC20 exchanges and introducing a Time-Weighted Average Price (TWAP) oracle. This version marked Uniswap's emergence as a pivotal player in the DeFi space, significantly increasing its market attention and user base.

(continued)

Table 5-3. (*continued*)

V3	In May 2021, Uniswap V3 was introduced, bringing the innovative concept of concentrated liquidity. This allowed liquidity providers to allocate capital within specific price ranges, optimising capital efficiency and providing better income opportunities. V3 also improved the TWAP oracle's efficiency and introduced multiple fee tiers, catering to different risk preferences among liquidity providers.
V4	The evolution continued with the development of Uniswap V4, which aims to further enhance flexibility and gas efficiency. It introduces customisable pools through hooks, allowing developers to augment the concentrated liquidity model with new functionalities. This version also moves towards a singleton contract approach for all pools, significantly reducing the deployment cost and gas fees associated with pool creation and trades. Moreover, V4 reintroduces native ETH support, simplifying transactions and potentially reducing gas costs.

Each version of Uniswap has progressively addressed the limitations of its predecessors, introducing new features that have significantly impacted the DeFi ecosystem. From facilitating simple ERC20/ETH trades to enabling complex, concentrated liquidity positions and customisable pool functionalities, Uniswap's evolution mirrors the broader growth and increasing sophistication of the DeFi sector. This continuous innovation has solidified Uniswap's position as a key infrastructure component in DeFi, supporting a wide range of applications and services while providing users with more efficient, flexible and cost-effective trading solutions.

CHAPTER 5   THE RISE OF DECENTRALISED FINANCE (DEFI)

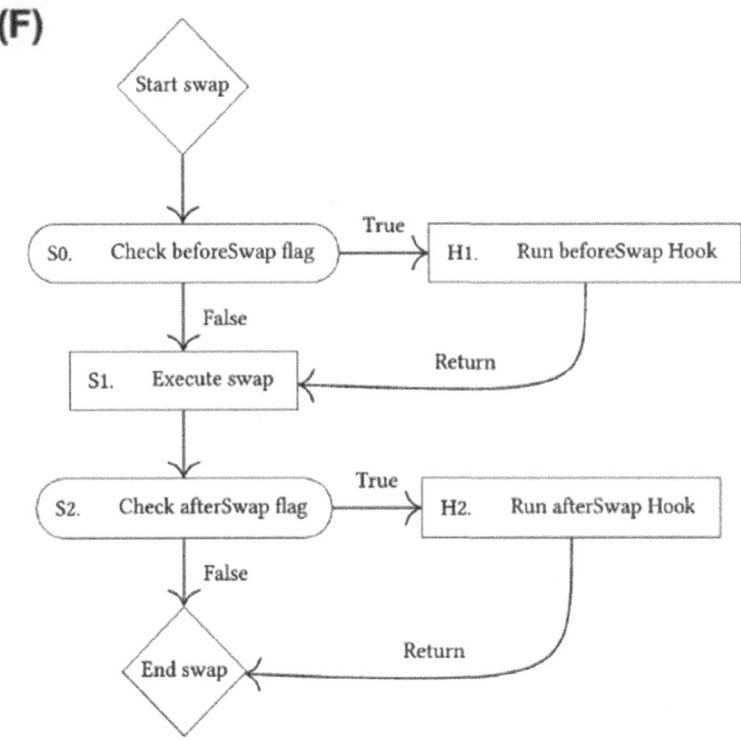

Figure 5-1. *Swap Hook Flow*[11]

Uniswap V4's 'hooks' feature provides developers the ability to implement specialised functionalities at certain stages of the protocol's processes. This includes capabilities such as the Time-Weighted Average Market Maker (TWAMM) for executing large orders over time without significant price impact and on-chain limit orders which allow users to set specific price points for trades. Additionally, dynamic fee adjustments based on volatility and mechanisms to capture Maximum Extractable Value (MEV) for liquidity providers can be created using these hooks.

The introduction of hooks is a significant enhancement from Uniswap's previous versions, aiming to afford developers the tools necessary to build more sophisticated and efficient financial products while also optimising the platform's transaction processes and fee structures. This demonstrates Uniswap's continuous push towards innovation and adaptability in the DeFi space.

Table 5-4. Uniswap: Redefining Access and Efficiency in DeFi[12]

Challenges in Traditional Finance	Uniswap Solutions
Centralisation: Market access and trade pairings are tightly controlled by centralised entities.	**Decentralisation**: Uniswap's open protocol allows anyone to create or trade on any pair, increasing market inclusivity.
Limited Liquidity: Traditionally, large institutions dominate market making and liquidity provision.	**Democratised Liquidity**: Uniswap enables individual liquidity providers to contribute to pools and earn fees, democratising access to market making.
Trading Inefficiencies: Trades can be slow due to reliance on intermediary parties for clearing and settlement.	**Instant Settlement**: Utilising smart contracts, Uniswap allows for near-instant trades without the need for intermediaries.
Restrictive Asset Exchange: Swapping assets across different platforms can be cumbersome and restrictive.	**Cross-Protocol Exchange**: Uniswap facilitates the seamless exchange of a vast array of assets, promoting a more integrated DeFi ecosystem.
Opacity in Operations: Traditional systems often lack transparency in operations, leading to trust issues.	**Transparent Processes**: With open source code and on-chain transactions, Uniswap provides complete visibility into its operations.

In conclusion, Uniswap addresses fundamental inefficiencies in traditional finance by leveraging decentralised, blockchain-based solutions. By promoting a permissionless and transparent environment, it provides unparalleled access and flexibility, which is reshaping the financial ecosystem. Uniswap stands as a testament to the potential of DeFi to offer a more inclusive and efficient alternative to conventional financial systems.

Aave

Aave is an open source and non-custodial liquidity protocol where users can earn interest on deposits and borrow assets. It has evolved through several versions, each introducing more sophisticated features that advance the DeFi lending landscape.

Aave V1 was the genesis of the protocol, launched in 2017 with a pooled risk model and support for two assets. It allowed users to earn interest on deposits and engage in peer-to-peer lending.

Aave V2, released in 2019, brought major improvements like the addition of more assets, including DAI, USDC and others. It introduced a protocol-based liquidation system and other features like debt tokenisation, stable and variable debt and the pioneering flash loans. These flash loans allow for collateral swapping, debt refinancing and leverage opportunities within a single transaction block.

Aave V3 continued this trajectory of innovation when it was launched in 2021. This version introduced a single-borrowable asset model for more secure lending, the Portal feature for cross-blockchain asset transfers and isolation mode to protect users' wallets. Additionally, Aave V3 introduced dynamic interest rates, adjusting loan rates based on market demand and supply, ensuring a more capital-efficient system.[13]

Each version aimed to improve user experience, reduce gas costs and provide more secure and versatile lending options. Aave has been a key player in DeFi lending by offering features that are responsive to the needs of its users and the market, advancing the capabilities of decentralised finance significantly beyond traditional finance.

Aave's significant TVL growth reflects its impact and popularity. By providing flexible, decentralised financial options, Aave is challenging traditional financial practices, enabling users to gain more control over their financial transactions in a transparent and efficient manner. With each version, Aave has aimed to simplify the complexities of lending and borrowing in the blockchain space, bringing a higher level of sophistication and security to DeFi.

Table 5-5. Addressing Traditional Finance Limitations with Aave's DeFi Innovations[12]

Challenges in Traditional Finance	Aave Solutions
Centralisation Risk: Financial systems are often controlled by a few entities, leading to single points of failure and lack of inclusion.	**Decentralisation**: Aave's protocol is open source and non-custodial, reducing centralisation risks and increasing financial inclusion.
Limited Yield Opportunities: Traditional finance generally offers lower yield opportunities, particularly for smaller investors.	**Higher Yields**: Aave enables users to earn higher yields on deposits through its lending pools and interest-bearing aTokens.
Restricted Access: Investment and borrowing are often restricted by credit checks and institutional barriers.	**Open Access**: Aave's protocol is permissionless, allowing anyone to lend, borrow or earn interest regardless of their location or status.
Liquidity Issues: Traditional lending can be illiquid, with long lock-up periods and cumbersome processes to access funds.	**Liquid Markets**: Aave offers instant loans and borrowing, providing high liquidity without long-term lock-ups.
Lack of Transparency: Traditional finance often has opaque practices with hidden fees and complex terms.	**Transparency**: Aave operates on the blockchain, offering full transparency on transactions, fees and contract terms.

(continued)

Table 5-5. (*continued*)

Challenges in Traditional Finance	Aave Solutions
Inflexible Terms: Loans in traditional finance come with fixed terms and rates that might not suit all borrowers.	**Flexible Terms**: Aave provides variable and stable interest rate options, as well as features like rate switching and flash loans for flexibility.
Interoperability: Assets in one financial institution are not easily transferable to another, leading to siloed ecosystems.	**Interoperability**: Aave's protocol is compatible with various other DeFi applications, enabling seamless asset transfer across platforms.

Aave presents a robust alternative to traditional financial systems by leveraging DeFi innovations to overcome common challenges. Its decentralised structure promotes financial inclusivity, while the protocol's transparency ensures users can trust the system they're engaging with. Aave offers greater flexibility in terms of yield, access and liquidity, which traditional finance systems often lack. With features like instant loans, a variety of interest rate options and seamless interoperability with other DeFi platforms, Aave addresses many of the pain points experienced by users of conventional financial services. As a result, Aave is not only a pioneering force in the DeFi space but also a viable competitor to the incumbent financial institutions, providing solutions that redefine borrowing and lending in the digital age.

MakerDAO

MakerDAO is a pivotal project in the DeFi space, recognised for the creation of DAI, a stablecoin that is pegged to the US dollar, and for its Maker Protocol, a decentralised credit platform operating on the Ethereum blockchain. The protocol allows users to generate DAI by using their cryptocurrency as collateral in a smart contract system known as a Vault.

CHAPTER 5   THE RISE OF DECENTRALISED FINANCE (DEFI)

The Maker Protocol uses a dual-token model comprised of its governance token, MKR, and its stablecoin, DAI. The system maintains the stability of DAI through a dynamic system of collateralised debt positions (CDPs), autonomous feedback mechanisms and appropriately incentivised external actors.

DAI maintains its peg to the US dollar through a series of smart contracts that incentivise external actors to maintain the balance of supply and demand. Maker Vaults allow users to deposit collateral in exchange for generating DAI, which creates a debt that accrues interest over time known as the Stability Fee. To reclaim their collateral, users must repay their DAI debt along with the Stability Fee.

The MakerDAO is governed by MKR token holders who vote on critical decisions affecting the system. This includes choices about the types of collateral accepted, risk parameters and system upgrades. The governance model is an example of 'scientific governance', where MKR holders manage the protocol and financial risks to ensure DAI's stability, transparency and efficiency.

MakerDAO's protocol has a significant impact on the DeFi ecosystem, providing a decentralised and stable medium of exchange. Its resilience against volatility makes it a trusted asset and a building block for other DeFi applications. The platform's Total Value Locked (TVL) signifies its central role and users' trust in the system.

The protocol has undergone several upgrades, each introducing more safety features, increasing efficiency and enhancing governance. These include the introduction of Multi-Collateral DAI, which allows various types of assets to be used as collateral, and improvements in the governance system to enable more decentralised and efficient decision-making processes.

MakerDAO's scientific governance involves Executive Voting and Governance Polling, allowing MKR holders to actively participate in the protocol's risk management and strategic planning. Furthermore, the Maker Protocol includes features such as the DAI Savings Rate (DSR), which provides a savings mechanism for DAI holders to earn interest on their holdings.

CHAPTER 5   THE RISE OF DECENTRALISED FINANCE (DEFI)

Table 5-6. *Reshaping Finance: MakerDAO's Approach to Traditional Challenges*[12]

Challenges in Traditional Finance	MakerDAO Solutions
Interest Rate Centralisation: Rates largely dictated by central banks like the Federal Reserve.	**Decentralised Rate Setting**: Interest rates are governed by MKR holders in a transparent manner.
Gatekept Financial Services: Many loan and credit services are only accessible to those with certain financial standings.	**Open-Access Finance**: MakerDAO enables equal access to financial services through decentralised governance.
High Loan Costs: Traditional loans can have high processing fees and administrative costs.	**Cost-Efficient Loans**: MakerDAO provides loans with minimal processing fees through smart contracts.
Rigid Financial Systems: Traditional financial systems are inflexible and slow to adapt to individual needs.	**Flexible Financial Tools**: MakerDAO's DAI Savings Rate (DSR) and other features offer customisable user experiences.
Financial Exclusion: A significant portion of the global population is unbanked or underbanked.	**Financial Inclusion**: MakerDAO provides global, borderless access to its stablecoin, DAI, regardless of banking status.
Currency Volatility: Traditional currencies can be volatile, affecting savings and purchasing power.	**Stable Currency**: DAI is soft-pegged to the USD, offering a stable medium of exchange and store of value.
Lack of Transparency: Traditional finance often lacks clarity on how money is managed and invested.	**Transparent Operations**: MakerDAO's operations are fully transparent and verifiable on the blockchain.

In summary, MakerDAO stands as a cornerstone of DeFi, with its innovative stablecoin, DAI, and the Maker Protocol. It has addressed the volatility typically associated with cryptocurrencies and has introduced a system that not only rivals traditional banking but also represents a significant advancement in decentralised finance. Through its robust governance and innovative features, MakerDAO continues to play a critical role in the ecosystem, fostering transparency, efficiency and inclusion.

Total Value Locked (TVL)

Total Value Locked (TVL) is an essential metric in the DeFi sector, offering a measure of the total assets committed to DeFi protocols and platforms. It serves as a key indicator of the sector's health and activity, reflecting the confidence and commitment of users in these decentralised services. TVL includes all assets that are staked, borrowed or serving as collateral.

To calculate TVL, one must aggregate the current market value of all assets deposited in a DeFi protocol. This involves multiplying the quantity of each locked asset by its current market price. For example, if a protocol has 100 Ethereum (ETH) and the current market price of ETH is $2,000, the TVL for that portion of assets would be $200,000.

TVL is significant for several reasons:

1. It reflects the adoption level of DeFi platforms – a higher TVL suggests a larger number of users engaging with the platform, implying trust and stability.

2. It provides a sense of the liquidity available within the ecosystem, which is crucial for the efficiency of various financial activities such as trading, lending and borrowing.

3. A high TVL can attract new users, as it implies a thriving platform with robust participation.

Despite its importance, TVL should not be the sole metric for assessing DeFi projects as it can fluctuate with market conditions and may not fully represent the utility or risk profile of the underlying protocols.

Data aggregators play a critical role in presenting TVL data, offering a centralised view of asset values across various DeFi protocols. These platforms help users track overall growth, assess potential investment opportunities and understand the dynamic landscape of decentralised finance.[14, 15, 16]

When evaluating the performance of DeFi platforms like Uniswap, Aave and MakerDAO, TVL provides insight into user adoption rates, liquidity and overall market presence. Substantial growth in TVL across these platforms indicates an increasing shift towards decentralised financial solutions and a broader acceptance of blockchain-based financial mechanisms over traditional financial systems. This growth not only signifies the amount of financial capital flowing into these protocols but also underscores their innovative capabilities in reshaping financial access and services.

5.3 Risks and Challenges of DeFi

DeFi, while innovative and transformative, faces a spectrum of risks and challenges that can potentially hinder its growth and adoption. Here's a deeper look into these issues.

Security Risks

The open source nature of DeFi's smart contracts is a double-edged sword; it fosters transparency and community-driven innovation but also exposes vulnerabilities. The decentralised nature means that once a smart contract is deployed, it can be challenging to alter, making any existing vulnerabilities potentially exploitable. High-profile incidents, such as the

DAO hack in 2016 and more recent exploits like the Flash Loan attacks, serve as case studies of such vulnerabilities. These incidents demonstrate the need for rigorous security protocols, including formal verification, extensive code auditing and real-time security monitoring to ensure the integrity of DeFi applications.

Regulatory Challenges

DeFi operates in a regulatory grey area. Traditional financial systems are heavily regulated with clear compliance procedures for AML (anti-money laundering) and KYC. DeFi's decentralised nature complicates the enforcement of these regulations. There's an ongoing debate on how to reconcile DeFi's ethos of openness and anonymity with the global regulatory landscape's demands. Regulations could provide legitimacy and protection for users, but overly strict policies might stifle innovation or push DeFi into the shadows, limiting its potential benefits.

The Ethereum Name Service (ENS) emerges as a bridge between the anonymity of blockchain and the necessity for identity verification in DeFi. ENS provides human-readable names for Ethereum addresses, which enhances the user experience but also has the potential to serve as a form of decentralised identity (DID). This decentralised identity can potentially be linked to a verifiable off-chain identity, creating a bridge between the user's on-chain activities and their real-world identity without sacrificing the decentralised ethos of blockchain technology.

Here's how ENS could interplay with KYC challenges in DeFi:

- **ENS As DID**: ENS names are unique and owned by individuals, similar to a domain name, but for blockchain addresses. This aligns with the principles of self-sovereign identity (SSI), where individuals have ownership and control over their identity without relying on a central authority.

- **Regulatory Compliance**: Integrating ENS with KYC processes could enable users to prove their identity in a privacy-preserving manner. ENS names could be associated with credentials verified by third parties without exposing the underlying personal data on the blockchain, allowing DeFi platforms to remain compliant with regulations.

- **Reducing Friction for Users**: ENS can make interactions with DeFi protocols less cumbersome by reducing the need for managing long, hexadecimal wallet addresses. Instead, users can engage with DeFi products using their ENS names, which could also be linked to their verified identities.

- **Enhanced Trust and Security**: With ENS names serving as DIDs, it becomes easier to establish trust within the DeFi ecosystem. Verified ENS names can help mitigate the risk of fraud and improve the reputation of DeFi services.

- **KYC and AML Integration**: ENS names could act as pointers to off-chain identity verification processes that meet AML and KYC requirements. This integration would maintain the integrity of DeFi's decentralised model while ensuring compliance with global financial regulations.

To conclude, ENS offers a promising path for aligning DeFi with the necessary regulatory frameworks while maintaining user autonomy and privacy. It stands as a testament to the innovation within blockchain technology, striving to balance the decentralised principles of the technology with the practicalities of regulatory compliance.

Scalability and Interoperability

Currently, many DeFi applications are built on the Ethereum network, which has struggled with high transaction fees and network congestion due to its popularity. These issues highlight the need for scalable solutions. Layer 2 solutions, sharding and alternative blockchains are being developed to address these problems. Moreover, interoperability is crucial for creating a seamless DeFi ecosystem, where assets and data can flow freely between different blockchains and platforms without the need for intermediaries.

Market Risks and Volatility

DeFi markets are often more volatile than traditional markets due to their relative infancy, lower liquidity and speculative nature. Participants are exposed to market risks, including significant financial loss due to rapid price fluctuations. Moreover, the use of leverage in DeFi can amplify losses, leading to the liquidation of collateralised positions. Users must navigate impermanent loss, particularly in liquidity pools, and the risk of systemic failures precipitated by the cascading effects of interdependent protocols.

Understanding and mitigating these risks requires a concerted effort from developers, users, regulators and other stakeholders in the DeFi space. Implementing robust security practices, establishing clear regulatory frameworks, improving network infrastructure and educating users on market risks are essential steps towards a resilient and sustainable DeFi ecosystem.

CHAPTER 5   THE RISE OF DECENTRALISED FINANCE (DEFI)

5.4 Summary

This chapter provides an in-depth exploration of Decentralised Finance (DeFi), its foundational concepts, and its transformative impact on the traditional financial system (TradFi). It begins by examining the core components of DeFi, such as smart contracts, permissionless platforms, and the advantages of decentralisation. DeFi's primary innovations, including decentralised exchanges (DEXs), lending platforms, stablecoins, insurance protocols, and prediction markets, are explored in detail, showcasing how they revolutionise traditional financial services by eliminating intermediaries and providing global access to financial tools.

The chapter also offers a comprehensive analysis of key DeFi protocols such as Uniswap, Aave, and MakerDAO, highlighting their contributions to liquidity provision, lending, and stablecoin issuance. The role of Total Value Locked (TVL) as a crucial metric for evaluating DeFi platforms is discussed, providing insight into the sector's health and user engagement.

Finally, the chapter addresses the risks and challenges associated with DeFi, such as security vulnerabilities, regulatory uncertainties, scalability issues, and market volatility. While DeFi offers a new, more inclusive financial paradigm, it also requires participants to navigate a complex and evolving landscape, balancing innovation with emerging risks.

5.5 Notes

1. Born, A., Gschossmann, I., Hodbod, A., Lambert, C., & Pellicani, A. (2022). Decentralised finance – a new unregulated non-bank system? European Central Bank. www.ecb.europa.eu/press/financial-stability-publications/macroprudential-bulletin/focus/2022/html/ecb.mpbu202207_focus1.en.html (Accessed: 9 April 2024).

2. Casey, M. (2002). 'DeFi' and 'TradFi' must work together. IMF. www.imf.org/en/Publications/fandd/issues/2022/09/Point-of-View-Defi-Tradfi-must-work-together-Michael-Casey (Accessed: 9 April 2024).

3. Advanced Applications of DeFi: Complete Guide (2024). Blockpit. www.blockpit.io/blog/advanced-defi-applications (Accessed: 9 April 2024).

4. Dappgrid (2023). List of DeFi Apps – Top DeFi Apps – Dappgrid. https://dappgrid.com/defi-apps/ (Accessed: 9 April 2024).

5. Anwar, H. (2023). 30+ Best Decentralized Finance Applications. 101 Blockchains. https://101blockchains.com/decentralized-finance-applications/ (Accessed: 9 April 2024).

6. George, B. (2022). What Is a DEX? How Decentralized Crypto Exchanges Work. Coindesk. www.coindesk.com/learn/what-is-a-dex-how-decentralized-crypto-exchanges-work/ (Accessed: 9 April 2024).

7. Geroni, D. (2024). A Beginner's Guide to Decentralized Exchanges (DEX). 101 Blockchains. https://101blockchains.com/decentralized-exchanges/ (Accessed: 9 April 2024).

8. Nexus Mutual | The Crypto Insurance Alternative (2024). https://nexusmutual.io/ (Accessed: 9 April 2024).

9. Opyn Markets | Uniswap, but for perps (2024). www.opyn.co/ (Accessed: 9 April 2024).

10. Capital, L. (23 June 2023). The Evolution of UNisWaP: Opportunities and Impacts of V4. Medium. https://ld-capital.medium.com/the-evolution-of-uniswap-opportunities-and-impacts-of-v4-2c706c055a4e (Accessed: 9 April 2024).

11. Owen, J. (2023). What is Uniswap? v1, v2, v3, v4? – James Owen – Medium. Medium. https://medium.com/@jamesowen.dev/what-is-uniswap-v1-v2-v3-v4-563440e0885f (Accessed: 9 April 2024).

12. Harvey, C. R. (2021). DeFi and the Future of Finance. John Wiley & Sons.

13. Wehodl (5 November 2023). Aave V1, V2, and V3: A Comparison of Three Generations of DeFi Lending. Medium. https://blog.wehodl.finance/aave-v1-v2-and-v3-a-comparison-of-three-generations-of-defi-lending-9573eec663e2 (Accessed: 9 April 2024).

14. George, B. (2024). Why TVL Matters in DeFi: Total Value Locked Explained. Coindesk. www.coindesk.com/learn/why-tvl-matters-in-defi-total-value-locked-explained/ (Accessed: 9 April 2024).

15. Total Value Locked (TVL) | DeFi Pulse Docs (2024). https://docs.defipulse.com/methodology/tvl (Accessed: 9 April 2024).

16. Thrive. (6 February 2023). Understanding Total Value Locked (TVL) in DeFi. thrive.fi. https://thrive.fi/blogs/defi/total-value-locked-tvl-in-defi (Accessed: 9 April 2024).

CHAPTER 6

Tokenised Real-World Assets (RWA) and Decentralised Physical Infrastructure Networks (DePIN)

6.1 Introduction to RWA

RWAs encapsulate both tangible and intangible assets that exist in the physical world but can be digitally represented through tokenisation on blockchain or other distributed ledger technologies (DLTs). These assets cover a wide array, including cash, commodities, equities, bonds, real estate, art and intellectual property. RWAs play a crucial role in bridging the gap between traditional financial systems and the rapidly evolving digital economy, promising a pathway to more accessible, transparent and efficient asset management and investment opportunities.

- **From the Cryptocurrency Perspective**: In the crypto realm, the logic surrounding RWAs is centred on transferring the income rights of income-generating assets, such as US Treasuries, fixed income and stocks, onto the blockchain. It involves leveraging off-chain assets for on-chain collateralised loans and bringing various RWAs online for trading (e.g. minerals, real estate, gold). This unilateral demand from the crypto world for RWAs encounters numerous regulatory hurdles, illustrating a complex yet burgeoning interest in integrating the tangible with the digital.

- **From the Traditional Finance (TradFi) Perspective**: From the TradFi viewpoint, RWA tokenisation is seen as a bidirectional bridge towards DeFi. It is considered a revolutionary tool that combines the reliability and vastness of traditional assets with the efficiency and innovation of blockchain technology. For TradFi institutions, asset tokenisation using DeFi protocols opens new avenues for enhancing liquidity, reducing operational costs and addressing long-standing inefficiencies within the system. It represents an evolution towards a more integrated financial system that utilises blockchain for transparent, efficient and inclusive asset markets.[1]

CHAPTER 6 TOKENISED REAL-WORLD ASSETS (RWA) AND DECENTRALISED PHYSICAL INFRASTRUCTURE NETWORKS (DEPIN)

The Blockchain As Ideal Infrastructure

Blockchain technology stands as the epitome of a 'computational system' within the financial domain, primarily due to its ability to automate and secure financial transactions and asset management through smart contracts and decentralised consensus mechanisms. This contrasts sharply with 'non-computational systems' found in traditional finance (TradFi), which rely heavily on manual processes, intermediaries and regulatory frameworks based on trust in centralised institutions.

Computational systems, like blockchain, excel in executing repetitive processes and delivering verifiable outcomes without the need for trust or direct human intervention. They are characterised by their transparency, immutability and the capacity to facilitate direct ownership, fractionalisation of assets and global access. This automation of trust and execution not only reduces operational inefficiencies but also opens up new avenues for financial innovation, such as the tokenisation of RWAs.

On the other hand, **non-computational systems** in TradFi encompass those aspects of finance that remain largely outside the purview of automation and digital trust. These include the nuanced decisions based on human judgement, such as credit assessments, which rely on interpersonal trust, historical financial behaviour and regulatory compliance. While blockchain can streamline many aspects of financial transactions, it cannot fully replace the human elements and the existing legal and regulatory frameworks that underpin non-computational systems.

The tokenisation of RWAs showcases the convergence of computational and non-computational systems, bringing tangible and intangible assets onto the blockchain. This process not only enhances the liquidity, accessibility and efficiency of asset management but also underscores the critical need for an integrated approach that respects the legal, regulatory and human contexts of asset ownership and transfer.

In essence, the future of finance and asset management lies in a harmonious integration of blockchain's computational capabilities with the non-computational aspects of traditional financial systems. This synergy promises to unlock unprecedented levels of efficiency, transparency and inclusivity in global finance, provided that challenges related to regulatory compliance, security and the seamless interaction between digital and physical assets are effectively addressed.

The Disruptive Impact of RWA Tokenisation on TradFi

The tokenisation of RWAs heralds a transformative shift in the financial sector, marrying the robust, time-tested value of tangible and intangible assets with the cutting-edge technology of blockchain. This fusion not only enhances the traditional financial landscape but also sets the stage for a radical departure from long-standing norms thanks to the inherent benefits of blockchain technology: decentralisation, transparency and immutability. The core of this disruption lies in the application of computational finance through decentralised finance (DeFi) innovations, fundamentally redefining how assets are managed, traded and conceptualised.

- **Enhanced Liquidity and Global Accessibility**: One of the cornerstone benefits of RWA tokenisation is the unprecedented liquidity and accessibility it introduces to assets once bound by the constraints of traditional markets. Digital tokens representing RWAs can be traded 24/7 on global platforms, transcending geographical boundaries and the limitations of standard market operating hours. This continuous trading cycle not only increases liquidity but also broadens market participation, democratising access to investment opportunities that were previously limited to a select few.

- **Inherent Transparency and Security**: Blockchain's inherent transparency acts as a beacon of trust, significantly boosting investor confidence. This technology mitigates the risks associated with fraud and ownership disputes, laying a clear trail of asset ownership and transaction history that is immutable and verifiable by all parties involved. Furthermore, the utilisation of smart contracts automates and secures the management and transaction processes of tokenised assets, ensuring each step is executed reliably and without tampering, thereby reinforcing the security of digital asset transactions.

- **Operational Efficiency and Cost Reduction**: The process of tokenising RWAs on a blockchain infrastructure notably streamlines asset management, removing the costly and cumbersome layers associated with intermediaries, legal proceedings and extensive paperwork. This efficiency not only makes high-value investments more accessible to a wider audience but also reduces the operational costs involved in asset transactions, fostering a more inclusive financial ecosystem.

- **Computational Finance and the Paradigm Shift in TradFi**: At the heart of RWA tokenisation's disruptive potential is the distinction between computational and non-computational systems within the realm of finance. Blockchain, a computational system, excels in executing complex algorithms and maintaining an immutable ledger of transactions, providing a solid foundation for the automation and innovation DeFi brings to financial services. This new paradigm facilitates a fully automated environment for executing traditional financial operations such as lending, borrowing and asset management without manual intervention, signifying a profound shift towards more efficient, secure and accessible financial services.

- **Programmability and Transparency in Financial Products**: Moreover, tokenisation introduces a layer of programmability into financial operations, especially benefiting sectors like the derivatives market and SME financing. This feature allows for the creation of innovative financial products, enhancing liquidity, and access to capital while maintaining transparency and minimising risks. The programmability inherent in tokenised RWAs not only simplifies the creation and management of financial products but also ensures these processes are conducted with a higher degree of transparency and security.

The integration of RWA with blockchain and DeFi innovations marks a pivotal moment in the evolution of traditional finance. By capitalising on the efficiencies of computational finance, the DeFi ecosystem is set to streamline, expand and revolutionise financial services, rendering them more accessible, efficient and secure for all. As such, the disruptive impact of RWA tokenisation on traditional finance is not merely a speculative future but an unfolding reality that promises to reshape the financial landscape in profound ways.

6.2 Overview of DePIN

DePINs herald a new era where blockchain's inherent properties – security, transparency and collective control – converge with the physical infrastructures that underpin our society. This synergy is set to redefine the creation, operation and utilisation of our core physical systems. DePINs are much more than a blockchain adaptation of existing services; they are a re-envisioning and an evolutionary leap in infrastructure management. These networks are designed to be self-regulating, robust and inherently protected against the vulnerabilities that centralised systems often face. The vision for DePINs extends towards a future where infrastructure is not only shared but also collectively nurtured, leading to ecosystems that are equitable, sustainable and adaptable to the collective will of their participants.[2,3]

Core Components of DePINs

- **Blockchain and Smart Contracts**: At the core of DePINs lies blockchain technology, serving as the immutable ledger that records all transactions and interactions within the network. Smart contracts automate the execution of these transactions, facilitating trustless and secure exchanges of services and resources.

- **Internet of Things (IoT)**: IoT's role in DePINs is indispensable as it equips the network with data-gathering capabilities, ensuring constant communication between the physical and digital realms. The data collected from sensors and devices are fed into the blockchain, enabling real-time monitoring and management.

- **Tokenomics and Incentives**: A robust incentive model is vital for encouraging participation in DePINs. Tokenomics involves creating a digital currency or token system that rewards contributors for their role in building, maintaining or utilising the network, aligning individual incentives with the network's health.

- **Interoperability Protocols**: DePINs require seamless interaction between different blockchain platforms and traditional systems. Interoperability protocols ensure that information and value can be exchanged across diverse networks without friction.

Real-World Applications

- **Energy Grids**: DePINs can revolutionise energy distribution by facilitating P2P energy trading, allowing individuals with solar panels to sell excess energy directly to neighbours or back to the grid.

- **Telecommunications**: In the realm of telecommunications, DePINs can create decentralised networks where individuals contribute to the network's coverage by hosting nodes, enhancing connectivity and reducing reliance on traditional providers.

- **Transportation and Logistics**: DePINs can track goods in real time across the supply chain, ensuring transparency and authenticity. In transportation, they can support decentralised ride-sharing networks or vehicle data marketplaces.

CHAPTER 6 TOKENISED REAL-WORLD ASSETS (RWA) AND DECENTRALISED PHYSICAL INFRASTRUCTURE NETWORKS (DEPIN)

- **Urban Development and Real Estate**: In urban development, DePINs can play a role in smart city initiatives, integrating various infrastructural elements into a cohesive, responsive and efficient whole. They can also streamline real estate transactions, making property ownership more accessible and secure.

DePINs can be categorised into two distinct types based on the nature of the resources they deal with: Physical Resource Networks (PRNs) and Digital Resource Networks (DRNs). Table 6-1 shows an analytical comparison of the two.

Table 6-1. PRNs vs. DRNs

Aspect	Physical Resource Networks (PRNs)	Digital Resource Networks (DRNs)
Resource Nature	Tangible, immovable assets	Intangible, virtual resources
Localisation	Services and resources are location-specific and non-portable	Services are not location-bound and can be accessed globally
Interchangeability	Non-fungible; resources are unique to their function and location	Fungible; resources can be replicated and are not unique to a location
Deployment	Involves physical installation, which can be capital and labour-intensive	Deployment is software based, requiring minimal physical intervention
Capital Requirements	Typically higher due to the need for physical hardware and infrastructure	Lower initial capital needed; resources are digital and more easily distributed

(*continued*)

Table 6-1. (*continued*)

Aspect	Physical Resource Networks (PRNs)	Digital Resource Networks (DRNs)
Scalability	Scalability is constrained by physical factors like geography and infrastructure	Highly scalable without the constraints of physical geography
Maintenance	Physical upkeep is necessary, potentially leading to higher long-term costs	Mainly requires software maintenance, which can be managed remotely
Service Scope	Localised to specific service areas due to the physical nature of resources	Global service provision is possible due to the digital nature of resources
Examples	Helium (decentralised wireless networks), Power Ledger (peer-to-peer energy trading)	Filecoin (decentralised storage), IoTeX (decentralised machine network)
Service Continuity	Can be affected by physical damage or local disruptions	Generally more resilient to local disruptions; continuity is maintained as long as the network is operational
Regulatory Environment	May face more stringent regulations due to the physical aspect of the infrastructure and its impact on the environment and communities	Regulation can be more challenging due to the intangible nature and rapid evolution of digital assets and services

CHAPTER 6   TOKENISED REAL-WORLD ASSETS (RWA) AND DECENTRALISED PHYSICAL INFRASTRUCTURE NETWORKS (DEPIN)

Table 6-1 summarises the fundamental distinctions between PRNs and DRNs within the DePIN framework. While PRNs deal with physical, often infrastructural resources that are bound to a specific location, DRNs handle virtual resources that are more versatile and globally accessible. Each has its own set of benefits and challenges, making them suitable for different types of decentralised applications.

The Dynamics of DePIN Flywheel

DePINs operate through a symbiotic cycle that marries the technological prowess of blockchain with the utility of physical infrastructure. This cycle, known as the DePIN Flywheel, showcases the interaction between various stakeholders and the network, driving growth and value in the ecosystem.[4]

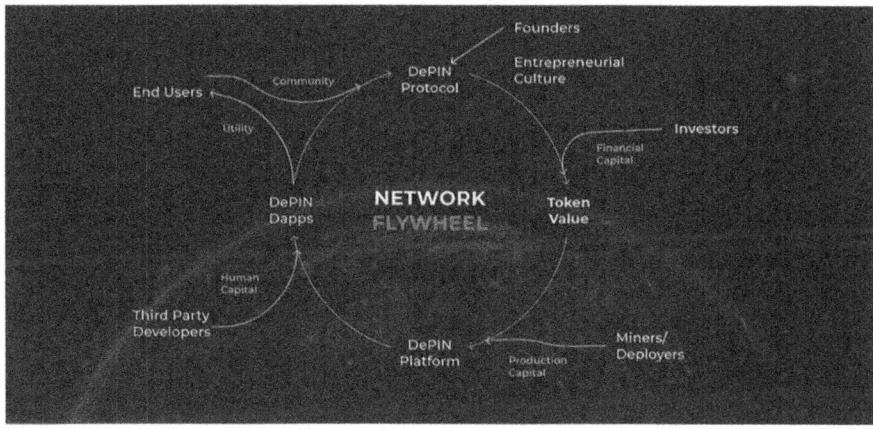

Figure 6-1. *DePIN Flywheel*

Figure 6-1 illustrates how different elements within the DePIN ecosystem feed into each other to create a self-sustaining model. Here's a breakdown:

1. **Founders and Investors**: The cycle begins with founders who establish the DePIN protocol, supported by investors who provide the financial capital. This capital is vital for developing the infrastructure and incentivising early adopters.

2. **Token Value and Miners/Deployers**: The financial capital helps to establish the token value, which is fundamental in remunerating miners or deployers. These participants contribute production capital by providing the necessary hardware or services.

3. **DePIN Platform and Third-Party Developers**: With the hardware in place, the DePIN platform becomes operational, attracting third-party developers. These developers contribute human capital by creating decentralised applications (DApps) that utilise the platform.

4. **DePIN DApps and End Users**: The DApps provide utility to end users who engage with the platform, benefiting from the decentralised services it offers.

5. **Community Engagement**: A thriving user base fosters a robust community around the DePIN, feeding back into the protocol and completing the flywheel. This community engagement is crucial for long-term sustainability and growth.

The flywheel concept emphasises the importance of each participant's role and the interconnectedness of their contributions. By ensuring that incentives are aligned across the board, DePINs aim to maintain a balanced growth trajectory where network participants are rewarded, and end users enjoy increasing utility.

Such a model presents a transformative approach to building and managing infrastructure that is participatory, incentivised and decentralised. It shifts the control from centralised entities to a distributed network of stakeholders, each contributing to and benefiting from the network's growth.

As DePINs continue to evolve, they could potentially disrupt traditional infrastructure management systems, providing a more efficient, transparent and equitable framework for service provision across various sectors like energy, telecommunications, health and more.

Scalability and Sustainability

Scalability and sustainability are twin pillars essential for the success and longevity of DePINs. To optimise for scalability, DePINs must employ blockchain protocols that can handle a high number of transactions and data throughput without compromising performance. This could involve adopting or developing more efficient consensus mechanisms that use less energy, such as proof of stake (PoS) rather than proof of work (PoW), or integrating Layer 2 solutions that can offload transaction processing from the main blockchain.

For sustainability, DePINs should focus on creating network architectures that minimise energy consumption, perhaps by integrating renewable energy sources or by designing systems that incentivise energy-efficient operations. This not only aligns with the global push towards greener technologies but also ensures that the network remains cost-effective in the long run.

CHAPTER 6   TOKENISED REAL-WORLD ASSETS (RWA) AND DECENTRALISED PHYSICAL INFRASTRUCTURE NETWORKS (DEPIN)

Tokenomics plays a critical role in ensuring that incentives within the network promote healthy growth. The economic model must be constructed to reward contributors fairly while avoiding the creation of economic bubbles. This means devising mechanisms that align the interests of all stakeholders – from miners and users to developers and investors – ensuring that the value of tokens is tied to the actual utility and demand rather than mere speculation.

In this context, it's not just about building the infrastructure but also about nurturing a robust ecosystem around it. This includes having a solid governance model in place that can adapt to the network's evolving needs and challenges. Moreover, it involves creating an environment where innovation can thrive, fostering developments that enhance the network's capabilities and services.

In the narrative of DePINs, sustainability also means maintaining an adaptable framework that can respond to changing market conditions, technological advancements and regulatory landscapes. For DePINs to truly flourish, they need to demonstrate resilience not just in the face of technical challenges but also in economic and environmental sustainability.

The focus must also be on ensuring that the physical and digital components of DePINs are able to expand in harmony. This requires careful coordination between the deployment of physical resources and the scalability of the digital infrastructure underpinning them.

By focusing on these areas, DePINs can potentially revolutionise how we approach infrastructure, moving from a centralised, top-down model to a distributed, bottom-up one that empowers individuals and communities while maintaining harmony with our environment and resources.

6.3 Synergy Between RWA and DePIN: Opportunities and Complexities

RWA tokenisation and DePIN are two transformative forces in the crypto space, both serving to bridge the gap between traditional financial markets and the blockchain ecosystem. RWA refers to the process of converting rights to real-world physical assets into digital tokens on a blockchain network, while DePIN stands for decentralised networks that use blockchain to manage and improve physical infrastructure systems. Together, they signify a potent combination for revolutionising digital asset transactions and the management of physical resources.

DePINs can be seen as a subset of RWA, where the tokenisation of physical infrastructure plays a pivotal role. Projects that fall under DePIN use token rewards to motivate community-driven construction and management of physical networks. For instance, a DePIN project could incentivise users to share data from a mobile device's camera, contributing to a larger network of geospatial information. Through tokenisation, such networks can finance expensive infrastructure, encourage public participation and democratise the ownership of these resources.

The Solana Edge in DePIN Projects

Solana's architecture offers several unique advantages over Ethereum that are particularly beneficial for DePIN projects, where scalability and rapid data transactions are critical.

Solana's transaction throughput is significantly higher, capable of processing up to 2,000–3000 transactions per second (TPS), while Ethereum currently processes around 10–15 TPS. This stark contrast in performance is largely due to Solana's innovative proof of history (PoH) consensus mechanism, which timestamps transactions to streamline the order of events, thus enabling this higher throughput without the delays and backlogs often experienced on Ethereum during periods of congestion.

Moreover, Solana's stateless architecture does not require the network's entire state to be updated with each transaction, which helps to reduce memory consumption and allows for transactions to be processed sequentially with greater efficiency. This feature, along with the Turbine block propagation protocol, aids in breaking down data for easier network transfer and contributes to Solana's scalability at the base level, without the need for Layer 2 scaling solutions.

Another important aspect is cost-effectiveness. Solana maintains much lower transaction fees compared to Ethereum, making it an attractive platform for users and developers looking for an efficient and affordable transaction experience. For instance, Solana's fees are measured in fractions of a cent, whereas Ethereum's can vary widely and soar during peak usage times due to network congestion.

Solana also introduces Sealevel, a system that allows for the parallel running of smart contracts, thereby optimising network efficiency and the handling of multiple transactions simultaneously, which is a significant advantage over Ethereum where smart contracts cannot operate in parallel.

These features underpin Solana's edge in DePIN projects, providing a high-speed, scalable and cost-efficient environment that supports complex infrastructure models and the high-frequency data transactions required to run them effectively.

Despite these advantages, it's important to note that Solana does have centralisation trade-offs and has faced network downtime issues, which raises concerns about its robustness and reliability compared to Ethereum, which, despite its scalability challenges, has a strong track record of uptime and security due to its decentralised nature.

Both networks continue to evolve, with Ethereum making strides towards improving its scalability and efficiency through Ethereum 2.0 upgrades, including a transition to a proof-of-stake (PoS) consensus, which aims to address current bottlenecks and enhance the network's performance.

In conclusion, while Solana offers a specialised set of features that are conducive to DePIN projects, it's crucial for stakeholders to weigh these against the broader context of network stability, security and decentralisation when choosing a blockchain platform for development.[5,6,7,8]

Challenges

1. **Regulatory Hurdles**: RWA and DePIN initiatives often face stringent regulatory environments that can limit their ability to operate freely across different jurisdictions. The integration of traditional financial assets and blockchain technology presents complex legal challenges, especially in terms of compliance, asset custody and cross-border transactions.

2. **Interoperability Issues**: Ensuring seamless interoperability between different blockchain platforms and between blockchain and traditional financial systems is critical. This includes the technical challenges of developing standardised protocols that allow for efficient and secure asset tokenisation, transfer and settlement across diverse platforms.

3. **Scalability Concerns:** As DePIN projects grow, they must handle increasing transaction volumes without compromising performance or security. This is particularly challenging for blockchain networks that struggle with scalability, where higher transaction throughput can lead to congestion and increased transaction fees.

4. **Data Privacy and Security:** Safeguarding sensitive financial data and ensuring privacy in transactions while maintaining transparency and compliance with regulations like GDPR is a significant challenge. This includes protecting against data breaches and unauthorised access to personal and financial information.

5. **Asset Valuation and Liquidity:** Accurately valuing RWAs and ensuring their liquidity once tokenised on the blockchain poses challenges. This includes developing reliable mechanisms for price discovery, asset appraisal and managing liquidity pools to facilitate trading and lending.

Solutions

1. **Regulatory Engagement and Compliance:** Building a framework for regulatory compliance from the outset is crucial. This involves working closely with regulatory bodies to ensure that DePIN initiatives comply with existing financial regulations and are prepared for potential future regulatory developments.

2. **Interoperability Solutions**: Developing and adopting cross-chain technologies and standards can address interoperability issues. This includes leveraging protocols like Cosmos or Polkadot for cross-chain transactions and employing common standards for tokenisation to ensure assets can move seamlessly between chains.

3. **Scalability Enhancements**: Implementing Layer 2 solutions, such as rollups or sidechains, can significantly improve scalability. Additionally, exploring newer consensus mechanisms that offer a balance between security, decentralisation and throughput can help DePIN projects scale effectively.

4. **Privacy-Preserving Technologies**: Utilising cryptographic techniques like zero-knowledge proofs (ZKPs) can help protect data privacy while ensuring compliance. These technologies enable the verification of transactions and asset ownership without revealing sensitive information.

5. **Advanced Oracle Networks**: As previously discussed in Section 5.1, oracles serve as essential conduits for data between the Web2 and Web3 realms, crucial for the accurate and timely delivery of real-world information to the blockchain. Enhancing oracle networks to offer secure, tamper-proof data feeds is imperative for precise asset valuation and the operational integrity of

smart contracts reacting to real-world stimuli and market fluctuations. The advancement of oracle technology, as seen with platforms like Chainlink and Pyth, underscores the importance of developing sophisticated oracle networks. These networks, equipped with safeguards and diversified data inputs, address the 'oracle problem' by reducing the risk of data manipulation and safeguarding the fidelity of information within DePIN projects. This progress reflects a significant leap towards mitigating centralisation risks and ensuring the secure, reliable and decentralised execution of smart contracts across various DeFi applications, including prediction markets, lending platforms and insurance contracts, thereby fostering trustless interaction with real-world data and catalysing the growth and stability of the DeFi ecosystem.

In the envisioned future of the Web3 ecosystem, the integration of RWA and DePIN represents a transformative shift towards a more interconnected, efficient and accessible digital world. Drawing insights from the documents provided, it's clear that the synergy between RWA and DePIN extends far beyond financial transactions, permeating various facets of the Web3 landscape, from data authenticity to decentralised governance.

In this envisioned future, every tangible asset, whether real estate, artworks, or commodities, is tokenised into digital representations that seamlessly circulate within blockchain networks supported by robust Decentralised Physical Infrastructure Networks (DePIN). This transition not only democratises access to asset ownership and investment opportunities but also ensures a level of transparency and efficiency previously unimaginable.

The pivotal role of oracles in bridging the gap between off-chain data and on-chain applications becomes increasingly significant. By ensuring that smart contracts operate with accurate and timely data, oracles enable a myriad of applications—from automated insurance claims and dynamic NFTs to real-time supply chain tracking—thus broadening blockchain's impact across multiple sectors.

Moreover, DePINs enhance physical infrastructure by supporting and augmenting digital representations of Real-World Assets (RWAs), fostering an environment where the physical and digital realms converge. This convergence enables innovative solutions in sectors such as IoT, where blockchain provides secure and immutable data management, enhancing operational efficiency and driving new business models.

The widespread tokenisation of RWAs, combined with the expansion of DePINs, catalyses the development of a more inclusive Web3 ecosystem. It empowers individuals and communities by providing tools for direct participation in economic activities, governance, and decision-making processes. This decentralised approach not only challenges traditional power structures but also promotes a more equitable distribution of wealth and resources.

Ultimately, the full potential of Web3—decentralisation, trustlessness, and permissionless access—reaches its pinnacle, transforming not just finance, but various aspects of daily life. The integration of RWAs and DePINs thus marks a crucial step towards a future where technology lays the foundation for a more equitable, transparent, and participatory global society, enabling individuals to actively shape the digital landscape of tomorrow.

6.4 Summary

This chapter examined the tokenisation of Real-World Assets (RWAs) and the transformative potential of Decentralised Physical Infrastructure Networks (DePINs). It highlighted how blockchain technology enables secure, efficient, and transparent management of physical and digital assets. By linking physical infrastructure with decentralised technologies, DePINs create opportunities for innovative applications in sectors such as energy, telecommunications, and logistics. Furthermore, oracles play a critical role in connecting off-chain data with on-chain applications, enhancing the functionality of smart contracts. The integration of RWAs and DePINs opens the door to a more inclusive and efficient Web3 ecosystem. This shift empowers individuals and communities by facilitating direct participation in economic and governance processes, while also challenging traditional financial systems and power structures. In this new landscape, decentralisation, transparency, and permissionless access redefine how assets are managed and traded, paving the way for a more equitable global society.

6.5 Notes

1. RWA 资产通证化未来蓝图研报:底层逻辑全景式梳理与大规模应用实现路径 - 深潮TechFlow (2023). TechFlow. www.techflowpost.com/article/detail_14359.html (Accessed: 9 April 2024).

2. Decentralized physical infrastructure network (DePIN), explained (2024). Cointelegraph. https://cointelegraph.com/explained/decentralized-physical-infrastructure-network-depin-explained (Accessed: 9 April 2024).

3. Graves, S., & Elliott, S. (6 March 2024). What is DePIN? Bringing Physical Infrastructure to Blockchain. Decrypt. https://decrypt.co/resources/what-is-depin-physical-infrastructure-blockchain (Accessed: 9 April 2024).

CHAPTER 6   TOKENISED REAL-WORLD ASSETS (RWA) AND DECENTRALISED PHYSICAL INFRASTRUCTURE NETWORKS (DEPIN)

4. Agbo, J. (2024). What Is the Decentralized Physical Infrastructure (DePIN) Narrative in Crypto? CoinGecko. www.coingecko.com/learn/depin-crypto-decentralized-physical-infrastructure-networks (Accessed: 9 April 2024).

5. CoinMarketCap (2022). Solana vs Ethereum: A Detailed Comparison. CoinMarketCap Academy. https://coinmarketcap.com/academy/article/solana-vs-ethereum-a-detailed-comparison (Accessed: 9 April 2024).

6. Rosic, A. (3 February 2024). Solana vs Ethereum: A Comprehensive Comparison for 2024. Blockgeeks. https://blockgeeks.com/guides/solana-vs-ethereum/ (Accessed: 9 April 2024).

7. Vasile, I. (2022). Solana vs. Ethereum: An Ultimate Comparison. BeInCrypto. https://beincrypto.com/learn/solana-vs-ethereum/ (Accessed: 9 April 2024).

8. Chichyan, L. (2022). Solana vs Ethereum [The Ultimate Guide 2023]. CoinStats Blog. https://coinstats.app/blog/solana-vs-ethereum/ (Accessed: 9 April 2024).

CHAPTER 7

Non-fungible Tokens (NFTs) and Digital Art

7.1 Understanding NFTs: Mechanisms and Market Dynamics

Non-fungible tokens (NFTs) represent a groundbreaking shift in the digital ownership paradigm, leveraging blockchain technology to certify uniqueness and ownership of digital assets. Unlike fungible tokens, such as cryptocurrencies, which are interchangeable and hold the same value (one Bitcoin is always equal to another Bitcoin), each NFT is unique or 'non-fungible' and cannot be exchanged on a like-for-like basis. This uniqueness and indivisibility make NFTs the perfect vehicle for digitally representing ownership of unique items, from digital art to virtual real estate.

Unique Properties and Underlying Technology

Non-fungible tokens (NFTs) leverage the transformative power of blockchain technology to bring unparalleled levels of authenticity, provenance and ownership to digital assets. Predominantly built on

Ethereum, with other blockchains like Solana and Flow gaining traction, NFTs represent a significant departure from traditional digital and physical asset management systems.[1]

- **Authenticity**: Blockchain technology secures the authenticity of NFTs through cryptographic hash functions. Each NFT is associated with a unique digital signature, which acts as an unforgeable certificate of authenticity. Unlike traditional digital files that can be easily copied or modified without trace, the blockchain's immutable ledger ensures that once an NFT is minted, its authenticity can be verified by anyone at any time. This starkly contrasts with traditional digital assets, where determining an item's originality often requires extensive manual verification and trust in issuing authorities.

- **Provenance**: Provenance, or the history of ownership and transfer of an NFT, is transparently and permanently recorded on the blockchain. Each transaction associated with the NFT, from its creation by the artist to every subsequent transfer or sale, is timestamped and stored on the blockchain. This comprehensive historical record is publicly accessible, providing clear evidence of the item's journey through various owners. Traditional systems, on the other hand, rely on physical certificates or centralised databases, which can be prone to loss, forgery or alterations, making the provenance of artworks or collectibles difficult to establish unequivocally.

- **Ownership**: Blockchain technology provides an unprecedented level of certainty regarding the ownership of digital assets. When an NFT is purchased, the transaction is recorded on the blockchain, and the buyer's digital wallet address becomes indelibly linked to the NFT as its current owner. This process ensures that ownership is easily verifiable and cannot be disputed, as the blockchain ledger is immutable and distributed across numerous nodes, making unauthorised alterations practically impossible. In contrast, traditional digital assets, such as downloads or licences, do not have this level of secure ownership attribution. Physical assets, while possibly having legal documents or receipts to prove ownership, do not offer the same immutable, instantly verifiable proof of ownership that blockchain technology enables for NFTs.

The integration of blockchain technology into the realm of digital assets through NFTs addresses long-standing challenges in establishing authenticity, provenance and secure ownership of digital items. By providing a decentralised, tamper-proof ledger that records every aspect of an NFT's existence and transaction history, blockchain technology offers a revolutionary solution that is vastly superior to traditional methods. This paradigm shift not only enhances security and trust in the digital economy but also opens up new possibilities for artists, creators and collectors in the digital age.

Applications of NFTs

Non-fungible tokens (NFTs) have ushered in a new era of digital ownership and utility, reaching far beyond their initial association with digital art and high-profile sales, such as Beeple's iconic *Everydays: The First 5000 Days*. The versatility of NFTs is demonstrated across various domains, from gaming and real estate to digital identity management and GameFi, showcasing their potential to revolutionise how we interact with digital and physical assets.

- **Gaming and GameFi**: In the gaming industry, NFTs are redefining user interaction by enabling true ownership of in-game assets. Players can now own, trade or sell their unique in-game items, characters or parcels of land in virtual worlds, thanks to NFTs. This has also given rise to the concept of GameFi, where gaming meets decentralised finance, allowing players to earn real-world rewards through gameplay. In GameFi ecosystems, NFTs play a critical role by representing assets that can accrue value, be staked or used to interact with decentralised applications (DApps), further blurring the lines between entertainment and finance.

- **Real Estate**: The tokenisation of real estate through NFTs is transforming property transactions by digitising property rights and ownership documents. This application facilitates transparent, efficient and fraud-resistant property transactions, enabling buyers and sellers to transfer ownership without the cumbersome paperwork and intermediaries traditionally involved. By representing real estate as NFTs, the entire history of a property, including previous transactions and ownership details, is accessible on the blockchain, enhancing trust and liquidity in the real estate market.

- **Digital Identities**: A profound application of NFTs lies in their capability to manage and verify digital identities in a secure and decentralised manner. This is especially evident in the implementation of the

Ethereum Name Service (ENS), highlighted in Section 5.3, which tokenises domain names as NFTs on the Ethereum blockchain. ENS allows users to assign readable names to their cryptocurrency addresses, streamlining transactions and interactions within the decentralised web. This mechanism not only simplifies digital communication by replacing complex addresses with human-readable names but also grants users full control over their digital presence and identity. The convergence of digital identity management with ENS highlights the utility of NFTs in enhancing online security, privacy and user experience. By leveraging NFTs for digital identity, users gain a robust tool for identity verification that circumvents the pitfalls of centralised identity management systems, heralding a new age of privacy and control in digital interactions.

The expansive applications of NFTs, from GameFi and real estate tokenisation to digital identity management and decentralised web services like ENS, underscore the versatility of NFTs as a technology. As NFTs continue to evolve, they promise to reshape numerous aspects of our digital and physical lives, offering innovative solutions to long-standing challenges in ownership, identity and online interaction.

Distribution Models: From Standard Mints to Dutch Auctions

As the NFT market evolves, distribution models such as Standard Mints and Dutch Auctions have emerged as key mechanisms for creators to release their digital assets. Each model offers distinct advantages but also faces specific challenges related to market inclusivity and integrity. The progression from Standard Mints to Dutch Auctions reflects an ongoing effort within the NFT community to refine these models for fairer price discovery and more equitable access while also grappling with broader market challenges:

- **Standard Mints: A Straightforward Beginning**

    Standard Mints serve as the bedrock of NFT distribution, favoured for their simplicity and straightforwardness. Creators set a fixed price for each NFT, enabling an uncomplicated entry point for buyers. This model's ease of understanding and accessibility has popularised it among emerging artists and creators in the digital space. However, its rigidity in price setting can lead to challenges in accurately gauging market demand, potentially resulting in either the rapid sell-out of undervalued NFTs or the sluggish sales of overpriced ones. Such issues highlight the need for models that better adapt to market dynamics, ensuring that both creators and collectors engage in fair and rewarding transactions.

- **Dutch Auctions: Dynamic Price Discovery**

    The introduction of Dutch Auctions marked a significant shift towards dynamic price discovery. By starting at a high price that decreases over time, Dutch Auctions allow the market to play a more active role in determining the value of NFTs. This model aims to mitigate the price discovery issues inherent in Standard Mints by adapting to real-time demand, potentially leading to a more accurate reflection of an NFT's market value. However, while Dutch Auctions offer a solution to some of the pricing challenges, they also introduce new concerns regarding market speculation and the accessibility for genuine collectors, particularly those with limited resources who may be priced out in the initial high-demand phases.

Addressing Market Challenges: Inclusivity and Integrity

The transition from Standard Mints to Dutch Auctions underscores a broader dialogue within the NFT community about inclusivity and integrity in the market. While both models strive to improve upon previous limitations, they also reflect ongoing challenges:

- **Inclusivity**: Ensuring equitable access to NFTs remains a concern. Whitelists and presales have emerged as methods to reward early supporters and community members with guaranteed or early access, but these mechanisms can inadvertently exclude newcomers and casual collectors from participating in high-demand releases. The challenge lies in designing distribution methods that balance rewarding loyal community members while keeping the market open and accessible to all.

- **Integrity**: Market integrity issues such as wash trading – where transactions are artificially inflated to manipulate perceived value and liquidity – pose significant challenges. Wash trading not only distorts the true value and demand of NFTs but also undermines trust in the NFT market. Both Standard Mints and Dutch Auctions, while primarily focused on price discovery and sale efficiency, must be part of a larger strategy to combat such practices. This involves implementing robust detection and prevention mechanisms and fostering a market culture that values transparency and genuine engagement.

Market Dynamics

The non-fungible token (NFT) market has experienced a surge in growth, transforming it into a multi-billion-dollar arena that attracts a wide array of participants, from art collectors and investors to digital enthusiasts. This expansive growth, however, comes with its share of volatility, characterised by periods of intense demand followed by significant market corrections. The liquidity of NFTs, which significantly varies across assets, is largely influenced by factors like rarity, demand and prevailing market sentiment, underlining the complex dynamics at play as the market continues to mature.

The mechanisms for pricing, buying and selling NFTs are evolving to accommodate the burgeoning ecosystem, with innovations such as Dutch Auctions and refined Standard Mints emerging to offer more dynamic and equitable transaction models. These developments are in response to the market's need for efficient, transparent and accessible means to connect creators with collectors, thereby shaping the future landscape of the NFT space.

NFTs extend well beyond the realm of digital art, demonstrating potential applications across various sectors, including entertainment, media, real estate and identity verification. This broad applicability underscores NFTs' role as a new form of digital ownership and value exchange, capable of significantly impacting how we interact with digital assets. The evolution of distribution models like Dutch Auctions and Standard Mints reflects the market's ongoing quest for solutions that balance efficiency, fairness and accessibility.

As the technology and market mechanisms behind NFTs continue to advance, they promise a pivotal role in the digital economy, reshaping our engagement with digital and physical assets alike. The journey from niche curiosity to a critical component of digital interaction highlights the transformative potential of NFTs, poised to drive innovation and change across the digital landscape.

7.2 The Evolution and Future Trends of NFT Markets

The NFT landscape is undergoing significant transformation, driven by the evolution of distribution models and the broadening of application horizons. From the simple beginnings of Standard Mints to the more dynamic Dutch Auctions, and now to the integration of whitelists and presales, the trajectory of NFTs highlights a robust pursuit of inclusivity, integrity and innovation within the market. These developments, while promising, underscore the imperative for continuous evolution and collaboration among stakeholders to forge a more equitable and transparent future for NFT trading.

Towards More Equitable and Transparent Distribution Models

The journey from Standard Mints to Dutch Auctions, complemented by the inclusion of whitelists and presales, signifies a dedication to overcoming the challenges of accessibility and market fairness. The exploration of hybrid models stands as a testament to this commitment, suggesting a future where distribution strategies are as diverse as the NFTs they aim to sell. These hybrid models, by merging various elements from existing methodologies, aspire to cater to the nuanced needs of both creators and collectors, ensuring that every release finds its ideal audience.

Enhanced transparency in distribution mechanisms is another critical area of advancement. By offering clear insights into the mechanics of sales, including participation criteria and pricing strategies, the NFT community aims to build a foundation of trust and openness. This level of transparency not only demystifies the buying and selling process but also plays a crucial role in mitigating the risks of market manipulation, ensuring that the value exchange is genuine and reflective of true market dynamics.

Community governance emerges as a pivotal theme in the evolution of NFT markets. By involving the broader NFT community in decision-making processes, there's a significant opportunity to ensure that distribution models are inclusive and reflective of a broad spectrum of interests and priorities. This collaborative approach could pave the way for a market that is not only vibrant and diverse but also resilient against the challenges that have historically plagued digital and physical asset trading.

Market Volatility and Liquidity Concerns

As NFTs continue to captivate a global audience, market volatility and liquidity emerge as significant concerns, highlighting the delicate balance between demand and supply. The fluctuating nature of the NFT market, while indicative of its dynamic and innovative spirit, also points to the need for more stable and predictable trading environments. Addressing these concerns involves not just refining distribution models but also enhancing the underlying infrastructure that supports NFT trading, from blockchain technology to market platforms, ensuring that liquidity is maintained without compromising the integrity of transactions.

Beyond Digital Art: The Expanding Applications of NFTs

The potential of NFTs extends far beyond the realm of digital art, promising to revolutionise industries such as entertainment, media, real estate and identity verification. This expansion of applications underlines the versatile nature of NFTs as tools for digital ownership and value exchange. In the entertainment and media industries, for example, NFTs offer novel ways to monetise content and engage audiences, while in real estate, the tokenisation of property rights could streamline transactions and reduce fraud. Furthermore, in the domain of identity verification, NFTs present innovative solutions for secure and user-controlled personal data management, challenging traditional centralised systems.

As NFTs venture into these new territories, the principles of equitable distribution, market stability and transparency will remain central to their success. The future trends of the NFT market, therefore, hinge not only on technological advancements but also on the community's ability to adapt, innovate and collaborate. Together, these efforts will shape a future where NFTs redefine our interaction with digital assets, heralding a new era of digital ownership and creativity.

7.3 Creating and Trading NFTs: A Step-by-Step Guide

Creating and listing an NFT on OpenSea involves a sequence of well-defined steps. Although this guide focuses on creating an NFT from an image, it's important to note that NFTs can encapsulate a wide range of digital formats, including but not limited to videos, audio files, digital art and even text documents. The choice of an image in this instance serves as a practical example due to its simplicity and the visual appeal of images on NFT marketplaces. However, the principles and steps outlined here can be adapted to other digital formats with some modifications, particularly in the file preparation and metadata specification stages. Let's delve into the process.

Step 1: Generate a Random Image with Python

```
import numpy as np
import matplotlib.pyplot as plt
from matplotlib import cm
import random
import json
import time

# Number of images to generate
m = 20

# Generate n steps for Brownian motion
n = 8888

# Define colormap options
colormap = [plt.cm.binary, plt.cm.gist_yarg, plt.cm.gist_gray,
plt.cm.gray,
            plt.cm.bone, plt.cm.pink, plt.cm.spring, plt.
            cm.summer, plt.cm.autumn,
            plt.cm.winter, plt.cm.cool, plt.cm.Wistia, plt.
            cm.hot, plt.cm.afmhot,
            plt.cm.gist_heat, plt.cm.copper]

# Define color names for metadata
color_names = ['binary', 'gist_yarg', 'gist_gray', 'gray',
'bone', 'pink', 'spring', 'summer', 'autumn', 'winter', 'cool',
'Wistia', 'hot', 'afmhot', 'gist_heat', 'copper']
```

```python
metadata = {}

for i in range(m):
    x = np.cumsum(np.random.randn(n))
    y = np.cumsum(np.random.randn(n))
    k = 10   # Interpolation factor
    x2 = np.interp(np.arange(n * k), np.arange(n) * k, x)
    y2 = np.interp(np.arange(n * k), np.arange(n) * k, y)

    fig, ax = plt.subplots(figsize=(8, 8))
    cmap_idx = random.randint(0, len(color_names) - 1)
    ax.scatter(x2, y2, c=range(n * k), linewidths=0,
    marker='o', s=3, cmap=colormap[cmap_idx])
    ax.axis('equal')
    ax.set_axis_off()
    plt.savefig(f'BMTEST_IMAGE/{i+1}.png')

    metadata[i] = {
        'name': f'#{i+1}',
        'description': 'This is just a Brownian Motion
        Simulation Game.',
        'edition': i + 1,
        'date': time.time(),
        'attributes': [
            {'trait_type': 'X Starting Point', 'value':
            f'{x2[0]:..2f}'},
            {'trait_type': 'X Ending Point', 'value':
            f'{x2[-1]:..2f}'},
            {'trait_type': 'Y Starting Point', 'value':
            f'{y2[0]:..2f}'},
```

```
            {'trait_type': 'Y Ending Point', 'value':
            f'{y2[-1]:.2f}'},
            {'trait_type': 'Color', 'value': color_
            names[cmap_idx]}
    ],
    'compiler': 'Hugo'
}
```

Before running the provided code, it's crucial to ensure that a folder named 'BMTEST_IMAGE' has already been created in the working directory. This preparation step is essential because the generated images will be saved in this folder before being uploaded to IPFS. The purpose of uploading images to IPFS is to ensure they are stored on a decentralised network, which aligns with the ethos of blockchain and NFTs, providing permanence and integrity for the digital assets.

The variable **m** in the script denotes the number of images (and consequently, NFTs) you intend to generate. While this example generates 20 images, it's common in the NFT space to create collections of 10,000 or 20,000 items to ensure a sufficiently large pool for community tokens. Such large collections help in fostering a sense of exclusivity and belonging among holders. However, for demonstration purposes and simplicity, this script is set to produce 20 unique images.

The variable **n** is set to dictate the complexity and uniqueness of the Brownian motion paths generated for each image. This parameter ensures that each resulting image, although not necessarily artistic in a traditional sense, exhibits distinct patterns that underscore the uniqueness critical to NFTs. This uniqueness is pivotal in demonstrating how even simple algorithmic processes can produce varied outcomes, enabling readers to generate distinct images for their experimentation with NFT creation.

The script incorporates the creation of five traits for each NFT, which are

1. **X Starting Point**: The initial x-coordinate of the Brownian path, adding spatial uniqueness.

2. **X Ending Point**: The final x-coordinate of the Brownian path, further contributing to the image's uniqueness.

3. **Y Starting Point**: The initial y-coordinate of the path, complementing the x-coordinates to define the path's origin.

4. **Y Ending Point**: The final y-coordinate, marking where the path concludes on the canvas.

5. **Color**: The randomly selected colour scheme used in the image, adding a visual trait that distinguishes each NFT.

These traits are stored in a metadata list for each generated image, capturing essential attributes that define and differentiate each NFT. This metadata is critical for potential collectors, as it provides verifiable details that contribute to the NFT's value and appeal. Subsequently, the information in the metadata list is converted into JSON files. This step is crucial for integrating the NFTs with blockchain and NFT marketplaces, as JSON is a widely accepted format for encoding NFT metadata, ensuring compatibility with platforms like OpenSea.

OpenSea's metadata standards allow for a rich representation of ERC721 or ERC1155 NFTs by providing detailed information beyond the unique identifier (tokenId). The metadata should be structured in a JSON format and made accessible via a URI returned by the **tokenURI** function in ERC721 or the **uri** method in ERC1155 contracts. This URI can point to an HTTP or IPFS URL, which, when queried, returns a JSON blob containing the NFT's metadata.

The JSON structure for NFT metadata typically includes several key properties:

- **image**: A URL to the image representing the NFT. It supports various image types and storage solutions, including IPFS and Arweave.
- **name**: The name of the item.
- **description**: A human-readable description of the item. Markdown is supported for formatting.
- **external_url**: A URL that will direct users to a page on your site for more details about the NFT.
- **attributes**: An array of properties that provide details about the item's traits or characteristics.

Your metadata can be hosted anywhere accessible via a URI, including decentralised storage solutions like IPFS, to align with the decentralised nature of NFTs. OpenSea supports IPFS and Arweave URIs directly, allowing for immutable and permanent hosting of metadata, ensuring that the digital asset cannot be altered once minted.

By adhering to these metadata standards and structuring your NFT's metadata accordingly, you ensure that your digital asset is represented on OpenSea in the best possible way. This includes showcasing high-quality images, detailed descriptions and unique attributes that highlight the distinctiveness of your NFT, thereby attracting potential buyers and collectors on the platform.

After generating your digital assets for NFTs, an essential next step is to securely upload them to a storage solution. While IPFS (InterPlanetary File System) is a popular choice due to its decentralised nature, ensuring the permanence and integrity of your files, you are not limited to this option. Your digital assets and NFT metadata can be stored on any platform that provides a direct link to the files, such as Google Drive or Dropbox.

Step 2: Upload the Asset to a Storage Solution

IPFS is one of several methods you can use to store your digital assets. As a decentralised storage system, it distributes your files across a global network of nodes, ensuring that the data remains accessible and resistant to censorship. This is particularly advantageous for NFTs as it links your digital asset with a unique, immutable URI in the NFT's metadata, confirming that the asset cannot be altered or removed.

Alternatively, centralised solutions like Google Drive or Dropbox can also be used to store NFT data if they provide a direct URL to the files. While these platforms may offer convenience and user-friendly interfaces, they do not inherently provide the same level of decentralisation and security as IPFS. When using centralised services, it's crucial to ensure that the URLs are permanent and directly accessible, as any changes in the URL structure could make the metadata links in your NFTs ineffective.

Option 1: Setting Up Your Own IPFS Node

Setting up your own IPFS node involves installing IPFS on your machine, initialising your IPFS repository and starting the IPFS daemon to connect your node to the IPFS network. This method gives you full control over your content's hosting but comes with increased complexity and responsibility. You'll need to manage your node's availability and connectivity to ensure your assets remain accessible. This approach might involve

- Downloading and installing IPFS
- Initialising your IPFS node with **ipfs init**
- Starting the IPFS daemon using **ipfs daemon**
- Adding your files to IPFS using **ipfs add -r /path/to/your/folder**

While running your own node offers a high degree of control and direct engagement with the IPFS network, it requires a good understanding of IPFS and might not be the most straightforward option for beginners or those looking for quick and easy solutions.

Option 2: Using Third-Party Services like Pinata

For many users, especially those new to IPFS or seeking convenience, third-party services like Pinata offer an easier way to upload and manage content on IPFS. Pinata simplifies the process by providing a user-friendly interface and additional features like pinning services to ensure your content remains readily available on the IPFS network.

To use Pinata for uploading your NFT assets:

1. **Create an Account**: Sign up on Pinata.cloud and log in to your account.

2. **Upload Content**: Navigate to the 'Upload' section and choose to upload a folder. Select the **BMTEST_IMAGE** folder containing your generated images. Pinata will automatically pin your uploaded content, ensuring its availability on the IPFS network.

3. **Retrieve IPFS Hashes**: Once uploaded, Pinata will provide an IPFS hash (CID) for your folder and each contained file. These hashes serve as permanent, immutable links to your assets, which you'll include in your NFTs' metadata.

For this tutorial, considering we have 20 images and subsequently 20 JSON documents for metadata, Pinata's free tier, which offers 100 free pins, is sufficient. Uploading the entire folder not only simplifies the process but also maintains the organisational structure of your assets, making it easier to reference and manage them as you proceed with NFT minting.

CHAPTER 7 NON-FUNGIBLE TOKENS (NFTS) AND DIGITAL ART

While setting up your own IPFS node offers a hands-on approach and complete control, it entails a steeper learning curve and ongoing management responsibilities. In contrast, using a third-party service like Pinata provides a straightforward, user-friendly solution, making it an attractive option for creators looking to streamline their NFT creation process. Regardless of the chosen method, the key objective is to ensure that your digital assets are securely uploaded to IPFS, paving the way for their transformation into NFTs.

After uploading your images to Pinata, which is a user-friendly interface for interacting with IPFS, you'll notice that each file has a corresponding CID (content identifier). This CID is a unique hash representing your file on the IPFS network and acts as a permanent pointer to its location.

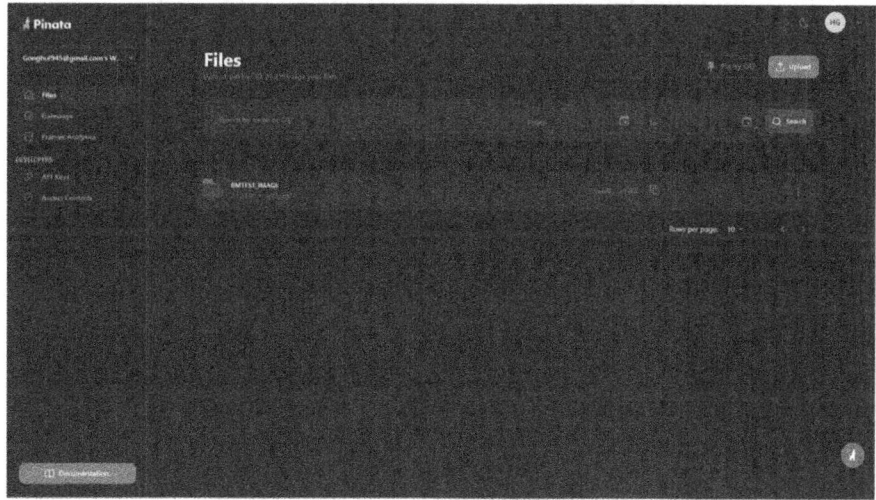

Figure 7-1. *Screenshots of Pinata – IMAGE*

When you upload an entire folder to Pinata, as shown in your screenshots, the service provides you with a CID for the entire folder as well. This is exceptionally useful when dealing with collections of files, such as a series of images for a 10k NFT collection, because you can

217

CHAPTER 7 NON-FUNGIBLE TOKENS (NFTS) AND DIGITAL ART

reference the folder's CID and append individual filenames to create complete URLs for each NFT's metadata.

Here's a breakdown of the steps to view and use the CIDs:

1. **Access Your Files on IPFS**: Once your **BMTEST_IMAGE** folder is uploaded, navigate to the 'Files' section on Pinata. You will see the folder listed with its size and upload date.

2. **Folder CID**: Click the folder, and you'll find an index of files, each with its own CID, similar to the second screenshot you've provided. This index is the folder's CID, and it will look something like **Qm...**, a string of letters and numbers.

3. **Individual File CID**: In the index view on IPFS, each file will have a link that includes the folder's CID and the file's name. For instance, the URL for the first image would be something like **ipfs://Qm... FolderCID/1.png**; see Figure 7-2.

Figure 7-2. Screenshots of File CID – IMAGE

CHAPTER 7   NON-FUNGIBLE TOKENS (NFTS) AND DIGITAL ART

4. **Utilising CIDs in Metadata**: These IPFS links are what you'll use in the metadata for your NFTs. When you create the JSON metadata file for each NFT, you'll specify the **image** field with the IPFS URL pointing to each image, ensuring that OpenSea or any other NFT marketplace can retrieve and display the image.

In summary, the use of IPFS for hosting the images and metadata of NFTs is advantageous because it ensures decentralised storage, aligning with the decentralised nature of blockchain and NFTs. Unlike centralised hosting solutions that depend on a single server or company, IPFS operates on a peer-to-peer network, making the content resistant to censorship and server outages, which in turn enhances the durability and availability of the NFTs' associated digital assets. This decentralised approach is not just a technical preference but a core principle of blockchain technology, offering a level of resilience and permanence in line with the immutable nature of NFTs themselves. Therefore, while centralised URLs could technically serve a similar purpose, they do not provide the same level of trustless assurance as IPFS does, which is why IPFS is often the preferred choice for NFT storage, as also highlighted in Section 3.3.

Step 3: Create Metadata Compliant with OpenSea's Standards

After uploading your digital assets to IPFS and obtaining their CIDs, the next critical step in the NFT creation process is generating metadata that complies with OpenSea's standards. Metadata in the context of NFTs is a JSON file that contains detailed information about each token, including its name, description and a link to the digital asset (typically an image or other multimedia files) on IPFS.

The metadata should be structured according to the specifications that marketplaces like OpenSea have set out. This structure not only includes basic identification properties but also allows for a variety of attributes that detail the NFT's traits, contributing to its uniqueness and collectability.

Before you execute the script to generate metadata files, make sure to create a folder named **BMTEST_JSON** in your working directory to store the final JSON documents. This organisational step ensures that all metadata files are systematically arranged and easily accessible for subsequent steps in the NFT minting process.

With your CID at hand (in this example, **QmcdEjixt5jJq8ynXYyyNWFgicbUs7xt4CygB5DxQ62KMc**), you will replace it with the actual CID obtained from your IPFS upload process. The Python script iterates through each digital asset, assigning the correct image URL and saving the metadata into individual JSON files:

```
for k in range(m):
    metadata[k]['image'] = f'ipfs://QmcdEjixt5jJq8ynXYyyNWFgicbUs7xt4CygB5DxQ62KMc/{k+1}.png'
    with open(f'BMTEST_JSON/{k+1}.json', 'w') as fp:
        json.dump(metadata[k], fp)
```

Once the script has run, the **BMTEST_JSON** folder will contain 20 JSON files, each representing the metadata for one NFT. These files will detail the stored location and traits of each corresponding digital asset. This metadata plays a crucial role when minting NFTs as it tells the blockchain where the NFT's associated digital asset can be found and how it should be represented on platforms like OpenSea.

Compliance with metadata standards is not merely a technical requirement but a means to ensure that the NFTs will be fully compatible with OpenSea's user interface and feature set. It allows for rich displays, filtering and sorting options within the marketplace, enhancing the user's experience and the discoverability of the NFTs.

CHAPTER 7 NON-FUNGIBLE TOKENS (NFTS) AND DIGITAL ART

By carefully preparing and structuring your metadata, you contribute to the overall narrative and value proposition of your NFT collection. This structured data not only informs potential buyers about the unique characteristics of each NFT but also serves as the backbone for how these assets are interacted with and perceived within the digital ecosystem.

Once you have generated the JSON metadata files for each of your NFTs, the final step in this phase is to upload these files to Pinata, just as you did with the image files. This will assign a unique CID to the entire **BMTEST_JSON** folder and individual CIDs to each JSON file within it; see Figure 7-3.

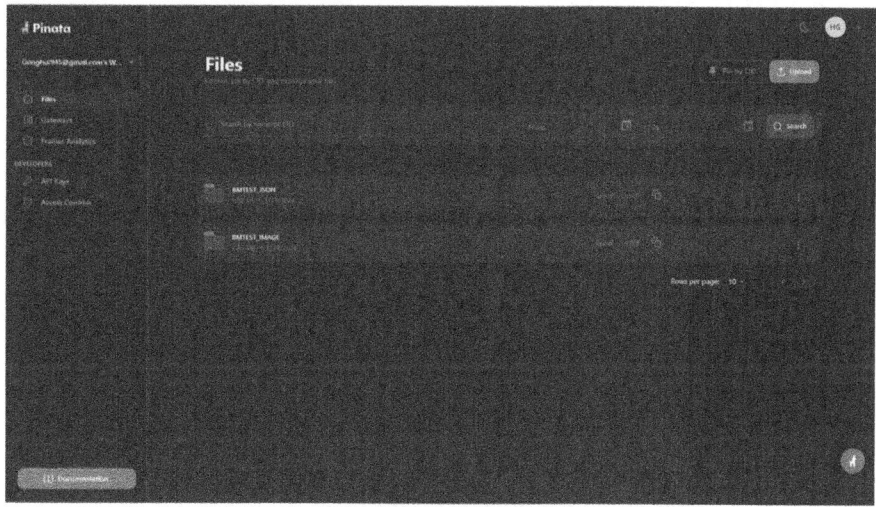

Figure 7-3. *Screenshots of Pinata – JSON*

After the upload, you can view your JSON files on Pinata or directly through the IPFS gateway; see Figure 7-4. By uploading your JSON metadata to Pinata, you are effectively pinning your NFT descriptions to the IPFS network, ensuring they are as permanently and immutably stored as the image files themselves. Each JSON file now has a dedicated CID that can be used within the NFT's metadata to point to its description, traits, and other attributes.

221

This step is crucial as it completes the NFT's data structure, ensuring that all components – visual and descriptive – are decentralised and resistant to changes. It maintains the integrity of the NFT by securing its associated information in a way that is consistent with the decentralised and permanent nature of blockchain assets.

With both the images and their metadata now securely uploaded to IPFS and their CIDs known, you have all the necessary components to mint your NFTs on the blockchain, ensuring that they are ready for integration with NFT marketplaces such as OpenSea.

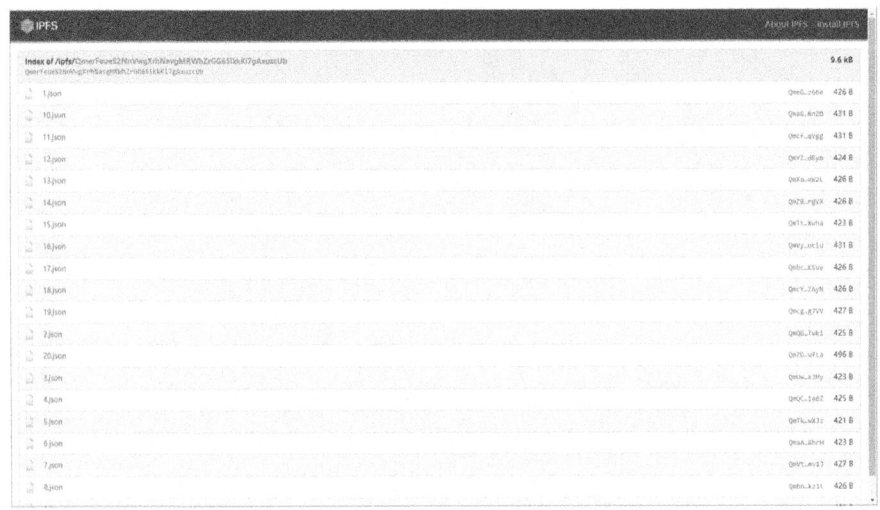

Figure 7-4. Screenshots of File CID – JSON

Step 4: Mint the NFT on the Blockchain

Using a development environment like Remix, you write and compile your ERC721 smart contract. The contract should include functions to mint NFTs and set base URI, which points to the location of your metadata on IPFS. You may use the example from Section 3.3 or the following example which has been modified based on the code provided by the YouTube influencer Hashlips:

```
// SPDX-License-Identifier: GPL-3.0

// Amended by HUGO

pragma solidity >=0.7.0 <0.9.0;

// Importing ERC721Enumerable from OpenZeppelin Contracts
// ERC721Enumerable is an extension of ERC721 standard that includes
// functionalities for enumerating tokens. It is widely used due to its
// robustness and thorough testing, making OpenZeppelin a trusted standard
// in the development of Ethereum smart contracts.
import "github.com/OpenZeppelin/openzeppelin-contracts/blob/v4.8.0/contracts/token/ERC721/extensions/ERC721Enumerable.sol";

// Importing Ownable from OpenZeppelin Contracts
// Ownable is a contract module which provides basic authorization control functions.
// This simplifies the implementation of "user permissions" or "ownership" making it easier
// to restrict access to certain functions to only the owner of the contract.
import "github.com/OpenZeppelin/openzeppelin-contracts/blob/v4.8.0/contracts/access/Ownable.sol";

// Note: It is crucial to import smart contract libraries and modules from reputable and
// verified sources only. Using unverified or poorly reviewed code can lead to serious
// security vulnerabilities and potential loss of funds. Always ensure the source of any
// imported code is trustworthy and secure.
```

CHAPTER 7   NON-FUNGIBLE TOKENS (NFTS) AND DIGITAL ART

```
contract NFT is ERC721Enumerable, Ownable {
  using Strings for uint256;

  string public baseURI;
  string public baseExtension = ".json";
  uint256 public cost = 0.01 ether;
  uint256 public maxSupply = 10000;
  uint256 public maxMintAmount = 20;
  bool public paused = false;
  mapping(address => bool) public whitelisted;

  constructor(
    string memory _name,
    string memory _symbol,
    string memory _initBaseURI
  ) ERC721(_name, _symbol) {
    setBaseURI(_initBaseURI);
    mint(msg.sender, 20);
  }

  // internal
  function _baseURI() internal view virtual override returns
  (string memory) {
    return baseURI;
  }

  // public
  function mint(address _to, uint256 _mintAmount) public
  payable {
    uint256 supply = totalSupply();
    require(!paused);
    require(_mintAmount > 0);
    require(_mintAmount <= maxMintAmount);
    require(supply + _mintAmount <= maxSupply);
```

CHAPTER 7 NON-FUNGIBLE TOKENS (NFTS) AND DIGITAL ART

```solidity
  if (msg.sender != owner()) {
     if(whitelisted[msg.sender] != true) {
       require(msg.value >= cost * _mintAmount);
     }
  }

  for (uint256 i = 1; i <= _mintAmount; i++) {
    _safeMint(_to, supply + i);
  }
}

function walletOfOwner(address _owner)
  public
  view
  returns (uint256[] memory)
{
  uint256 ownerTokenCount = balanceOf(_owner);
  uint256[] memory tokenIds = new uint256[](ownerTokenCount);
  for (uint256 i; i < ownerTokenCount; i++) {
    tokenIds[i] = tokenOfOwnerByIndex(_owner, i);
  }
  return tokenIds;
}

function tokenURI(uint256 tokenId)
  public
  view
  virtual
  override
  returns (string memory)
{
  require(
    _exists(tokenId),
```

CHAPTER 7   NON-FUNGIBLE TOKENS (NFTS) AND DIGITAL ART

```
      "ERC721Metadata: URI query for nonexistent token"
  );

  string memory currentBaseURI = _baseURI();
  return bytes(currentBaseURI).length > 0
      ? string(abi.encodePacked(currentBaseURI, tokenId.
      toString(), baseExtension))
      : "";
}

//onlyowner
function setCost(uint256 _newCost) public onlyOwner {
  cost = _newCost;
}

function setmaxMintAmount(uint256 _newmaxMintAmount) public
onlyOwner {
  maxMintAmount = _newmaxMintAmount;
}

function setBaseURI(string memory _newBaseURI) public
onlyOwner {
  baseURI = _newBaseURI;
}

function setBaseExtension(string memory _newBaseExtension)
public onlyOwner {
  baseExtension = _newBaseExtension;
}

function pause(bool _state) public onlyOwner {
  paused = _state;
}
```

CHAPTER 7   NON-FUNGIBLE TOKENS (NFTS) AND DIGITAL ART

```
function whitelistUser(address _user) public onlyOwner {
    whitelisted[_user] = true;
}

function removeWhitelistUser(address _user) public
onlyOwner {
    whitelisted[_user] = false;
}

function withdraw() public payable onlyOwner {
    // This will pay Hugo 2.5% of the initial sale.
    // You can remove this if you want, or keep it in to
    support Hugo.
    // ===========================================================
    // ===========================================================
    (bool hs, ) = payable(0x979390763254C21986D24139818a052
    C9D934fb8).call{value: address(this).balance * 25 /
    1000}("");
    require(hs);
    // ===========================================================

    // This will payout the owner 97.5% of the contract
    balance.
    // Do not remove this otherwise you will not be able to
    withdraw the funds.
    // ===========================================================
    (bool os, ) = payable(owner()).call{value: address(this).
    balance}("");
    require(os);
    // ===========================================================
}
}
```

227

CHAPTER 7   NON-FUNGIBLE TOKENS (NFTS) AND DIGITAL ART

This is a smart contract for an ERC721 token, which is a standard for representing ownership of non-fungible tokens, commonly used for digital assets such as NFTs. The contract includes several important elements and features which are standard for NFTs but also introduces some custom functions and modifiers:

1. **Variables**
    - **baseURI**: Stores the base part of the URI used to access the token's metadata
    - **baseExtension**: The file extension appended to the **tokenURI**
    - **cost**: The cost to mint each NFT
    - **maxSupply**: The maximum number of tokens that can be minted
    - **maxMintAmount**: The maximum number of tokens that can be minted in a single transaction
    - **paused**: A boolean that can pause the minting function when **true**
    - **whitelisted**: A mapping that keeps track of addresses that are whitelisted to mint tokens, possibly without paying the cost or with other benefits
2. **Constructor**: When the contract is deployed, it sets the initial **baseURI** and mints 20 tokens to the contract deployer.
3. **Minting**: The **mint** function allows a user to mint new tokens. It includes checks for whether minting is paused, if the mint amount is appropriate and

CHAPTER 7   NON-FUNGIBLE TOKENS (NFTS) AND DIGITAL ART

if the supply cap has not been exceeded. It also handles whether the sender is required to pay for minting based on their whitelist status.

4. **Helper Functions**

    - **walletOfOwner**: Returns an array of tokenIds that the owner has

    - **tokenURI**: Returns the full URI to the metadata of the given tokenId

5. **Owner-Only Functions**: There are several functions that can only be called by the owner of the contract, enabling them to change the minting cost, the maximum minting amount, the base URI and the base extension. The owner can also pause or unpause minting, whitelist users and withdraw funds collected from minting.

6. **Withdraw Function**: The **withdraw** function allows the owner to withdraw funds from the contract. It includes a feature to pay 2.5% of the withdrawal to the address presumably belonging to Hugo (as a royalty or developer fee) and the rest to the owner's address.

This contract provides a customisable and ready-to-use implementation for an NFT project with the flexibility to set various parameters and maintain control over the minting process. By deploying this contract to the Ethereum blockchain, a project can start minting NFTs that are compliant with the ERC721 standard and OpenSea's metadata standards, provided the metadata URIs point to valid JSON metadata files.

Then, choose a network to deploy your contract. For testing purposes, as mentioned, the Sepolia Testnet can be used to avoid real transaction costs. After compiling the contract, deploy it to the Sepolia Testnet. This will require some test Ether, which you can obtain from a faucet specific to Sepolia. Upon successful deployment, you will receive a contract address which is unique to your NFT collection.

When deploying the smart contract, it is important to ensure that you input the correct details for the NFT's name, symbol and the base URI of the metadata.

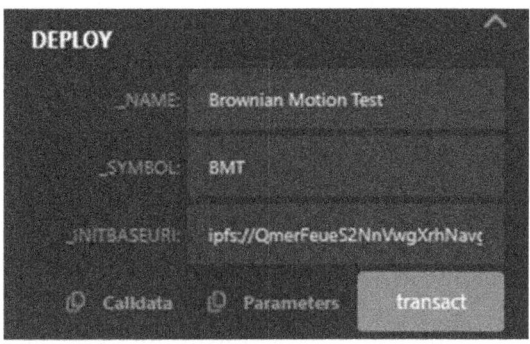

Figure 7-5. Smart Contract Deployment Information

The name (_NAME) is typically a descriptive title for the collection of NFTs, such as 'Brownian Motion Test' in this case. The symbol (_SYMBOL) is an abbreviation that represents your NFT collection, like 'BMT' for Brownian Motion Test.

For the base URI (_INITBASEURI), this should be the IPFS URI that points to the location where your metadata JSON files are stored. It is essential to use the CID provided by Pinata for the folder containing your JSON files, which in your example is **ipfs:// QmerFeueS2NnVwgXrhNavgMRWhZrGG65ikkKi7gAxuzcUb/**.

CHAPTER 7   NON-FUNGIBLE TOKENS (NFTS) AND DIGITAL ART

The trailing slash '/' is crucial because your smart contract appends this base URI to the token IDs to form the full URI for each token's metadata, as indicated by the **baseURI** and **baseExtension** variables in the contract:

```solidity
string public baseURI; string public baseExtension = ".json";
```

With the base URI set to **ipfs://QmerFeueS2NnVwgXrhNavgMRWhZrGG65ikkKi7gAxuzcUb/** and the base extension set to **.json**, the contract will automatically generate the correct metadata URI for each NFT. For example, if you mint an NFT with a token ID of 1, the contract will concatenate the base URI with the token ID and the base extension to form the full metadata URI:

ipfs://QmerFeueS2NnVwgXrhNavgMRWhZrGG65ikkKi7gAxuzcUb/1.json.

This full URI is where OpenSea and other platforms will look to retrieve the NFT's metadata, which includes the name, description, image and attributes of the NFT. Getting this right is essential for the proper display and functioning of your NFT on marketplaces and ensures that all the metadata associated with your NFTs is accessible and correctly linked.

After deploying your NFT contract to the blockchain using Remix or another development environment, you'll see a series of functions that you can interact with directly in the Remix interface, as shown in Figure 7-6. These functions allow you to manage various aspects of your NFT collection.

Here's an expanded explanation of the post-deployment steps you can take:

1. **Minting NFTs**

    - Use the **mint** function to create new NFTs. Specify the recipient's address (**_to**) and the number of tokens (**_mintAmount**) you want to mint.

231

- The **mint** function will also require that the cost set in the contract is paid if the minter is not the owner or not whitelisted, ensuring that the smart contract's rules for minting are followed.

2. **Setting Prices and Limits**

   - The **setCost** function allows you to update the minting price (**_newCost**) for each NFT if needed.

   - Use the **setmaxMintAmount** function to adjust the maximum number of tokens that can be minted in a single transaction (**_newmaxMintAmount**). This is useful for managing the flow of new tokens and preventing spamming of the network.

3. **Managing Whitelist**

   - The **whitelistUser** function enables the contract owner to add an address to the whitelist, potentially giving that address the ability to mint without paying the minting cost or giving them early access to minting.

   - Conversely, the **removeWhitelistUser** function removes an address from the whitelist.

4. **Controlling Contract Behaviour**

   - The **pause** function can be toggled to temporarily halt all minting activity, which can be useful in various situations, such as when updating contract parameters or in the event of discovering a critical bug.

CHAPTER 7   NON-FUNGIBLE TOKENS (NFTS) AND DIGITAL ART

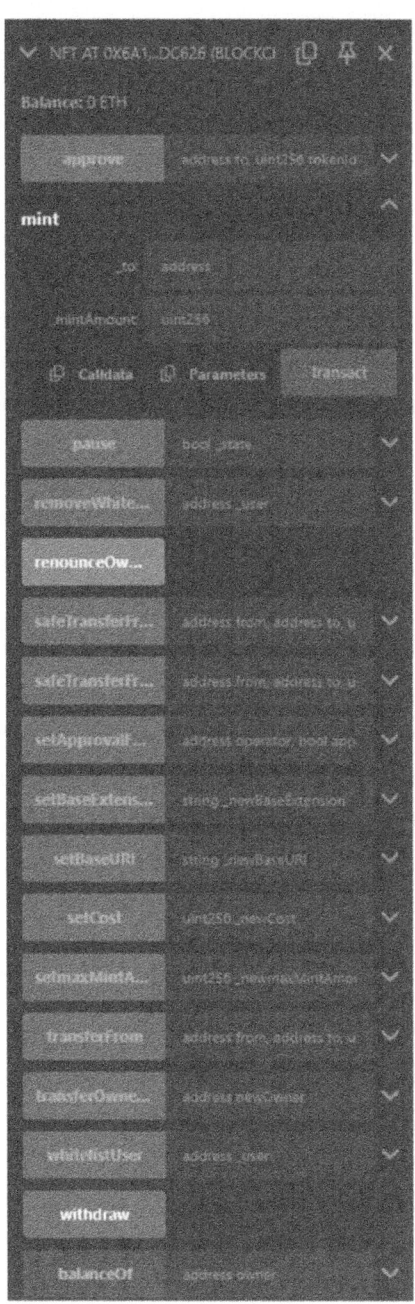

Figure 7-6. *Smart Contract Functions*

- The **withdraw** function allows the contract owner to transfer all the collected Ether to their address, less any percentage predefined in the contract to pay royalties or developer fees.

5. **Adjusting Metadata Settings**

    - If you need to change the location where your NFT's metadata is stored, you can use the **setBaseURI** function to update the base URI that is prepended to token IDs to form the full metadata URI.

    - The **setBaseExtension** function can be used to change the extension of the metadata files if needed (e.g. from **.json** to another format).

It's important to note that while the contract provides a range of controls for managing your NFT collection, interacting with these functions requires a transaction on the blockchain and will consume gas. Additionally, functions that are marked as **onlyOwner** can only be called by the account that deployed the contract, providing a level of administrative control over the NFT collection.

This interface allows you to effectively manage your NFT project directly from the blockchain without the need for additional front-end development. Whether it's minting new tokens, adjusting the cost, managing the whitelist or withdrawing funds, you have direct control over these aspects through the deployed smart contract's functions.

After minting your NFTs, you can confirm that the transaction has been processed successfully by checking the transaction details on a blockchain explorer like Etherscan, even for Sepolia testnet transactions; see Figure 7-7. The transaction receipt provides a wealth of information, including the transaction hash, status and the number of tokens transferred, among other details.

CHAPTER 7 NON-FUNGIBLE TOKENS (NFTS) AND DIGITAL ART

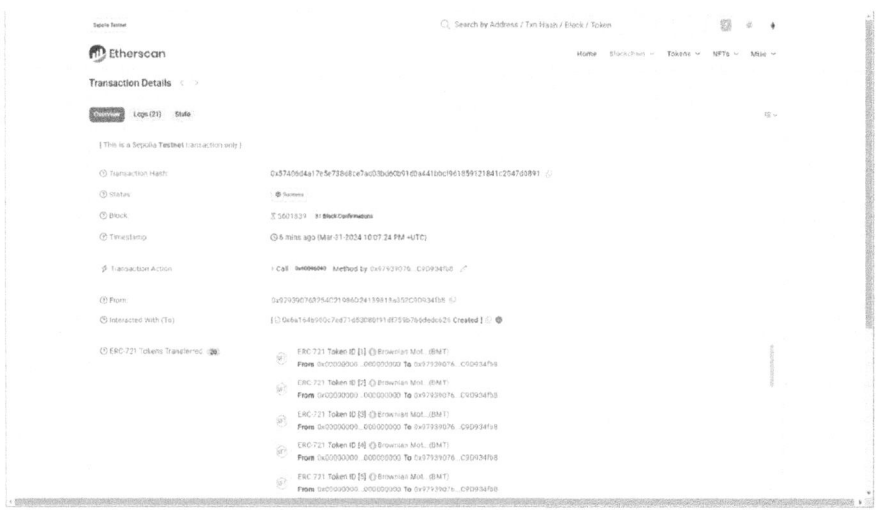

Figure 7-7. *View the ERC721 Smart Contract*

Step 5: List the NFT for Sale on OpenSea

Visit OpenSea's testnet (https://testnets.opensea.io/) and log in using your wallet. This wallet should be the one you used for minting and should have Sepolia Testnet selected. In the Studio section of OpenSea, you'll see your minted NFTs. If your NFTs do not show up immediately, you may need to refresh the page or wait a short period for the blockchain to propagate the changes.

Click one of your NFTs to view its details. Figure 7-8, illustrated in your first screenshot, will display the NFT's image, description and all the traits associated with it.

CHAPTER 7   NON-FUNGIBLE TOKENS (NFTS) AND DIGITAL ART

Figure 7-8. BMT NFT on OpenSea

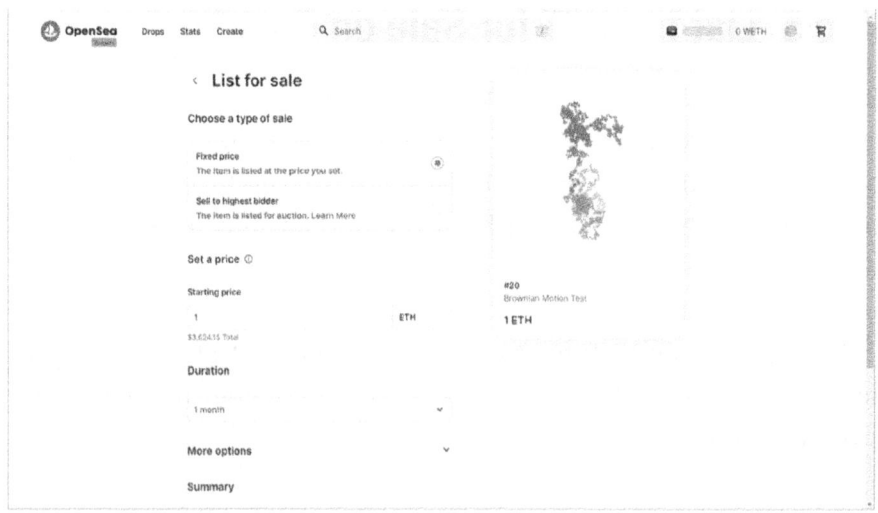

Figure 7-9. NFT List for Sale

Listing for Sale

- Click the 'List for sale' button. You'll be taken to a page where you can set the terms of the sale; see Figure 7-9.

- Choose the type of sale: a fixed price where buyers can purchase immediately at your set price or an auction where you can sell to the highest bidder.

- Set your price. Input the starting price for your NFT in ETH. Keep in mind the current market trends when setting your price.

- Determine the duration. Decide how long the listing will be active. You can choose from a day up to several months, depending on how quickly you are looking to sell.

Once you have configured all the sale details, review your listing. It's essential to double-check all the information as once you confirm, it will be recorded on the blockchain. Post your listing by clicking the confirmation button. This action will trigger a MetaMask transaction, and you'll need to pay a gas fee to complete the listing process.

After doing this, your NFT is now officially up for sale. Buyers can view and make offers on your NFT if they find it appealing. You can also share the listing link on social media or with potential buyers directly to attract more visibility.

Through the steps of generating digital assets, uploading them to IPFS, creating and configuring metadata, minting NFTs on the blockchain and finally listing them for sale on OpenSea, creators embark on a comprehensive journey that showcases the robust capabilities of NFT technology. This process allows for the tokenisation of a vast array of digital creations, providing a secure way to claim ownership and transact in the digital realm.

From the initial artistic conception to the final act of selling on a global marketplace, NFTs offer an unparalleled level of flexibility and security for creators to monetise their work. The technology behind NFTs fundamentally alters how digital art and content are valued and traded, enabling artists to directly connect with collectors without intermediaries.

This transformative process not only brings a new dimension of recognition to digital creativity but also fosters a decentralised and inclusive economy for digital assets. As NFTs continue to evolve, they will likely unlock even more possibilities for creators across all forms of media, from static visuals to interactive and multimedia experiences. The NFT movement is a testament to the innovation happening at the intersection of art, technology and commerce, heralding a new era for creators and collectors alike.

7.4 Summary

This chapter provides an in-depth exploration of Non-Fungible Tokens (NFTs) and their pivotal role in the digital economy. It begins by explaining the unique characteristics of NFTs, including their indivisibility and uniqueness, which differentiate them from fungible tokens like cryptocurrencies. Built on blockchain technology, NFTs offer solutions to long-standing challenges in the digital world, such as ensuring authenticity, provenance, and secure ownership of digital assets.

The chapter also discusses the growing applications of NFTs beyond digital art, extending into gaming, real estate, and digital identity management. NFTs are shown to redefine asset ownership by enabling true ownership and transferability of in-game items, property, and even personal data in a decentralised manner. This transformation is complemented by various distribution models like Standard Mints and Dutch Auctions, which play a crucial role in how NFTs are released and traded.

Finally, the chapter outlines a step-by-step guide for creating and trading NFTs, from generating digital assets, uploading them to decentralised storage solutions like IPFS, and minting them on the blockchain, to listing NFTs on marketplaces such as OpenSea. It highlights the technical aspects of NFT creation, including metadata standards and smart contract functionalities, ensuring that creators and developers can successfully mint and sell NFTs in a secure and transparent manner.

7.5 Note

1. Yan, T. (2024). From Dutch Auctions to Open Editions: A Deep Dive into NFT Distribution Models. Delphi Digital. `https://members.delphidigital.io/reports/from-dutch-auctions-to-open-editions-a-deep-dive-into-nft-distribution-models` (Accessed: 9 April 2024).

CHAPTER 8

DEX and Market Cap Management

8.1 How DEXs Work

Decentralised exchanges (DEXs) represent a significant shift from traditional financial exchange mechanisms, embodying the ethos of decentralisation central to blockchain technology. By facilitating peer-to-peer transactions without intermediaries, DEXs offer a level of transparency, security and accessibility not typically found in centralised exchanges (CEXs).

Principles of Operation

At the core of most DEXs, including platforms like Uniswap, is the Automated Market Maker (AMM) model. Unlike traditional exchanges that rely on order books to match buyers and sellers, AMMs use liquidity pools for asset trading.[1] These pools are funded by liquidity providers (LPs) who deposit pairs of tokens in a smart contract. In return, LPs earn trading fees based on the proportion of the pool they provide.

CHAPTER 8   DEX AND MARKET CAP MANAGEMENT

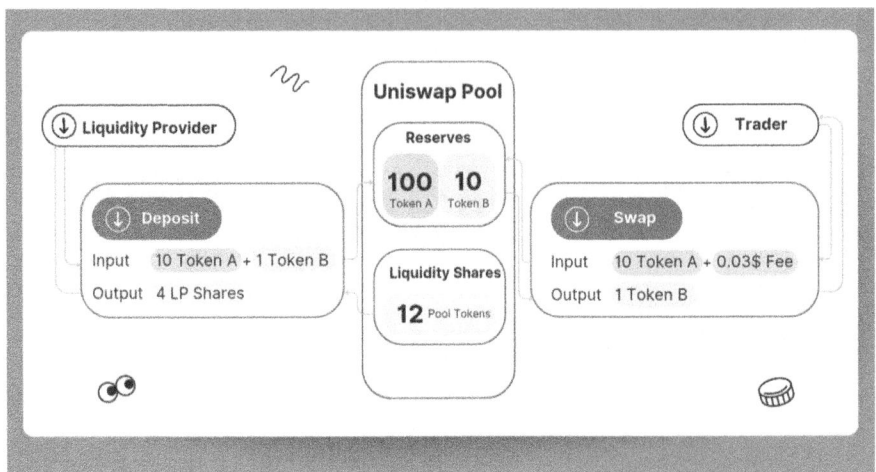

Figure 8-1. How DEXs Work

Figure 8-1 illustrates the core operations of a decentralised exchange (DEX) like Uniswap, utilising an Automated Market Maker (AMM) protocol.

LPs deposit pairs of tokens into a liquidity pool, and these pairs must be in equivalent value to maintain the balance of the pool. In the provided image, an LP deposits '10 Token A + 1 Token B' into the Uniswap Pool and receives '4 LP Shares' in return. This mechanism is critical as it allows the pool to have sufficient funds to facilitate trades for other users.[2]

The AMM protocol automates price discovery without the need for a traditional order book. The image represents this with a 'Swap' operation where '10 Token A' is swapped for '1 Token B'. A nominal fee (in this case, $0.03) is included in the transaction, which is shared among LPs as a reward for providing liquidity.

The AMM leverages the concept of liquidity pools, which consist of reserves of paired tokens. These reserves are what traders transact against. The liquidity shares, represented in the image as '12 Pool Tokens', denote the proportional ownership of the pool's total liquidity by the LPs.

When an LP contributes liquidity, they receive pool tokens, which can be redeemed later for their share of the pool, along with a portion of the transaction fees accrued over time.

The most commonly used pricing mechanism in AMMs is the constant product formula, represented as '$x * y = k$', where 'x' and 'y' are the respective quantities of the two assets in the liquidity pool, and 'k' is a constant. This formula ensures that the product of the quantities of the two assets always remains the same, maintaining the pool's balance after trades. The image does not explicitly show this formula, but it underlies the swap operation depicted.

Traders interact directly with the liquidity pool via their wallets. They can swap tokens by interacting with the smart contract that governs the liquidity pool, as shown in the 'Swap' section of Figure 8-1. The fees and slippage are calculated automatically by the AMM based on the current state of the liquidity pool.

A key principle of DEXs is their decentralised nature. Unlike centralised exchanges, DEXs do not hold users' funds, and all trades are executed via smart contracts directly on the blockchain. This minimises counterparty risk and provides transparency in the execution of trades.

For liquidity providers, the primary implication is the potential for earning transaction fees. However, they are also exposed to risks like impermanent loss, which occurs when the price of tokens in the pool changes significantly after they have deposited their assets.

For traders, DEXs offer the advantage of direct and immediate token swaps with potentially lower fees than centralised exchanges. They also benefit from the security provided by blockchain technology, as there is no central point of failure.

CHAPTER 8   DEX AND MARKET CAP MANAGEMENT

Token Listing and Liquidity Pools

Listing your token and establishing a liquidity pool, as exemplified with Uniswap here, is a foundational step for enabling trading and carving out an initial marketplace for your token. This approach is generally applicable across various DEX platforms.

- **Step 1: Prepare Your Token**

    Before you begin, make sure your ERC20 token contract is deployed to the Ethereum mainnet, and you've sent your tokens to your MetaMask wallet.

- **Step 2: Access Uniswap Interface**

    Go to the Uniswap interface. The first screenshot shows the 'Add Liquidity' page on Uniswap. Here, you'll start the process of creating a liquidity pool for your token.

- **Step 3: Connect Your Wallet**

    Using MetaMask or another compatible wallet, connect to Uniswap. Your wallet address will appear in the top-right corner once it's connected.

- **Step 4: Add Liquidity**

    Click the 'Pool' tab and then select 'Add Liquidity'. In the interface, you'll select the token pair you wish to provide liquidity for. This is where you would select your token and a pair like ETH, as seen in Figure 8-2.

CHAPTER 8   DEX AND MARKET CAP MANAGEMENT

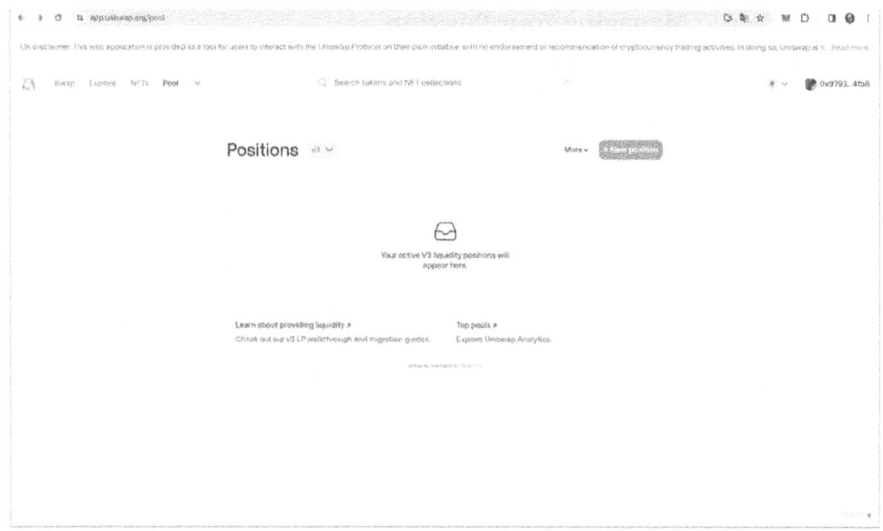

Figure 8-2. *Add Liquidity – 1*

- **Step 5: Set Up Token Pair and Initial Price**

    Upon clicking 'Select a token', input your token's contract address and select it. Then, decide how much of your token and its pair (e.g. ETH) you want to deposit. The ratio of these tokens will set your initial token price. For instance, if you input 1 ETH and 1000 of your token, you are essentially saying 1 ETH = 1000 of your token.

- **Step 6: Approve and Supply Liquidity**

    After setting the amounts, you'll need to approve the transaction through MetaMask, confirming you want to deposit these tokens into the liquidity pool. This is followed by clicking the 'Supply' button, where you will finalise the creation of the pool and deposit your tokens.

CHAPTER 8   DEX AND MARKET CAP MANAGEMENT

- **Step 7: Managing Your Position**

    Figure 8-3 illustrates the 'Positions' tab, where you can view and manage your active liquidity positions. Once you've added liquidity, your position will appear here, and you'll see details such as your pool share, accrued fees and the ability to add or remove liquidity.

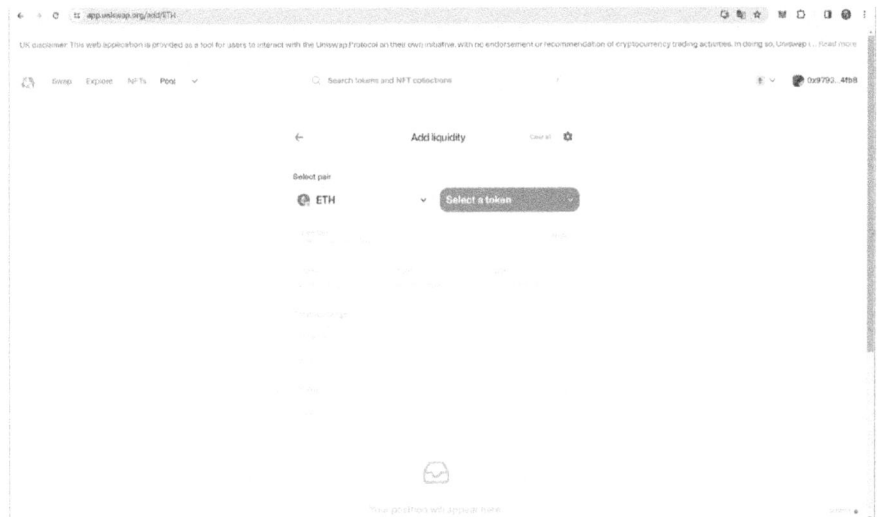

Figure 8-3. *Add Liquidity – 2*

- **Step 8: Monitoring and Adjustments**

    It's essential to monitor your liquidity pool and adjust your position as needed, especially in response to market changes or if you want to collect fees or reallocate your capital.

Decentralisation, Security and Governance

Decentralised exchanges (DEXs) like Uniswap leverage a decentralised infrastructure that enables trading via automated smart contracts. This not only minimises the risk of security breaches commonly associated with centralised custody but also empowers users with full control over their funds. The non-custodial nature of DEXs means that users interact directly with the contract, maintaining ownership of their private keys and thus their assets at all times. However, the autonomy granted by smart contracts comes with the responsibility of due diligence; users must recognise the potential for vulnerabilities within these contracts. Therefore, regular audits and rigorous security checks are crucial to uphold the integrity and trust in these platforms.

The governance structure of DEXs often manifests through decentralised autonomous organisations (DAOs), where community involvement is facilitated via token-based voting systems. Unlike traditional corporate governance, which is typically hierarchical, DAOs promote a flat and inclusive structure. Token holders participate directly in the decision-making processes, influencing vital aspects of the platform's operations, such as fee structures, token support, protocol upgrades and even treasury management.

This democratic governance model is foundational to the ethos of decentralisation, ensuring that the power dynamics are balanced and that the community can steer the platform in alignment with shared interests and values. The transparent and consensus-driven nature of DAOs stands in stark contrast to the closed-door decision-making and top-down directives often seen in corporate settings.

In essence, the convergence of decentralisation, security and DAO-based governance in DEXs fosters an ecosystem where security, transparency and community empowerment are intertwined. This paradigm shift from centralised authority to collective governance is a distinctive feature of DEXs and a significant evolution in the landscape of digital asset exchanges.

8.2 Tokens' Market Cap Management Strategies

Market capitalisation is not just a mere representation of a crypto-asset's current value; it is the bedrock upon which investor confidence is built and market stability is assessed. This section expands on methods for managing market cap effectively, particularly for tokens listed on decentralised exchanges (DEXs).

Token Burn

Token burn is a deflationary mechanism where tokens are permanently removed from circulation, often by sending them to an irretrievable address, known as a 'dead' wallet. This strategy can be likened to a company buying back shares – it reduces supply and can potentially drive up the value of the remaining tokens, assuming demand is unchanged or increases. The concept is akin to monetary policy tools that manipulate supply to impact value and velocity, with the additional benefit of signalling long-term commitment to token economy health.

Liquidity Provision

Providing liquidity is pivotal for maintaining the seamless operation of DEXs and the stability of a token's price. In the context of Uniswap and similar protocols, liquidity pools enable trading and yield generation for participants, serving as a robust indicator of token health and ecosystem vibrancy. Liquidity provision acts as a cushion against volatility, ensuring that large trades do not significantly impact prices, thus preserving market cap from erratic swings.

Partnership and Integration

Forging strategic partnerships and integrating tokens into wider ecosystems can create a multifaceted demand, which in turn may enhance market cap. Collaborative efforts range from achieving interoperability between various blockchain platforms to embedding tokens into decentralised finance (DeFi) protocols. Such integrations expand utility, often creating a positive feedback loop that sustains and grows the user base, reinforcing the asset's valuation.

Mechanism and Fiscal Policy Design

Market-making strategies that provide liquidity across multiple exchanges are essential for managing the token's presence and performance in the market. Such strategies can mirror liquidity, creating seamless trading experiences and aligning prices across exchanges, which in turn affects market cap perceptions. Furthermore, fiscal incentives like staking rewards encourage holding, reducing velocity and increasing the perceived value of the token.

Algorithmic Market Making

Algorithmic trading can be utilised to optimise liquidity provision, enhance order book depth and manage risk more effectively. Through high-frequency trading and utilising computational models, DEXs can offer better price stability for tokens, which is a key factor in market cap management. These algorithms can react to market conditions much faster than manual trading, adjusting orders to maintain optimal liquidity levels and spreads.

CHAPTER 8   DEX AND MARKET CAP MANAGEMENT

Strategic Distribution

A well-thought-out token distribution strategy is critical for ensuring a wide and even spread of tokens, which can reduce volatility and encourage a healthy trading environment. Techniques such as airdrops can serve as both marketing tools and mechanisms for increasing the number of token holders, thereby potentially stabilising and increasing market cap.

Monetary Policies: Burn-and-Mint Equilibrium

Incorporating burn-and-mint mechanisms can help manage the token's velocity and its market cap. By burning tokens during transaction processing and minting new tokens in alignment with ecosystem growth, a dynamic equilibrium is established. This approach can stabilise the token's supply-demand dynamics, promoting sustainable growth in market cap over time.

The strategies highlighted earlier are not exhaustive but provide a foundational understanding of the complexities involved in market cap management for crypto-assets on DEXs. These strategies must be employed judiciously, with a deep understanding of the token economics, market trends and the unique attributes of each crypto-asset. It is through this multifaceted approach that a token can achieve a balanced and robust market cap, reflecting its true value and utility within the digital economy.

8.3 Future Development of DEXs

In the future development of decentralised exchanges (DEXs), the trajectory is set to address crucial challenges and leverage emerging technologies. While scalability solutions such as Layer 2 have been previously discussed in Section 4.3 and regulatory concerns along with decentralised identity (DID) aspects in Section 5.3, they continue to underpin the evolution of DEXs. Here, our focus areas are the integration with traditional finance and addressing challenges such as Just-in-Time (JIT) Liquidity Attacks and Sandwich Attacks, which have been problematic for users and liquidity providers (LPs). These foundational aspects will seamlessly blend with future initiatives, ensuring DEXs are well equipped to navigate the complexities of a maturing digital economy.

Integration with Traditional Finance

Integration with traditional finance is a pivotal area in the evolution of DEXs.[3] DEXs are expected to bridge the gap with traditional finance through several initiatives:

1. **Tokenisation of Assets**: DEXs will likely expand to include a wider array of tokenised assets, such as real estate, stocks or commodities, allowing traditional assets to be traded in a decentralised environment.

2. **Hybrid Financial Products**: With Uniswap V4, hooks enable more customisation and can cater to complex interactions with various DeFi protocols, potentially attracting traditional financial players to the decentralised space by mimicking familiar financial instruments.[4]

3. **Increased Regulatory Compliance**: While maintaining decentralisation and privacy, DEXs will likely incorporate regulatory frameworks that align with global standards to foster institutional adoption.

CHAPTER 8   DEX AND MARKET CAP MANAGEMENT

Addressing JIT Liquidity and Sandwich Attacks

JIT Liquidity Attacks, where adversaries manipulate liquidity pools for profit, are a concern in DEXs. However, with Uniswap V4, there is an emphasis on enhanced security measures that could mitigate such risks:

1. **Singleton Contract**: This contract reduces the need for multiple transactions, thus potentially decreasing the opportunities for JIT Liquidity Attacks.

2. **Flash Accounting**: By combining multiple actions, such as swaps and liquidity additions, Uniswap V4 aims to reduce the chance of JIT Liquidity Attacks by settling all debts at the end of the transaction.[5]

Sandwich Attacks, which involve manipulating market prices to profit from trades queued in a mempool, have also been problematic. To counteract these:

1. **Time-Weighted Average Market Maker (TWAMM)**: Uniswap V4 will implement TWAMM to protect users from price manipulation, as it executes large orders over time to minimise market impact.

2. **Better Oracles**: With built-in oracles, Uniswap V4 will make it more difficult and costly for attackers to manipulate market prices.

3. **Countermeasures**: Solutions like the introduction of 'flashbot transactions' by platforms like 1inch, which are not visible in the mempool, could be adopted widely to prevent front-running attacks such as Sandwich Attacks.[6]

TWAMM vs. CFMM

Time-Weighted Average Market Maker (TWAMM) is a new concept introduced in Uniswap V4, designed to combat certain inefficiencies in traditional Automated Market Makers (AMMs), especially the Constant Function Market Maker (CFMM).

TWAMM allows large orders to be executed over a longer period, thus minimising the immediate impact on the market price. It achieves this by breaking up a large transaction into smaller pieces and executing these pieces at regular intervals over time. This gradual execution can prevent the drastic price slippage often seen with large orders in CFMMs.

CFMMs, like those used in Uniswap V2 and V3, rely on a formula to ensure that the product of the quantities of two assets remains constant. They allow liquidity providers to create a pool by depositing two assets, which traders can then use to swap one asset for another. While this design ensures liquidity, it has certain drawbacks:

1. **Slippage**: Large trades can significantly alter the ratio of assets in a pool, leading to substantial price impact.

2. **Impermanent Loss**: Liquidity providers may suffer losses when the price of assets in a pool changes after they've contributed liquidity.

3. **Capital Efficiency**: CFMMs often require more capital to provide liquidity effectively across a wide range of prices.

The TWAMM design in Uniswap V4 provides several advantages:

1. **Minimised Market Impact**: By breaking up and spreading out trades, TWAMM reduces the likelihood of large trades creating significant price slippage.

2. **Reduced Arbitrage Opportunities**: The gradual execution of large orders over time diminishes the potential for arbitrage that can occur in the wake of large trades in CFMMs.

3. **Long-Term Order Fulfilment**: TWAMM is advantageous for traders or entities looking to execute substantial trades without immediately affecting the market, similar to dollar-cost averaging strategies in traditional finance.

Table 8-1. *TWAMM and CFMMs: Comparison Table*

Aspect	CFMM (like Uniswap V2/V3)	TWAMM (Uniswap V4)
Trade Execution	Immediate, based on the current pool ratio	Over time, reducing immediate impact
Market Impact	High for large trades	Reduced impact due to time distribution
Capital Efficiency	Varies depending on the price range	Potentially higher due to optimised execution
Arbitrage	Opportunities arise from price slippage	Reduced opportunities due to gradual execution
Implementation Complexity	Relatively simple	More complex due to time-weighted execution
User Experience	Instant swaps	Orders executed over a duration

By incorporating TWAMM, Uniswap V4 aims to provide a more sophisticated, efficient and user-friendly trading experience for both traders and liquidity providers. The key innovation here is to combine the immediacy and simplicity of CFMMs with a time-distributed approach to order execution, which could lead to a more stable and predictable market, especially beneficial for DeFi protocols.

Encouraging Liquidity Providers

To encourage LPs, Uniswap V4 and other DEXs are expected to provide better incentives:

1. **Lower Gas Fees**: By consolidating liquidity pools into a single contract, gas fees will be significantly reduced, making it cheaper for LPs to participate.

2. **Dynamic Fees**: LPs could have more control over the fees they charge, which could maximise their returns on providing liquidity.

3. **Customised Pools**: Hooks in Uniswap V4 will allow LPs to create pools with specific features, attracting different types of traders and potentially increasing fee revenue.[7]

With innovations like Uniswap V4's singleton contract, TWAMM, better oracles and hooks, DEXs are positioned to revolutionise digital asset trading and investment, making the platform more attractive to both retail and institutional participants. These advancements will cater to the needs of LPs by reducing costs, mitigating risks and offering new revenue opportunities, further cementing the role of DEXs in the future of finance.

8.4 Summary

This chapter provides a detailed exploration of Decentralised Exchanges (DEXs) and the strategies for managing the market capitalisation (market cap) of tokens traded on these platforms. It begins by explaining how DEXs operate, using the Automated Market Maker (AMM) model, which replaces the traditional order book mechanism with liquidity pools. Liquidity providers (LPs) contribute tokens to these pools, earning fees while enabling seamless token swaps for traders. This decentralised system offers transparency, security, and user control over assets, distinguishing it from centralised exchanges (CEXs).

The chapter also delves into various market cap management strategies, including token burn mechanisms, liquidity provision, partnerships, and algorithmic market making. These strategies are crucial for maintaining token value, stabilising prices, and encouraging investor confidence. The role of monetary policies, such as burn-and-mint equilibrium, is highlighted as a method for managing token supply and demand dynamics.

Additionally, the future of DEXs is explored, with a focus on integration with traditional finance and addressing key security concerns, such as Just-in-Time (JIT) liquidity attacks and sandwich attacks. Innovations like Uniswap V4's Time-Weighted Average Market Maker (TWAMM) and improved oracles are discussed as solutions for mitigating these risks, enhancing the trading experience, and encouraging liquidity provision.

In conclusion, DEXs are positioned to revolutionise the financial landscape by providing decentralised, transparent, and secure trading platforms, while offering sophisticated tools for managing market cap and liquidity.

8.5 Notes

1. George, B., & Bochan, T. (2024). Centralized Exchange (CEX) vs. Decentralized Exchange (DEX): What's the Difference? Coindesk. www.coindesk.com/learn/centralized-exchange-cex-vs-decentralized-exchange-dex-whats-the-difference/ (Accessed: 9 April 2024).

2. Decentralized Exchanges: Operating Principles and Distinctive Features (2024). https://bitsgap.com/blog/how-decentralized-exchanges-operate (Accessed: 9 April 2024).

3. Oliver Wyman Forum, DBS, Onyx by J.P. Morgan, & SBI Digital Asset Holdings. (2022). Institutional DeFi: The next generation of finance. www.jpmorgan.com/onyx/documents/Institutional-DeFi-The-Next-Generation-of-Finance.pdf (Accessed: 9 April 2024).

4. CyberArk Software (2024). What is Just-In-Time Access? CyberArk. www.cyberark.com/what-is/just-in-time-access/ (Accessed: 9 April 2024).

5. CyberArk Software (2024). What is Just-In-Time Access? CyberArk. www.cyberark.com/what-is/just-in-time-access/ (Accessed: 9 April 2024).

CHAPTER 8   DEX AND MARKET CAP MANAGEMENT

6. Sergeenkov, A. (2021). What Are Sandwich Attacks in DeFi — and How Can You Avoid Them? CoinMarketCap Academy. https://coinmarketcap.com/academy/article/what-are-sandwich-attacks-in-defi-and-how-can-you-avoid-them (Accessed: 9 April 2024).

7. Hoogendoorn, R. (2024). What is Uniswap V4, and How it Will Revolutionize DeFi. https://dappradar.com/blog/uniswap-v4-defi-guide-hooks-singleton-contract (Accessed: 9 April 2024).

PART IV

Advancing Web3: Integration, Innovation and Regulation

PART IV

Discussion and Conclusion

CHAPTER 9

Navigating the Future of Web3 and the Metaverse

9.1 Web3 and Metaverse: Foundations and Technologies

The metaverse, a term first coined in Neal Stephenson's 1992 science fiction novel *Snow Crash*, represents a collective virtual shared space, created by the convergence of virtually enhanced physical reality, augmented reality (AR) and the Internet. This digital universe allows users to interact with a computer-generated environment and other users. The concept has evolved from fictional imaginations to a significant focus of technological development, aiming to create immersive, digital worlds where people can work, play, socialise and participate in a variety of experiences that span across both the digital and physical worlds.

The need for Web3 in the development of the metaverse is critical due to the limitations of the current Internet infrastructure, Web2, which is characterised by centralised data control and limited user ownership over digital assets and identities. Web3, with its decentralised nature, blockchain technology and emphasis on user sovereignty, provides the foundational elements necessary for a truly immersive, interactive and user-owned metaverse.

The evolution of the Internet from Web1 to Web3 marks a significant transformation in how users interact with digital content, who controls that content, the underlying technologies that power these interactions and the roles users play within this ecosystem. Each iteration of the Web has built upon the previous, moving from a static collection of pages to a dynamic and interactive experience and now to a decentralised platform that emphasises user sovereignty and asset ownership. Table 9-1 shows a detailed comparison of these three stages, highlighting the core distinctions that define each era.

Table 9-1. *Web1, Web2 and Web3 Comparison*

Feature	Web1 (The Static Web)	Web2 (The Social Web)	Web3 (The Decentralised Web)
Interaction	Read-only, limited user interaction	Read and write, interactive applications and social networks	Read, write and own, emphasising user ownership and interaction with digital assets
Content Control	Content created and controlled by website owners	Content creation democratised but centrally controlled by platforms	Decentralised control, users own their content and data
Technology	Basic HTML, static pages	AJAX, JavaScript, enabling dynamic content and applications	Blockchain, decentralised applications (DApps), smart contracts
User Role	Consumers of content	Content creators and consumers, but with significant privacy and data ownership issues	Owners of their data and digital assets, participants in a decentralised economy

CHAPTER 9   NAVIGATING THE FUTURE OF WEB3 AND THE METAVERSE

Web1, often referred to as the 'Static Web', laid the groundwork for the digital age, offering users access to information but limited interaction. Web2, or the 'Social Web', revolutionised this model by enabling user-generated content and social networking, fostering an unprecedented level of interactivity and community creation. However, it also centralised control over data in the hands of a few major platforms, raising issues around privacy and data ownership. Web3 represents the next frontier, the 'Decentralised Web', which aims to address these concerns by leveraging blockchain technology to return control and ownership of data and digital assets back to the users themselves. This shift not only has technological implications but also deeply affects the socio-economic fabric of the digital ecosystem.

Table 9-1 showcases the progressive enhancement of user capabilities and autonomy over the Web's evolution. Web1 established the foundation of the Internet as a digital information repository. Web2 built upon this by making the Internet more interactive and social, yet it centralised power and control. Web3 seeks to redistribute this control back to users, ensuring they can own, control and profit from their content and contributions to the digital world. The transition to Web3 represents not just technological innovation but a reimagining of the Internet's potential to empower individuals and communities.

Core Foundational Elements of the Metaverse

The metaverse, a concept that has captivated the imagination of technologists, creators and consumers alike, stands on the brink of redefining the digital and physical realms. Its foundation is built upon a series of technological advancements that set it apart from the traditional

Internet and digital spaces we've grown accustomed to. Here, we delve into the core foundational elements that make the metaverse a unique and transformative platform for future generations:

- **Decentralised Architecture**: The metaverse leverages blockchain technology to ensure that data integrity, security and ownership are maintained across its vast digital landscape. Blockchain's inherent characteristics such as decentralisation, immutability and transparency provide a robust framework for creating a metaverse where users can trust in the security of their data and transactions. By decentralising the architecture, the metaverse ensures that no single entity has control over the entire ecosystem, thus democratising digital interactions and ownership.

- **Immersive Technologies**: At the heart of the metaverse experience are immersive technologies such as virtual reality (VR), augmented reality (AR) and 3D modelling. VR immerses users in digital environments where they can interact with the virtual world in a highly realistic manner. AR overlays digital information onto the physical world, enriching the user's environment with interactive digital elements. 3D modelling and simulation technologies enable the creation of complex, lifelike objects and environments within the metaverse. Together, these technologies create compelling, immersive experiences that blur the line between the digital and physical worlds.[1]

- **Digital Economy**: The metaverse introduces a digital economy where true ownership of digital assets is facilitated through non-fungible tokens (NFTs) and cryptocurrencies. NFTs represent unique digital items – ranging from art and collectibles to virtual real estate and more – while cryptocurrencies enable secure, transparent financial transactions within the metaverse. This economic model allows for the creation, buying, selling and trading of virtual goods and services, fostering a vibrant economy that mirrors the complexity and dynamism of real-world economies.

- **Interoperability**: A key feature of the metaverse is its ability to ensure that assets and identities can seamlessly move across different environments and platforms. This is achieved through the development and adoption of standards and protocols that facilitate interoperability. By enabling assets to be portable and persistent across various virtual spaces, the metaverse offers a unified, continuous experience that transcends individual platforms or applications.[2]

- **Spatial Computing**: Incorporating artificial intelligence (AI), machine learning and spatial technologies, the metaverse enables complex interactions and behaviours within its environments. Spatial computing allows for the understanding and manipulation of digital and physical spaces, enabling AI-driven avatars to navigate the metaverse, realistic simulations of physics and context-aware digital content. This level of computational intelligence is crucial for creating dynamic, responsive environments that adapt to user interactions and behaviours.[3]

These foundational elements collectively promise a future where the convergence of digital and physical realities opens up unprecedented opportunities for collaboration, creativity and interaction. The metaverse, powered by Web3 technologies, signifies a fundamental shift in how we perceive and interact with digital spaces, heralding a new era of digital existence.

9.2 Economic Models and Opportunities in Web3 and the Metaverse

In examining the evolving economic models and opportunities that Web3 and the metaverse present, it's clear that we are on the cusp of a fundamental shift in how economic systems are structured, how value is created and distributed and how individuals and organisations interact within digital realms. This expansion seeks to distil key insights into these transformative shifts, drawing upon broader concepts within the blockchain and digital asset spheres.[4, 5]

Decentralised Economic Systems

The move towards decentralised economic models in Web3 and the metaverse represents a departure from traditional shareholder-centric models towards systems where stakeholders have a more significant say and share in the economic outcomes. This paradigm shift expands the definition of capital to include digital assets, intellectual property and user engagement, thus democratising economic participation and benefit distribution. Let's delve into the **4D Metanomics** and explore their roles within decentralised economic systems:

CHAPTER 9   NAVIGATING THE FUTURE OF WEB3 AND THE METAVERSE

- **Digital Creation**: This dimension focuses on the production of digital content within the metaverse. It ranges from the creation of virtual worlds and digital goods to the generation of media such as music, art and literature. In a decentralised system, creators retain ownership and control over their works, utilising blockchain technology to protect intellectual property and manage rights. This empowerment not only fosters innovation but also ensures creators are fairly compensated.

- **Digital Assets**: Digital assets include anything from NFTs representing ownership of virtual items to tokens embodying stakes in digital ventures. These assets are unique in that they provide proof of ownership and can be traded or used across different platforms and services in the metaverse. Their interoperability and liquidity in digital markets signify a major shift from physical asset constraints, enhancing the velocity and volume of economic transactions in Web3.

- **Digital Market**: This is where digital assets are bought, sold or traded. Digital markets in the metaverse are designed to be open and global, operating 24/7 without the restrictions of geographical boundaries or centralised control. These markets rely on blockchain to facilitate trustless transactions, smart contracts for self-executing agreements and decentralised exchanges that enable peer-to-peer trading without intermediaries.

- **Digital Currency**: The lifeblood of transactional activity in the metaverse, digital currencies, such as cryptocurrencies, allow for the seamless transfer of value in the digital realm. Beyond mere transactional mediums, these currencies can also represent governance tokens, giving holders voting rights on decisions within decentralised autonomous organisations (DAOs) or other Web3 entities.

Decentralised economic systems in the context of 4D Metanomics imply a holistic ecosystem where each dimension interplays to create a robust and inclusive economy. Here, stakeholders are not just passive investors but active participants with significant agency over the creation, valuation, trading and use of digital goods and services. This inclusive and participatory economy has the potential to redefine wealth generation, distribution and economic empowerment on a global scale, opening up opportunities for broad-based wealth creation and distribution far beyond what traditional economic systems have offered.

Value Creation and Distribution

The process of value creation in the metaverse hinges on the utilisation of digital platforms where creators can innovate without the constraints of the physical world. Virtual real estate development, for example, allows for the creation of spaces for social interactions, commerce and entertainment. The development tools and platforms in Web3 are designed to be more accessible, which democratises the process of creation. Users are not just passive consumers but also become creators themselves, participating in and contributing to the metaverse's expansion and diversity.

The distribution of value in the metaverse is facilitated through blockchain technology, enabling a fair and transparent system where contributions and transactions are recorded and rewarded accordingly.

Smart contracts automate the distribution of revenues according to predefined rules agreed upon by stakeholders, ensuring that creators and participants receive their fair share of the profits generated from their contributions.

The monetisation strategies in the metaverse are as varied as the assets themselves. Creators can monetise digital art via NFTs, developers can sell virtual real estate, and gamers can earn through 'play-to-earn' models. The direct relationship between creators and consumers in the metaverse eliminates many of the middlemen present in traditional economies, allowing for a more efficient and equitable flow of funds.

The traditional market norms are upended in the metaverse, where scarcity is not dictated by physical limitations but by design and consensus. The metaverse economy thrives on the principles of abundance and network effects, where the value of a digital asset often increases with its usage and integration into different platforms and applications. This creates a more dynamic and fluid economic model, where value is not solely based on scarcity or traditional supply and demand dynamics.

The 4D Metanomics paves the way for innovative financial models, such as fractional ownership of digital assets and the emergence of micro-economies within the metaverse. These models provide opportunities for both small and large investors to participate in the growth of digital assets. Additionally, the integration of DeFi (decentralised finance) introduces new investment and funding mechanisms, like yield farming and liquidity mining, which are unique to the blockchain-based economy.

In this expanded digital economy, every interaction, every creation and every transaction has the potential to generate value that can be captured, distributed and monetised in ways that traditional markets have not envisioned. As these systems continue to evolve, they promise to offer more personalised, empowering and democratised economic experiences.

CHAPTER 9   NAVIGATING THE FUTURE OF WEB3 AND THE METAVERSE

Collaborative Work and Innovation

In the context of Web3 and the metaverse, the shift towards collaborative work and innovation heralds a new era of collective creativity and distributed entrepreneurship. This transformative approach reshapes the landscape of work, blurring the lines between creators, consumers and collaborators:

- **Crowdsourced Innovation**: Web3 platforms empower a crowdsourced model of innovation where ideas and projects can be sourced from a global community. Through mechanisms like DAOs and open source frameworks, individuals from different backgrounds can contribute to a project, pushing the boundaries of innovation beyond what might be possible within a single organisation or geography.

- **Decentralised Collaborative Platforms**: The metaverse provides platforms that allow for real-time collaboration in virtual environments. These platforms are not limited by geography, enabling real-time interactions and teamwork across the globe, which can lead to faster ideation and development cycles. Virtual spaces can simulate real-world conditions, or they can provide entirely new contexts for problem-solving and creativity.

- **Redefining Roles and Employment**: In the metaverse, traditional roles such as employee, contractor and consumer are being redefined. Users can simultaneously be creators, market participants and beneficiaries in the value chain. This multiplicity of roles fosters a dynamic environment where work, participation and consumption are intertwined.

- **Productivity in the Digital Economy:** Productivity metrics in the metaverse are reimagined, focusing on contribution and impact rather than traditional metrics like hours worked. In this environment, the efficiency of work can be vastly improved by digital tools and AI assistants that automate routine tasks, freeing human creativity for higher-level problem-solving and artistic endeavours.

- **Open Talent Networks:** The metaverse creates open talent networks where individuals can showcase their skills and be discovered by potential collaborators or employers. These networks support a gig economy on a global scale, with the potential to match talent with opportunities more efficiently than ever before.

- **Incentive Alignment:** In the metaverse, economic incentives can be aligned with contributions through tokenomics, ensuring that those who contribute value are rewarded. This direct incentive mechanism encourages active participation and continuous contribution, which is crucial for sustained innovation.

The metaverse and Web3 are not only changing where and how we work but also why we work. They provide a foundation for a more collaborative, innovative and inclusive economic structure that incentivises and rewards participation and contribution, laying the groundwork for a future where the pursuit of individual passions and collective goals can be one and the same.

CHAPTER 9   NAVIGATING THE FUTURE OF WEB3 AND THE METAVERSE

Tokenisation and Economic Incentives

Tokenisation serves as the bedrock of economic interaction within the Web3 and metaverse landscapes, revolutionising how we define and exchange value. It transforms various forms of assets and rights into tokens, allowing for a seamless representation of ownership and exchange. These tokens can be traded, staked or used to participate in governance processes, democratising access to economic activities and decision-making.

Incentives are intrinsic to this model, rewarding creators and users alike for their contributions and participation. For creators, tokenisation opens up new avenues for monetising content directly, offering an alternative to traditional revenue streams dominated by intermediaries. Users, on the other hand, gain from the enhanced liquidity and the potential for financial growth provided by the appreciating value of tokens in active markets.

The DeFi ecosystem particularly thrives on tokenisation, offering decentralised financial services like lending, trading and insuring assets, all without the centralised control of traditional banking systems. These services, powered by smart contracts, automate transactions and enforce agreements, providing a more inclusive and transparent financial infrastructure.

Overall, tokenisation encapsulates the essence of a decentralised economy, fuelling innovation and participation by aligning economic incentives with the values of openness and accessibility. It allows for a more flexible and equitable distribution of wealth and opportunities, reshaping our understanding of financial systems in the digital age.

The economic models and opportunities within Web3 and the metaverse represent a radical departure from traditional systems, paving the way for a more decentralised, equitable and inclusive economic landscape. With tokenisation at its core, this new paradigm allows for nuanced representations of ownership and participation, empowering creators, innovators and users with direct economic incentives and greater control over their digital interactions. Collaborative work is enhanced through global platforms that transcend geographical and organisational boundaries, fostering a culture of open innovation. The integration of DeFi further challenges conventional financial institutions by offering transparent, user-centric alternatives for financial services. This shift towards a digitised economy, characterised by its 4D Metanomic structure, heralds a future where the creation, distribution and exchange of value are more accessible, dynamic and aligned with the collective interests of a globally connected community.

9.3 Leading Platforms, Projects and Their Applications

In the expanding universe of Web3 and the metaverse, platforms like Decentraland and innovative practices from traditional financial institutions like JPMorgan offer clear case studies of adaptation and evolution in the digital economy.

Decentraland: A Case Study in User-Governed Virtual Real Estate

Decentraland represents a leading example of a self-governing, immersive virtual platform built on the Ethereum blockchain. It is a decentralised virtual world where users can create, enjoy and monetise content and applications. In Decentraland, users purchase plots of virtual land as NFTs, which they can then develop to create unique experiences ranging from games to educational services and interactive art exhibitions.

A significant milestone in Decentraland's evolution was the launch of Metajuku, a virtual analog to Tokyo's Harajuku shopping district. This development underscores the platform's commercial potential, illustrating how brands can establish a virtual presence to engage with their audience.

CHAPTER 9   NAVIGATING THE FUTURE OF WEB3 AND THE METAVERSE

For instance, a large virtual land parcel was purchased for development into a bustling commercial hub, indicative of the growing market value of virtual real estate and its appeal to both individual investors and corporate entities.[6]

JPMorgan's Foray into the Metaverse: Onyx Lounge and Beyond

JPMorgan has demonstrated a tangible belief in the metaverse's potential by opening the Onyx Lounge in Decentraland's Metajuku district. This virtual space, named after the bank's suite of permissioned Ethereum-based services, features a digital portrait of JPMorgan's CEO and a roaming tiger, symbolising the bank's pioneering spirit in uncharted digital territories.

Figure 9-1. JPMorgan Metaverse Lounge[6]

CHAPTER 9   NAVIGATING THE FUTURE OF WEB3 AND THE METAVERSE

However, JPMorgan's engagement in the metaverse isn't merely about creating a virtual space for visitors. The bank has released a whitepaper on metaverse opportunities, positioning itself as a thought leader in how businesses can navigate and capitalise on this new frontier. They have recognised that the dynamics of supply and demand are steering individuals into a burgeoning meta-economy that necessitates the development of new skills and creation of novel opportunities for the workforce.

By recognising the potential for virtual real estate to include credit, mortgages and rental agreements akin to the physical world, JPMorgan has signalled its readiness to finance the virtual land market. They point out the considerable investment in virtual lands and suggest that the same financial principles applying to physical real estate may soon govern the virtual equivalents.

JPMorgan's initiative in the metaverse serves as a beacon for other businesses, indicating that an investment in the digital space is not just speculative but strategic. The financial giant sees potential in offering metaverse-related financial services such as mortgages and credit facilities on virtual properties, viewing these services as future growth areas.

These case studies exemplify how both decentralised platforms and established corporations are embracing the metaverse's new economic landscape. Decentraland is pioneering the community-driven model for virtual experiences, while JPMorgan's venture demonstrates traditional financial institutions' ability to innovate and adapt within these digital realms. The initiatives and explorations by such entities provide valuable insights into how the metaverse can reshape interactions, offering new avenues for investment, commerce and community building.

9.4 Future Directions: Challenges and Preparations

In the final section of our exploration of Web3 and the metaverse, we must acknowledge that as much as these technologies represent transformative possibilities, they also present significant challenges and require careful preparation. The future of these digital spaces is contingent on the proactive management of various issues ranging from regulatory compliance to the very architecture of the platforms.

Regulatory and Ethical Considerations

The unprecedented nature of the metaverse and Web3 introduces a complex array of regulatory and ethical questions that must be addressed to protect consumers and ensure the stability of these new systems:

- **Data Privacy and Security**: As users increasingly conduct significant portions of their lives within digital realms, the protection of personal data against misuse and breaches is paramount. Legislation similar to the General Data Protection Regulation (GDPR) will need to be adapted to the unique nature of the metaverse.

- **Consumer Protection**: There must be mechanisms in place to prevent fraudulent activities and ensure the authenticity of digital assets. Clear guidelines and standards will be essential for transactions, particularly with NFTs and cryptocurrencies.

- **Content Moderation**: Ethical considerations around content, including the prevention of harmful activities and cyberbullying, require thoughtful moderation strategies that respect free expression while safeguarding users.

Future Directions: Challenges and Preparations

The trajectory of Web3 and the metaverse indicates that several technical and social hurdles must be overcome to realise their full potential:

- **Interoperability**: For a truly cohesive metaverse, different platforms must be able to work together seamlessly. Users should move across virtual spaces without friction, retaining their digital assets and identities.

- **Scalability**: The infrastructure supporting these spaces must be robust enough to support millions of concurrent users engaging in complex interactions, demanding significant advances in computing power and network architecture.

- **User Adoption**: Bridging the gap between early adopters and the broader public involves making these spaces accessible and user-friendly. There's a need to educate potential users on the value and workings of Web3 and the metaverse.

Preparations for the Road Ahead

To navigate these challenges, concerted efforts from multiple stakeholders are required:

- **Developing Standards and Protocols**: Cross-industry collaborations to establish universal standards and protocols will facilitate interoperability and user engagement across different metaverse platforms.

- **Building Robust Infrastructure**: Investment in the underlying technology, from server capacity to development tools, will enable scalable and sustainable growth.

- **Fostering a Collaborative Ecosystem**: Encouraging partnerships between tech companies, regulatory bodies and user communities will ensure that the metaverse develops in a way that is inclusive, ethical and beneficial to all stakeholders.

- **Creating a Clear Regulatory Framework**: Policymakers must work with technology providers to develop regulations that balance innovation with consumer protection and ethical considerations.

As the metaverse and Web3 continue to evolve, addressing these challenges proactively and preparing for the future will be crucial. It's a journey that requires the collective effort of creators, regulators and users to ensure that the next iteration of the Internet fulfils its promise of a more connected and immersive digital experience.

9.5 Summary

This chapter examines the convergence of Web3 and the metaverse, focusing on how these technologies are transforming digital experiences and economies. Key foundational technologies, such as blockchain, VR/AR, and spatial computing, enable immersive, decentralized environments where users can create, own, and trade digital assets.

The chapter also explores decentralized economic models, where tokenization, NFTs, and cryptocurrencies drive the metaverse's digital economy. It highlights case studies like Decentraland and JPMorgan's Onyx Lounge, illustrating how both decentralized communities and traditional finance are leveraging the metaverse for innovation.

CHAPTER 9 NAVIGATING THE FUTURE OF WEB3 AND THE METAVERSE

Finally, the chapter addresses future challenges, including regulatory concerns, scalability, and the need for interoperability. Collaboration between stakeholders and robust infrastructure are crucial for the future success of Web3 and the metaverse.

9.6 Notes

1. Milgram, P., & Kishino, F. (1994). A taxonomy of mixed reality visual displays. IEICE Transactions on Information and Systems, 77(12), 1321–1329.

2. Yang, L., Ni, S. T., Wang, Y., Yu, A., Lee, J. A., & Hui, P. (2024). Interoperability of the Metaverse: A Digital Ecosystem Perspective Review. arXiv preprint arXiv:2403.05205.

3. Zambonelli, F., & Mamei, M. (2004). Spatial computing: An emerging paradigm for autonomic computing and communication. In Workshop on Autonomic Communication (pp. 44–57). Berlin, Heidelberg: Springer Berlin Heidelberg.

4. 万向区块链. (2022). 肖风:元宇宙有十大经济规则. AI新智界. www.aixinzhijie.com/article/6795694 (Accessed: 9 April 2024).

5. 肖风, 万向区块链实验室创始人肖风:元宇宙的新经济规律 | 每经网. (2022). www.nbd.com.cn/articles/2022-09-26/2480200.html (Accessed: 9 April 2024).

6. Shevlin, R. (2022). JPMorgan Opens a Bank Branch in the Metaverse (But It's Not What You Think It's For). Forbes. www.forbes.com/sites/ronshevlin/2022/02/16/jpmorgan-opens-a-bank-branch-in-the-metaverse-but-its-not-for-what-you-think-its-for/?sh=44b1ec05158d (Accessed: 9 April 2024).

CHAPTER 10

The Integration and Evolution of AI in Web3

10.1 Blockchain Enhanced by Generative AI

In Section 1.1, we have briefly touched upon the relationship between blockchain and AI. Here, a profound analysis reveals a seemingly paradoxical yet inherently complementary relationship between blockchain technology and Artificial General Intelligence (AGI), also referred to as strong AI. Despite their contrasting value orientations, the juxtaposition of these two groundbreaking technologies heralds a symbiotic partnership pivotal for shaping the future of digital society and technological evolution.

At its core, AGI embodies the zenith of artificial intelligence development, characterised by its enigmatic internal mechanisms that remain largely inscrutable to human understanding. This intrinsic complexity of AGI poses a significant challenge for human oversight, rendering attempts to directly intervene or alter its internal processes not only futile but also potentially hazardous. It is within this context that blockchain technology emerges not as a rival but as an indispensable ally to AGI, offering a framework for ethical governance and accountability.

Blockchain technology, with its immutable ledger and decentralised architecture, provides the essential infrastructure for establishing a binding 'contract' between humanity and AGI. This contractual framework is critical for imposing external constraints on AGI, ensuring that its operations and decisions align with human values and societal norms. By codifying ethical guidelines and operational boundaries into blockchain-based smart contracts, we can create a robust mechanism for governing AGI's integration into various facets of human life, from economic systems and social networks to critical infrastructures and beyond.

The future envisioned at the intersection of blockchain and AGI is one of mutual dependency and balanced co-evolution. AGI, with its unparalleled efficiency and capacity for innovation, drives the advancement of productivity and technological progress. In contrast, blockchain serves as the ethical backbone, safeguarding fairness, transparency and trust in this rapidly evolving digital landscape. While AGI expands the horizons of what is technologically possible, blockchain ensures that these advancements are harnessed for the greater good, maintaining a protective boundary around human interests and societal welfare.[1]

Expanding on the discourse that blockchain and Artificial General Intelligence (AGI) serve as a dynamic duo in the technological landscape, we delve deeper into their complementary roles. AGI, with its vast capabilities, promises to drive innovation and efficiency across myriad sectors. Yet, the unchecked progression of AGI carries inherent risks, making blockchain's role in governance and ethical oversight ever more crucial. Here, we outline key points and provide examples to illuminate their symbiotic relationship:

1. **Automated Efficiency vs. Ethical Boundaries**: AGI's main allure lies in its potential to automate complex cognitive tasks, ranging from data analysis and decision-making processes to creative endeavours like writing and design. For instance, AGI could revolutionise healthcare by diagnosing diseases with higher accuracy and speed than human practitioners. However, the ethical implications of such automation, including patient privacy and consent, necessitate blockchain's intervention. Through smart contracts, blockchain can encode ethical guidelines and patient consent directly into the data processing algorithms, ensuring that AGI operates within agreed ethical boundaries.

2. **Decentralised Governance of AGI Operations**: Blockchain technology can decentralise the governance of AGI, distributing control and oversight across a network rather than centralising it within a single entity. This is crucial for preventing misuse and ensuring that AGI's actions align with collective human values. For example, a decentralised autonomous organisation (DAO) could oversee an AGI system managing a smart city's infrastructure, with blockchain smart contracts ensuring that AGI decisions, such as traffic management or energy distribution, are made transparently and in accordance with the residents' consensus.

3. **Immutable Record-Keeping for AGI Decisions:** Blockchain's immutable ledger offers a transparent and unalterable record of AGI's decisions and actions. This is invaluable for auditing and accountability purposes, allowing stakeholders to trace the rationale behind AGI's decisions. Consider an AGI system tasked with managing financial transactions; blockchain can record every decision made by the AGI, providing an audit trail for regulators and users to verify the integrity and fairness of the transactions.

4. **Smart Contracts As Mediators:** Smart contracts can mediate interactions between humans and AGI, ensuring that AGI's capabilities are utilised according to predefined agreements. For instance, in supply chain management, AGI could optimise logistics and inventory management. Smart contracts would ensure that AGI's optimisations respect contractual agreements with suppliers and customers, automatically executing payments or adjustments when certain conditions are met, thereby preventing potential conflicts or misunderstandings.

5. **Future-Proofing Labour and Automation:** As AGI takes on more roles traditionally performed by humans, the drafting and auditing of smart contracts emerge as critical human-centric tasks. These activities not only require a deep understanding of legal, ethical and technical domains but also embody the negotiation of trust between humans and machines. For example,

in creative industries, while AGI might generate new content, human experts would be essential for ensuring that the use of such content respects copyright laws and ethical standards, encoded within blockchain smart contracts.

In drawing these discussions to a close, the symbiosis between blockchain and generative AI heralds not an era of technological displacement but one rich with unparalleled collaborative promise. The emergence of AGI doesn't overshadow blockchain; instead, it magnifies its significance, casting blockchain in the vital role of an ethical compass that directs the responsible evolution and deployment of AI technologies. As we delve into the intricacies of this AI-enhanced future, the union of blockchain and AGI emerges as a powerful emblem of human resilience and creative spirit, ensuring that our digital creations are firmly rooted in principles of fairness, responsibility and collective well-being.

This exploration underscores the profound interdependence between blockchain and AGI, where blockchain isn't merely a supplementary framework but a foundational element providing the essential checks and balances needed to ethically channel AGI's groundbreaking capabilities. Together, they are set to transform the fabric of human labour, ethical governance and technological progress, heralding a new epoch of innovation that's approached with mindful caution. This dynamic alliance is shaping up to redefine our world, assuring that as we stride into the future, we do so with a commitment to maintaining the human values that underpin our societies.

10.2 AI and Web3 Synergy

The convergence of artificial intelligence (AI) and Web3 technologies encapsulates a significant shift in digital and physical interactions. AI and blockchain, while independently powerful, exhibit contrasting attributes: AI is often centralised, less transparent and energy-consuming; blockchain, on the other hand, is decentralised and transparent and paves the way for energy-efficient solutions and user monetisation.

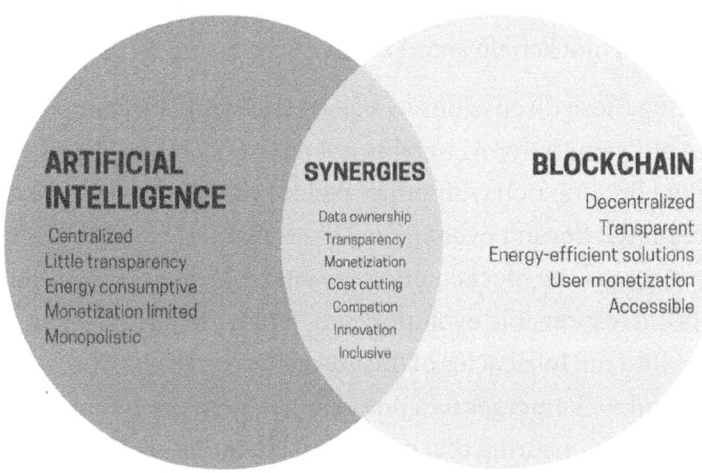

Figure 10-1. *Venn Diagram for AI and Blockchain*[2]

Figure 10-1 showcases the merging of these two fields and highlights the synergies created by their intersection. Central to this confluence is the idea that blockchain can mitigate some of the limitations of AI. It can decentralise data ownership, which is often monopolised by centralised AI entities, bringing transparency to AI's opaque processes and enabling new forms of monetisation beyond the traditional scope. This synergy can drive innovation, reduce costs through efficient processes and foster competitive markets that can challenge monopolistic tendencies.

AI encompasses a broad spectrum of algorithms developed not through explicit programming but by computational evolution, a process akin to the natural selection that led to human evolution. Despite their remarkable capabilities, the inner workings of AI algorithms often remain opaque. Within the context of AI's interaction with blockchain technology, four distinct roles for AI can be identified:

1. **AI As a Player in a Game**: AI operates as an active participant in blockchain-based protocols, responding to human-derived incentives and contributing to the mechanism's functionality.

2. **AI As an Interface to the Game**: AI assists users in navigating the crypto environment, interpreting complex information and ensuring that user actions reflect their true intentions, thereby avoiding scams.

3. **AI As the Rules of the Game**: Blockchain and DAOs may incorporate AI in a regulatory capacity, similar to 'AI judges', which requires cautious implementation due to the significant authority it entails.

4. **AI As the Objective of the Game**: The focus is on creating blockchain systems and DAOs with the express purpose of developing and sustaining AI, using the principles of cryptography to enhance training and protect against misuse of data.[3]

Each role presents varying levels of viability and risk, with AI as a player showing the most immediate promise and AI as the rules or objective of the game representing more complex, high-stakes applications that necessitate careful consideration and design.

Let's explore some practical examples of the power harnessed from the union of these technological titans.

CHAPTER 10   THE INTEGRATION AND EVOLUTION OF AI IN WEB3

Decentralised Finance (DeFi) and Predictive Analytics

The integration of decentralised finance (DeFi) and predictive analytics marks a transformative leap in the financial sector, one that harnesses the power of AI alongside the immutable trust of blockchain technology. This confluence not only democratises financial services but also imbues them with a level of sophistication and security previously unattainable.

Predictive analytics in DeFi leverages advanced AI algorithms capable of sifting through and analysing vast, complex datasets at an unprecedented scale. These algorithms scrutinise historical data, market movements, social media sentiment and economic indicators to forecast future market trends with remarkable accuracy. The predictive nature of these AI tools allows for the anticipation of market shifts, enabling proactive rather than reactive decision-making.

Within the DeFi ecosystem, AI-driven bots exemplify the practical application of predictive analytics. These bots, fuelled by AI's data processing capabilities, execute trades based on predictive models that anticipate market movements. For example, an AI bot might analyse patterns indicating an impending rise in a particular cryptocurrency's value and execute buy orders to capitalise on the anticipated increase. Conversely, it might identify signs of a potential market downturn and sell off assets before their value diminishes. These strategies, refined through machine learning and real-time data analysis, optimise investment portfolios, balance risk and potentially yield higher returns.

Risk management is another critical area where the synergy of DeFi and predictive analytics shines. AI algorithms assess the risk profile of various assets by evaluating factors such as volatility, market liquidity and credit risk. This analysis enables the dynamic adjustment of investment portfolios to mitigate risk, ensuring that investment strategies align with an individual's or institution's risk tolerance. Additionally, AI can detect anomalous patterns that may signify fraudulent activities or market manipulation, thereby safeguarding investments.

Blockchain technology underpins this AI-driven financial ecosystem, ensuring that all transactions executed by AI bots are recorded on a decentralised ledger. This ledger offers an immutable, tamper-proof record, providing a transparent audit trail for all activities. The decentralised nature of blockchain means that data integrity and transaction authenticity are maintained without the need for a central authority, thereby enhancing trust in DeFi platforms and services.

Moreover, smart contracts automate the execution of these transactions based on predefined criteria, further reducing the potential for human error or manipulation. These smart contracts, encoded on the blockchain, execute trades, enforce terms and manage assets autonomously, guided by the insights generated by AI's predictive analytics.

A practical example of AI and blockchain synergy in DeFi is in yield farming optimisation. Yield farming involves earning interest by lending crypto-assets. An AI-driven bot can analyse various DeFi platforms to identify the highest yielding opportunities across the ecosystem, adjusting the distribution of assets to maximise returns. Blockchain ensures that these transactions and the shifting of assets between platforms are secure, transparent and efficiently executed via smart contracts.

The intersection of decentralised finance and predictive analytics heralds a new era in financial services, one characterised by enhanced accessibility, efficiency and security. By leveraging AI's predictive power and blockchain's integrity, this integrated approach not only revolutionises investment strategies and risk management but also establishes a new standard for transparency and trust in financial transactions. As this synergy continues to evolve, it will undoubtedly unlock new potentials and paradigms in the financial sector, empowering both investors and service providers in the burgeoning DeFi landscape.

CHAPTER 10   THE INTEGRATION AND EVOLUTION OF AI IN WEB3

Healthcare: Patient Data and Personalised Medicine

The amalgamation of AI and Web3 technologies is poised to redefine the healthcare landscape, bringing forth unprecedented advancements in patient data management and the delivery of personalised medicine. At the heart of this transformation is the seamless integration of blockchain's robust security features with AI's sophisticated data analysis capabilities. This synergy not only promises to enhance the efficiency and effectiveness of healthcare services but also to significantly elevate patient care standards through highly customised treatment protocols.

Blockchain technology offers a decentralised framework for managing patient data, ensuring its security, integrity and accessibility. Unlike traditional centralised databases that are vulnerable to cyberattacks and unauthorised access, blockchain provides a secure, tamper-proof platform for storing patient health records. Each patient's data is encrypted and fragmented across multiple nodes in the network, making it virtually impossible for hackers to compromise the entire dataset. Moreover, blockchain's transparency allows for real-time audit trails, ensuring that any access or modification of patient data is permanently recorded and easily traceable.

The use of smart contracts further enhances patient data management by automating consent management and data access protocols. Patients have complete control over who can access their data, for what purpose and for how long, through digitally signed agreements. These smart contracts can automatically enforce privacy regulations and compliance standards, streamlining data sharing across institutions while safeguarding patient confidentiality.

AI's role in this integrated healthcare model is to sift through the vast amounts of patient data stored on the blockchain to identify patterns, correlations and insights that can inform personalised treatment plans.

Machine learning algorithms can analyse genetic information, clinical history, lifestyle factors and real-time health data from wearable devices to predict disease susceptibility, progression and response to various treatments.

For instance, in oncology, AI can help oncologists tailor cancer treatment by analysing the genetic make-up of a tumour. By comparing this information with data from thousands of other cancer cases and outcomes, AI algorithms can recommend the most effective treatment options for the specific genetic profile of the patient's cancer, potentially improving survival rates and reducing side effects.

The integration of AI and Web3 technologies addresses one of the most critical concerns in healthcare: data privacy and patient consent. Blockchain's secure environment ensures that patient data is stored anonymously, with sensitive information being accessible only to authorised individuals or systems. AI systems access this data based on permissions granted via smart contracts, which are explicitly approved by the patient. This setup not only ensures compliance with stringent data protection regulations but also empowers patients to be active participants in their healthcare journey.

A practical application of this integrated approach could be in managing chronic diseases such as diabetes. A blockchain-based patient data repository could securely store continuous glucose monitoring data, dietary information and medication records. AI algorithms could analyse this data to identify patterns and predict potential health risks or complications. Based on this analysis, personalised dietary recommendations, medication adjustments and exercise plans could be developed for the patient, dynamically adapting to their health status and lifestyle changes.

The convergence of AI and Web3 in healthcare heralds a new era of precision medicine, characterised by enhanced patient data security, personalised treatment plans and empowered patient involvement. By securely storing patient data on blockchain and leveraging AI for data analysis, the healthcare sector can achieve a level of personalisation and efficiency previously unattainable. This transformative approach not only improves patient outcomes but also optimises healthcare resources, paving the way for a more sustainable, patient-centric healthcare system.

Education: Tailored Learning Experiences

The integration of AI and Web3 technologies into the educational sector presents a transformative approach to personalised learning experiences. This synergy leverages blockchain's unparalleled security and transparency capabilities with AI's dynamic content customisation and analytical strengths. As a result, education systems can offer more tailored, efficient and student-centric learning pathways.

Blockchain technology offers a secure and immutable ledger for recording and storing educational achievements and records. This decentralised approach ensures that students' academic credentials, from course completions to degrees and certifications, are permanently and reliably documented. Unlike traditional systems, where records can be lost, falsified or subject to privacy breaches, blockchain's ledger provides a tamper-proof record, accessible to educational institutions, employers and students themselves. This not only streamlines the verification process for academic credentials but also empowers students to own and control their educational data.

Smart contracts on the blockchain can automate various administrative processes, such as enrolment, attendance tracking and even the release of financial aid, based on predefined criteria. This reduces administrative burdens and costs while ensuring processes are executed fairly and transparently.

AI plays a critical role in analysing students' learning habits, performance data and preferences to deliver a truly personalised education experience. Machine learning algorithms can sift through vast amounts of data to identify each student's learning style, strengths, weaknesses and pace of learning. This analysis allows for the customisation of learning materials and teaching methodologies to suit each student's unique needs.

For example, AI can dynamically adjust the difficulty level of quiz questions based on a student's performance, ensuring that they are continually challenged but not overwhelmed. It can also recommend additional resources for topics where a student might be struggling or suggest advanced materials when a student is ready to move ahead.

This AI and Web3 synergy makes education more accessible to a wider audience, including students in remote or underprivileged areas. Blockchain ensures that all students have access to their educational records and achievements, regardless of their geographic location. At the same time, AI can deliver customised learning experiences through digital platforms, breaking down barriers to education such as physical distance, economic constraints and even language barriers.

AI algorithms can also analyse student engagement levels, identifying when a student's attention may be waning and adapting content delivery in real time to re-engage them. This might include altering the format of the content, introducing interactive elements or suggesting a short break.

Consider an adaptive learning platform built on Web3 technology, where blockchain securely stores students' educational profiles, and AI customises the learning journey for each user. As students interact with the platform, AI continuously analyses their responses, engagement levels and performance to adapt the content, pace and teaching methods. Students struggling with a particular concept could be presented with different explanations or learning formats, such as videos, interactive simulations or gamified content, until they grasp the concept. Meanwhile, advanced students can be challenged with higher-level materials or projects to deepen their understanding and engagement.

The convergence of AI and Web3 in education represents a leap towards more personalised, secure and inclusive learning experiences. By combining blockchain's secure documentation of educational achievements with AI's ability to tailor learning experiences, this integrated approach not only enhances the quality of education but also makes it more accessible to learners worldwide. As we move forward, the potential of AI and Web3 to revolutionise the educational landscape continues to unfold, promising a future where learning is truly centred around the individual needs and potentials of each student.

Governance: Transparent Voting Systems

The integration of AI and Web3 technologies has the potential to redefine governance models by introducing transparent and secure voting systems. This transformative approach combines blockchain's inherent security and transparency features with AI's analytical prowess to create a voting mechanism that is not only invulnerable to tampering but also intelligent in its operation.

At the core of this innovative voting system is blockchain technology, which serves as a decentralised ledger that records votes in a manner that ensures integrity, confidentiality and accessibility. Unlike traditional voting systems that rely on centralised databases prone to hacking and manipulation, blockchain's distributed nature makes it nearly impossible for any single entity to alter recorded votes. Each vote is encrypted and stored across multiple nodes in the network, creating an immutable and verifiable record of every transaction. Furthermore, blockchain enables the verification of vote authenticity without revealing the voter's identity, preserving the principle of a secret ballot.

Smart contracts automate and enforce the rules of the voting process, from voter registration to vote counting, without the need for intermediaries. This reduces the possibility of human error or fraud and ensures that the election process is conducted according to predefined and transparent criteria.

While blockchain provides the framework for secure and transparent voting, AI contributes by enhancing the efficiency and security of the electoral process. AI algorithms can monitor the voting process in real time, analysing voting patterns to detect any anomalies or irregularities that could indicate fraudulent activities. For instance, a sudden surge in votes from a particular location that does not align with historical voting patterns could trigger an alert for further investigation.

AI can also optimise the allocation of polling resources based on predictive analytics. By analysing data on voter turnout, demographics and historical election data, AI can forecast which polling stations are likely to experience high volumes of voters and allocate resources accordingly to reduce waiting times and improve the voting experience.

Consider a municipal election where AI and blockchain technology are employed to facilitate the voting process. Blockchain securely records each vote, ensuring that the election results are transparent and tamper-proof. Concurrently, AI analyses early voting patterns and predicts potential bottlenecks at polling stations. In response, election officials can deploy additional voting machines or open new polling stations in real time, based on AI's recommendations, to accommodate the influx of voters and ensure a smooth voting process.

The fusion of AI and Web3 in governance also addresses issues of voter engagement and accessibility. AI-driven platforms can provide voters with personalised information on candidates and issues, based on their preferences and past voting behaviour, encouraging informed participation in the democratic process. Additionally, blockchain-enabled voting systems can facilitate remote voting, breaking down geographical barriers and making it easier for individuals who are unable to visit polling stations, such as the elderly or those living abroad, to cast their votes securely.

The integration of AI and Web3 technologies in governance through transparent and secure voting systems represents a significant advancement in promoting trust, integrity and participation in the democratic process. By leveraging blockchain for its security and transparency and AI for its analytical and optimisation capabilities, this innovative approach has the potential to make voting more accessible, efficient and resistant to fraud, heralding a new era in democratic governance where technology empowers citizens and strengthens democracy.

Supply Chain Management

The integration of artificial intelligence (AI) and Web3 technologies into supply chain management heralds a significant transformation in how goods are produced, tracked and delivered globally. This powerful synergy combines blockchain's unparalleled capabilities in ensuring transparency and traceability with AI's proficiency in predictive analytics and optimisation, thereby addressing some of the most persistent challenges in supply chain operations.

Blockchain technology serves as the backbone for a new era of supply chain management. By recording each transaction or movement of goods on a decentralised and immutable ledger, blockchain technology allows every stakeholder in the supply chain, from manufacturers to consumers, to verify the authenticity and provenance of products. This level of transparency is particularly valuable in industries where ethical sourcing and authenticity are of paramount concern, such as in the food and beverage sector, pharmaceuticals and luxury goods.

For instance, a blockchain ledger could record the entire life cycle of a pharmaceutical product, from the sourcing of raw materials to manufacturing processes, distribution and, finally, to its sale. This traceability not only helps in combating counterfeit products but also enables swift action in the event of a product recall.

AI complements blockchain's traceability with its ability to analyse complex datasets to forecast potential disruptions, optimise logistics and manage inventory more efficiently. By leveraging machine learning algorithms, AI can predict supply chain vulnerabilities, such as potential delays due to weather conditions, geopolitical tensions or supplier reliability issues, allowing companies to proactively adjust their strategies.

Moreover, AI can optimise routing and distribution strategies by analysing factors such as traffic patterns, fuel costs and delivery timelines, ensuring that products are delivered in the most efficient and cost-effective manner. In warehouse management, AI-driven robots and systems can streamline the picking and packing processes, reducing errors and improving operational efficiency.

The synergy between AI and Web3 technologies in supply chain management significantly enhances consumer confidence. Blockchain's transparent record-keeping allows consumers to verify the authenticity and ethical sourcing of the products they purchase, while AI's optimisation capabilities ensure that products are available when and where they are needed, at a reasonable cost. This is particularly impactful in sectors like food safety, where consumers are increasingly concerned about the origin and handling of their food. For example, a consumer could scan a QR code on a product package to access the blockchain ledger that documents the product's journey from farm to table, including information on organic certifications, fair trade compliance and even carbon footprint.

Consider the journey of coffee beans in a blockchain and AI-integrated supply chain. From the moment the beans are harvested, each step of their journey is recorded on the blockchain, including the farm's location, harvest date, transportation records and roasting processes. AI analyses historical data and current market demands to forecast coffee bean demand, optimising the distribution to retailers and cafes, reducing waste and ensuring freshness. Consumers purchasing the coffee can trace its journey, ensuring it meets their standards for ethical sourcing and sustainability.

The integration of AI and Web3 technologies in supply chain management offers a robust solution to the complexities of modern-day supply chains. By marrying blockchain's traceability with AI's predictive analytics and optimisation capabilities, this synergy not only streamlines supply chain operations but also plays a critical role in building a more sustainable, transparent and consumer-centric global trade ecosystem. As businesses and consumers alike demand greater accountability and efficiency, the AI- and Web3-powered supply chain stands as a testament to how technology can drive positive change.

Environmental Sustainability

The fusion of AI and Web3 technologies is poised to play a pivotal role in advancing environmental sustainability. This synergy harnesses AI's capabilities in predictive modelling and data analysis alongside blockchain's strengths in creating secure, transparent and immutable records. Together, they offer innovative solutions to some of the most pressing environmental challenges, such as deforestation, pollution and biodiversity loss, by enabling more informed decision-making and fostering accountability in environmental management.

AI's predictive modelling capabilities can analyse vast amounts of environmental data to forecast potential impacts resulting from various human activities or natural phenomena. For instance, machine learning algorithms can process satellite imagery, weather patterns and historical deforestation data to predict areas at high risk of illegal logging or forest fires. This allows for proactive intervention, directing conservation efforts where they are needed most.

Furthermore, AI can model the potential outcomes of different environmental policies or conservation strategies, helping policymakers and organisations make data-driven decisions. For example, AI models can simulate the effects of reforestation projects on carbon sequestration, biodiversity and local climates, providing valuable insights into the long-term impacts of such initiatives.

Blockchain technology complements AI's predictive insights by offering a platform to securely record and track environmental data and conservation efforts. Each transaction or intervention, such as the allocation of conservation credits or the verification of carbon offsets, is recorded on a blockchain ledger, ensuring data integrity and preventing tampering or falsification.

This transparency is crucial for building trust among stakeholders, including governments, NGOs, corporations and the public. It ensures that claims of environmental stewardship or sustainability achievements are backed by verifiable data. Moreover, blockchain enables the creation of transparent and accountable markets for environmental services, such as carbon trading platforms, where carbon credits are bought and sold. Smart contracts can automate the issuance and transfer of these credits, linking them directly to verified conservation activities.

A practical application of AI and Web3 technologies in environmental sustainability can be seen in efforts to combat deforestation. An AI system continuously analyses satellite images to monitor forest cover, detecting changes that may indicate illegal logging activities. When deforestation is detected, the system automatically updates a blockchain ledger with the location and extent of the affected area.

This information can then trigger smart contracts that allocate funding from conservation credits to reforestation projects in the impacted regions. Additionally, blockchain technology provides a transparent record of both the deforestation events and the subsequent reforestation efforts, allowing stakeholders to track progress and ensure that funds are used effectively.

Beyond monitoring and interventions, the integration of AI and Web3 can also empower local communities and indigenous populations. Blockchain platforms can facilitate the direct involvement of these groups in conservation efforts, recognising and rewarding their contributions through digital tokens or conservation credits. Meanwhile, AI-driven tools can provide communities with real-time data on environmental threats, enabling them to protect their ecosystems more effectively.

The synergy between AI and Web3 technologies offers a powerful toolkit for enhancing environmental sustainability. By leveraging AI's ability to forecast environmental impacts and blockchain's capacity for ensuring transparency and accountability, this integrated approach enables more effective and equitable environmental protection measures. As the world grapples with the escalating challenges of climate change and environmental degradation, the innovative use of AI and blockchain technology could be key to achieving a sustainable future for our planet.

In essence, the synergy between AI and Web3 is reshaping our world, promising a future where efficiency, transparency and personalisation converge across sectors like finance, healthcare, education, governance, supply chain and environmental sustainability. This integration not only enhances industry practices but also deeply aligns with societal values and individual needs, paving the way for a more equitable and sustainable global ecosystem. As we embrace this integrated future, the combined potential of AI and Web3 offers a hopeful blueprint for addressing complex challenges with innovative solutions.

10.3 From Meme to Mainstream: AI's Expanding Role in Web3 Culture and Creativity

The relationship between generative AI and meme culture within the Web3 ecosystem not only highlights the evolution of digital content creation but also underscores the significant role that memes play in shaping online communities and cultural trends.

The Power of Memes in Digital Currency Communities

Memes, characterised by their humorous, satirical and often viral nature, have become a central facet of digital currency communities, acting as a catalyst for widespread engagement and investment interest.[4] They transcend language and cultural barriers, leveraging social media as their primary vehicle for rapid dissemination. The influence of memes in these communities is profound, often affecting the perception and value of digital currencies, as seen in the notable rise of meme coins. These coins, often born out of viral Internet jokes or concepts, have seen significant market attention, driven by their ability to encapsulate and spread innovative or catchy ideas within the Web3 space.

Generative AI's Role in Meme Creation and Evolution

The advent of generative AI technologies, such as DALL·E Mini,[5] has ushered in a new era of meme creation, where AI's ability to generate images from textual prompts has become a source of both entertainment and introspection.[6] This AI-driven meme generation process has democratised content creation, allowing for the rapid production of visually engaging and contextually relevant memes that resonate with wide audiences. The phenomenon of AI memes exploding onto the Internet exemplifies the seamless integration of artificial intelligence into the creative process, challenging traditional notions of creativity and content ownership.[7]

CHAPTER 10   THE INTEGRATION AND EVOLUTION OF AI IN WEB3

The 'Make It More' Trend and the Expansion of AI Memes

A notable trend in the AI meme space is the 'make it more' movement, where users push the boundaries of generative AI by requesting increasingly exaggerated versions of an original concept or image.[8] This trend highlights the playful interaction between humans and AI, showcasing the limitless potential for creativity and humour in the digital age. It also reflects the growing comfort and familiarity of Internet users with AI as a tool for personal and communal expression.

The Cultural Impact and Future Directions

The integration of AI into meme culture within the Web3 ecosystem represents more than just technological advancement; it signals a shift in how digital communities communicate, share ideas and foster collective identities. As AI technologies continue to evolve, their role in cultural production and creativity is likely to expand, offering new avenues for artistic expression and social commentary. The symbiotic relationship between AI and memes, rooted in creativity and driven by community engagement, exemplifies the dynamic potential of Web3 to reshape digital culture and creativity.

In conclusion, the intersection of AI and Web3 in meme culture underscores a transformative shift towards more interactive, participatory forms of digital expression. As generative AI continues to redefine the boundaries of creativity, the meme culture within Web3 spaces serves as a vibrant testament to the innovative potential of this synergy, promising a future where digital creativity is boundless, inclusive and deeply integrated into the fabric of online communities.

10.4 Summary

This chapter explores the evolving relationship between Artificial Intelligence (AI) and Web3, focusing on how these technologies complement each other. It begins by discussing the integration of AI, particularly Artificial General Intelligence (AGI), with blockchain technology to ensure ethical governance and transparency in AI's decision-making processes. Blockchain's decentralised, immutable ledger provides a framework for monitoring and controlling AGI's actions in critical sectors such as finance, healthcare, and governance.

The chapter also highlights the role of AI in enhancing various Web3 applications, including decentralised finance (DeFi), predictive analytics, and supply chain management. AI's ability to analyse vast datasets helps improve decision-making and efficiency in these sectors, while blockchain ensures that transactions and operations remain secure and transparent.

Moreover, the chapter delves into AI's contribution to creative fields, such as meme culture and digital content creation, where generative AI tools are transforming how communities engage and create content in the Web3 ecosystem.

In conclusion, the integration of AI and Web3 promises to reshape multiple industries, fostering innovation while maintaining transparency and ethical governance.

10.5 Notes

1. 强人工智能时代,区块链还有戏吗?|界面新闻. (n.d.). https://m.jiemian.com/article/9134596.html (Accessed: 9 April 2024).

2. The promise and challenges of crypto + AI applications. (2024). https://vitalik.eth.limo/general/2024/01/30/cryptoai.html?ref=0xplayer.com (Accessed: 9 April 2024).

3. The promise and challenges of crypto + AI applications. (2024). https://vitalik.eth.limo/general/2024/01/30/cryptoai.html?ref=0xplayer.com (Accessed: 9 April 2024).

4. 万字全面解读 MEME 赛道_ MarsBIT. (2024). Mars Finance. https://news.marsbit.co/20240322084852093438.html (Accessed: 9 April 2024).

5. Borisdayma. (2022). GitHub - borisdayma/dalle-mini: DALL·E Mini - Generate images from a text prompt. GitHub. https://github.com/borisdayma/dalle-mini (Accessed: 9 April 2024).

6. Knight, W. (2022). Inside DALL-E Mini, the internet's favorite artificial intelligence meme machine. WIRED. www.wired.com/story/dalle-ai-meme-machine/ (Accessed: 9 April 2024).

7. Franzen, C. (2023). 'Make it more': generative AI memes explode onto the internet. VentureBeat. https://venturebeat.com/ai/make-it-more-generative-ai-memes-explode-onto-the-internet/ (Accessed: 9 April 2024).

8. Franzen, C. (2023). 'Make it more': generative AI memes explode onto the internet. VentureBeat. https://venturebeat.com/ai/make-it-more-generative-ai-memes-explode-onto-the-internet/ (Accessed: 9 April 2024).

CHAPTER 11

Legal Frameworks for Web3

11.1 Global Regulatory Divergence and Convergence in Token Definitions

Here, we embark on a comparative analysis of token definitions as articulated by leading financial regulatory bodies across the globe. The chosen regulators represent the financial epicentres of the modern world – entities that not only influence global financial trends but also signal the regulatory future of burgeoning technologies. This section underscores the importance of understanding token definitions, given their critical role in determining the scope of regulation, compliance requirements and the overarching legal treatment of digital assets.

United States – Securities and Exchange Commission (SEC)[1]

In the United States, the Securities and Exchange Commission (SEC) employs the Howey Test, a pivotal judicial tool stemming from a 1946 US Supreme Court decision, to determine whether a digital asset should be classified as a security. Under the Howey Test, an asset is considered a security if it involves an investment of money in a common enterprise with a reasonable expectation of profits predominantly from the efforts of others.

When this test is applied to tokens, it often becomes a contentious debate, particularly regarding the third and fourth criteria: the expectation of profits and the reliance on the effort of others. For example, while Bitcoin escapes the security classification due to its decentralised nature, tokens associated with a central entity that guides development or operations are more likely to be considered securities.

The SEC categorises digital assets broadly, which could be as securities, currencies, commodities or even property, depending on the specific nature of the asset. This categorisation significantly impacts how such assets are regulated. Digital assets deemed securities fall under the stringent requirements of the Securities Act of 1933 and the Securities Exchange Act of 1934, which include registration obligations and compliance with various disclosure and reporting standards. However, the SEC provides several exemptions, such as Regulation A, Regulation Crowdfunding and Regulation D, each with its conditions and limits, to facilitate capital-raising activities while still maintaining investor protections.

The significance of the SEC's approach lies in its influence as a leading financial regulator in one of the world's largest and most dynamic digital asset markets. The interpretation of token definitions by the SEC not only shapes the regulatory landscape within the United States but also serves as a benchmark for international regulators grappling with the evolving complexities of the digital asset space.

CHAPTER 11 LEGAL FRAMEWORKS FOR WEB3

United Kingdom – Financial Conduct Authority (FCA)[2,3]

In the United Kingdom, the Financial Conduct Authority (FCA) has established a taxonomy for crypto-assets that informs whether such assets fall inside or outside the regulatory perimeter. According to FCA guidance, there are three main categories:

1. **Security Tokens**: These tokens provide rights and obligations akin to specified investments as outlined in the Regulated Activities Order (RAO), excluding e-money. This category hasn't changed significantly from prior guidance and remains within the regulatory perimeter. Security tokens often exhibit characteristics akin to shares, debentures or units in a collective investment scheme and are thus treated as securities.

2. **E-money Tokens**: Tokens that meet the definition of e-money fall under this category and are subject to Electronic Money Regulations (EMRs). These tokens were previously classified under utility tokens but now form a distinct regulated category. Entities dealing with e-money tokens must comply with applicable rules and regulations and hold the correct permissions.

3. **Unregulated Tokens**: This category covers tokens that do not meet the definition of e-money or do not provide the same rights as other specified investments under the RAO. It includes utility tokens and exchange tokens, which can range from being issued centrally to being decentralised and

may serve various functions such as giving access to goods or services or being used as a means of exchange. These tokens are outside the regulatory perimeter and offer a degree of flexibility in usage and transferability.

The FCA has been active in providing further illustrative examples in their guidance to support this taxonomy. For instance, tokens referred to as 'bank' or 'settlement' tokens have been examined, as well as tokens that might shift between categories, especially with respect to transferability.

The importance of these distinctions is paramount for issuers navigating the UK's regulatory landscape, as they must determine if their offerings are subject to FCA regulations. With the crypto-asset market rapidly evolving, the FCA's taxonomy and guidance aim to offer clarity while accommodating the innovative nature of these assets. This approach reflects the FCA's attempt to align regulatory objectives with market developments, ensuring that policy objectives are achieved without stifling innovation.

Understanding these classifications is critical, especially for market participants who are either currently operating in the UK or considering entering the market. It helps in assessing the regulatory implications for various crypto-assets and in making informed decisions regarding compliance, risk management and business strategy.

For entities unsure about the regulatory treatment of their tokens, the FCA advises consultation with their guidance, seeking legal advice or using FCA's Innovate services, which support innovative financial products and services while ensuring they meet regulatory requirements.

CHAPTER 11   LEGAL FRAMEWORKS FOR WEB3

European Union – Markets in Crypto-Assets (MiCA)[4]

The Markets in Crypto-Assets (MiCA) regulation by the European Union represents a substantial step towards the harmonisation of crypto-asset activities across member states, establishing a clear framework aimed at protecting consumers and maintaining financial stability while fostering innovation. The MiCA framework is comprehensive, providing detailed definitions and categorisations of crypto-assets, particularly focusing on asset-referenced tokens (ARTs) and e-money tokens (EMTs), which are considered critical for their monetary substitution dimension and potential impact on financial systems.

According to the MiCA, an 'asset-referenced token' refers to crypto-assets intended to maintain a stable value by referencing any value or right, including one or more official currencies, addressing the store of value function of money. On the other hand, 'e-money tokens' are digital representations of value that have a direct reference to a single fiat currency and are primarily intended to be used as a means of payment, thus ensuring their value stability. E-money tokens are similar to electronic money, substituting coins and banknotes in the digital arena.

The MiCA regulation emphasises the importance of these tokens being backed by assets or claims recorded elsewhere, enabling value transfer between end users, possibly without a central third party's involvement, depending on the design. This aspect is crucial in classifying crypto-assets and their alignment with existing financial regulations, such as the Payment Services Directive (PSD2).

The European Central Bank (ECB) notes that the proposed MiCA regulation makes a clear distinction between crypto-assets and central bank money, aiming to avoid confusion regarding the legal nature of assets potentially issued by central banks compared to traditional central bank money.

Under MiCA, most stablecoin issuers will have to be legally established and authorised within the EU, and significant asset-referenced tokens may come under direct supervision by the European Banking Authority (EBA). The EBA, in collaboration with national competent authorities (NCAs), will be responsible for ensuring compliance with the MiCA regulation's requirements, thereby enforcing a dual supervisory arrangement that seeks to prevent regulatory arbitrage and enhance the oversight of significant e-money tokens.

This regulation responds to the gaps exposed by events like the collapse of the FTX exchange, underscoring the need for a legal environment that protects against the volatility, fraud and manipulation risks inherent in the crypto markets. By establishing uniform market rules, MiCA is expected to offer a more predictable and sounder legal environment for crypto-assets, providing clarity for issuers and security for investors while enabling a larger market within the EU for crypto-asset activities.

The MiCA framework is a clear indication of the EU's commitment to integrating crypto-assets into its financial system, recognising both their potential for innovation and their need for regulation. The convergence of regulatory efforts under MiCA signals the EU's dedication to shaping a sustainable digital finance ecosystem, leveraging advancements in technology to enhance financial services while maintaining a vigilant stance on consumer protection and market integrity.

Switzerland – Financial Market Supervisory Authority (FINMA)[5,6]

In Switzerland, the Financial Market Supervisory Authority (FINMA) plays a pivotal role in defining the regulatory landscape for Initial Coin Offerings (ICOs) and the broader realm of crypto-assets. FINMA distinguishes between three primary categories of tokens: payment, utility and asset tokens, each with distinct regulatory implications, especially concerning ICOs.

Payment tokens are synonymous with cryptocurrencies like Bitcoin and Ether. They are intended for use as a means of payment for acquiring goods or services or as a means of money or value transfer. Cryptocurrencies give rise to no claims on their issuer. In terms of regulation, payment ICOs that enable tokens to function as a means of payment and can already be transferred are subject to compliance with anti-money laundering regulations. However, FINMA does not classify such tokens as securities.

Utility tokens are designed to provide digital access to an application or service via a blockchain-based infrastructure. They are not treated as securities as long as their sole purpose is to confer digital access rights and can be used in this manner at the point of issue. If, however, a utility token also or solely serves an investment purpose, FINMA will treat such tokens as securities, similar to asset tokens.

Asset tokens represent assets such as a debt or equity claim on the issuer, akin to shares in future company earnings or future capital flows. As such, asset tokens are considered securities, meaning they are subject to securities law requirements for trading, as well as civil law requirements under the Swiss Code of Obligations, such as prospectus requirements.

This classification by FINMA is essential for understanding how ICOs are conducted within Switzerland's legal framework. It reflects the authority's nuanced approach to regulating the diverse range of crypto-assets, aiming to ensure market participant protection, fair and reliable trading and efficient price formation while also recognising the innovative potential of blockchain technology.

Such a regulatory approach underscores Switzerland's status as a leading global financial centre, actively adapting its legal framework to accommodate the evolving landscape of digital finance and fostering an environment conducive to technological innovation and investment.

CHAPTER 11   LEGAL FRAMEWORKS FOR WEB3

Singapore – Monetary Authority of Singapore (MAS)[7]

The Monetary Authority of Singapore (MAS) has made significant strides in regulating the digital payment token (DPT) sphere, marking a proactive approach towards ensuring user protection and stability within the digital token domain. Through the recent amendments to the Payment Services Act (PS Act) and its subsidiary legislation, MAS has notably expanded the regulatory scope to encompass a broader range of payment services, emphasising user protection and financial stability for DPT service providers.

This expansion brings under regulation the provision of custodial services for DPTs, the facilitation of DPT transmission between accounts, the facilitation of DPT exchanges and the facilitation of cross-border money transfers, regardless of whether the funds are accepted or received in Singapore. Crucially, this includes services where the provider does not directly handle the money or DPTs, marking a comprehensive approach to oversight.

Under the revised framework, MAS is empowered to enforce anti-money laundering, countering the financing of terrorism, user protection and financial stability requirements on DPT service providers. This shift is not just regulatory but also anticipatory, ensuring that as the digital token landscape evolves, protective measures grow alongside to guard both consumers and the broader financial system.

The amended regulations demand that entities engaged in activities now under the PS Act's expanded scope notify MAS within 30 days and submit a licence application within six months if they wish to continue these activities temporarily. This process includes submitting an attestation report on the entity's compliance with pertinent requirements, emphasising MAS's commitment to stringent oversight.

A significant addition to the regulations concerns the safeguarding of customer assets. Set to take effect six months from the enactment, these rules mandate the segregation of customers' assets in trust accounts, proper record-keeping and the implementation of robust systems and controls to ensure the integrity and security of these assets.

The MAS's recent amendments underscore Singapore's forward-looking stance on digital payment tokens. By extending its regulatory reach, MAS not only aims to protect users but also to foster a stable, trustworthy environment for the growth and innovation of digital payment services. This development marks a key step in Singapore's broader strategy to position itself as a global leader in fintech and digital finance, reflecting a nuanced understanding of the dynamic interplay between technological innovation and regulatory oversight.

Hong Kong – Monetary Authority (HKMA)[8]

In response to the evolving landscape of digital assets, the Hong Kong Monetary Authority (HKMA) has taken significant steps to enhance the security and integrity of crypto custodial services within the region. Through comprehensive guidelines outlined in their 'Expected Standards' document, HKMA has established rigorous protocols to ensure that firms offering custodial services for digital assets adhere to stringent risk management, client protection and operational resilience practices.

A key focus of the HKMA's guidance is the mandatory segregation of clients' digital assets from the custodial firm's own assets, ensuring that in the event of insolvency, clients' assets remain protected and distinct from those of the firm. This requirement not only safeguards client assets but also promotes trust and stability within the burgeoning digital asset sector.

Moreover, the HKMA expects authorised institutions to undertake thorough risk assessments and implement robust policies to manage and mitigate identified risks effectively. This comprehensive approach encompasses governance, operations and the management of potential conflicts of interest, highlighting the HKMA's commitment to maintaining high standards of practice within the industry.

Additionally, the guidance specifies the necessity for adequate resourcing, including expertise and manpower, to manage custodial services responsibly. It underscores the importance of staff and senior management possessing the requisite knowledge and skills to fulfil their roles effectively, ensuring that custodial activities are conducted with the highest level of competence and care.

The HKMA's guidelines also address the critical aspect of safeguarding client digital assets against theft, fraud, negligence and other forms of misappropriation. Firms are required to establish and maintain effective control measures to minimise the risk of loss, demonstrating the HKMA's proactive stance in protecting consumers and ensuring the resilience of custodial services.

In response to the collapse of major platforms such as FTX, Terra and Three Arrows, the HKMA's regulations serve as a timely and necessary measure to enhance the regulatory framework surrounding crypto custodial services in Hong Kong. By setting clear expectations and standards, the HKMA aims to foster a secure, reliable and transparent digital asset environment, reflecting Hong Kong's ambition to reclaim its status as a leading crypto hub.

The rationale for selecting these regulators emphasises their influential roles at the forefront of financial innovation. Their approaches to defining tokens significantly contribute to the discourse on the integration of digital assets within traditional financial systems and the anticipation of future regulatory frameworks. This comparative analysis aims to provide a structured understanding of the regulatory stance across key financial jurisdictions, illustrating the diversity in token classification and its implications for the global digital asset landscape.

Table 11-1. Token Definition in Different Jurisdictions

Jurisdiction	Regulatory Body	Token Definition Approach
United States	SEC	Utilises the Howey Test to determine if digital assets are securities, focusing on investment contracts
United Kingdom	FCA	Differentiates between regulated (security and e-money tokens) and unregulated tokens (exchange and utility tokens)
European Union	MiCA	Classifies tokens into e-money tokens and asset-referenced tokens, setting distinct regulatory standards for each
Switzerland	FINMA	Categorises tokens as payment, utility or asset tokens, with asset tokens considered securities
Singapore	MAS	Has expanded regulatory scope to include digital payment tokens, emphasising user protection and financial stability
Hong Kong	HKMA	Issues guidelines for crypto custodial services, focusing on security and robust risk management policies

Table 11-1 reveals a landscape where regulatory bodies are either moving towards a convergence on token standards or maintaining distinct, localised approaches. For instance, while the SEC's reliance on the Howey Test represents a functional approach to determining the nature of digital assets, MiCA's classification system reflects the EU's endeavour to harmonise regulatory standards across member states. Similarly, the FCA's bifurcation of tokens into regulated and unregulated categories highlights the UK's pragmatic approach to oversight, allowing for a degree of flexibility in the burgeoning crypto market.

The divergence in regulatory frameworks underscores the complexity of navigating the digital asset realm. Stakeholders, ranging from issuers to investors, must be adept at understanding these nuanced regulatory environments to effectively strategise and comply with varying legal requirements. This structured overview not only aids in demystifying the global regulatory stance on digital tokens but also underscores the importance of adaptive strategies in the face of evolving financial technologies. As the digital asset industry continues to mature, the dialogue between these regulatory perspectives will undoubtedly shape the future of digital finance, prompting a continuous assessment of legal frameworks in response to technological advancements.

11.2 Global Regulatory Strategies for Digital Assets

In the rapidly evolving domain of digital finance, the advent of Web3 and its associated digital assets has prompted a varied response from global financial regulators. This section aims to explore the nuanced regulatory frameworks established by entities such as the SEC and the FCA, shedding light on their strategies for navigating the complexities of digital asset regulation. The focus is on understanding the regulatory landscape without an exclusive emphasis on any single regulatory authority, thereby providing a panoramic view of global approaches to digital asset governance.

The SEC's Regulatory Compass

In the United States, the SEC plays a pivotal role in determining the regulatory fate of digital assets through the application of the Howey Test. This test, derived from a landmark 1946 Supreme Court ruling, evaluates whether a digital asset constitutes a security based on its investment structure and the expectation of profit derived from the efforts of others. The SEC's broad categorisation of digital assets – which may be classified as securities, currencies, commodities or property – fundamentally influences their regulatory treatment. Notably, the SEC's approach underscores a commitment to protecting investors while adapting to the intricacies of digital asset transactions. Through exemptions such as Regulation A, Regulation Crowdfunding and Regulation D, the SEC navigates the tension between fostering innovation and ensuring investor protection within the dynamic landscape of digital finance.

The FCA's Regulatory Blueprint

Across the Atlantic, the FCA's regulatory framework for digital assets distinguishes itself through a clear taxonomy, categorising tokens into security tokens, e-money tokens and unregulated tokens. This classification system plays a critical role in defining the regulatory perimeter for crypto-assets within the UK. Security tokens, akin to traditional financial instruments, fall squarely within the FCA's regulatory purview, necessitating compliance with established financial regulations. Conversely, unregulated tokens, which include utility and exchange tokens, operate outside this perimeter, offering a measure of operational flexibility. The FCA's proactive stance, exemplified by its sandbox programme, illustrates an effort to balance regulatory oversight with the promotion of financial innovation.

Navigating Cross-Border Regulatory Waters

The digital nature of Web3 and its assets inherently transcends national boundaries, presenting unique challenges for regulatory coherence and enforcement. International collaboration and standard-setting bodies like the Financial Action Task Force (FATF) and the Global Financial Innovation Network (GFIN) play critical roles in bridging regulatory divergences. Efforts to harmonise regulatory approaches are vital for managing the risks associated with digital asset transactions, particularly in areas such as anti-money laundering (AML) and countering the financing of terrorism (CFT).

Convergence and Divergence in Global Regulation

The exploration of the SEC and FCA's frameworks reveals both convergence and divergence in global regulatory approaches. While there is a shared emphasis on investor protection and market integrity, the methods and classifications employed by these regulators reflect their unique market environments and regulatory philosophies. The SEC's reliance on the Howey Test and the FCA's detailed crypto-asset taxonomy both aim to provide clarity and stability within their respective jurisdictions, yet their approaches to categorisation and exemption criteria differ.

Future Horizons

As the digital asset sector continues to mature, the dialogue among global regulators will likely deepen, potentially leading to more standardised or interoperable regulatory frameworks. The evolving landscape of digital finance demands a regulatory approach that is both adaptable and forward-looking, capable of addressing emerging challenges while fostering innovation.

This section has traversed the global regulatory maze of digital assets, offering insights into the strategies employed by the SEC and FCA. In doing so, it emphasises the importance of a nuanced understanding of regulatory environments in navigating the complex and dynamic world of digital finance.

11.3 Digital Asset Custody and User Protection

The custody of digital assets and the protection of users stand as paramount concerns for regulators worldwide. This section delves into the mechanisms and regulatory frameworks developed to ensure the safekeeping of digital assets and safeguard investors from potential risks associated with digital finance. By examining global practices and guidelines, this narrative aims to illuminate the efforts undertaken to fortify the security and integrity of digital asset transactions.

The Essence of Digital Asset Custody

Custody of digital assets involves the secure storage and management of cryptocurrencies, tokens and other forms of digital value. As the digital finance ecosystem expands, the importance of robust custodial services becomes increasingly critical. These services not only protect assets from theft, hacking and unauthorised access but also play a crucial role in the operational integrity of digital finance, ensuring transactions are executed as intended.

Regulatory Approaches to Custody and Protection

Globally, financial regulators have recognised the need for stringent custodial standards to protect digital asset holders. These standards often encompass requirements for the segregation of client assets, the implementation of comprehensive security measures and regular audits to ensure compliance.

- **Security Measures and Technological Safeguards**: Regulators mandate the adoption of advanced security protocols, including encryption, multi-signature wallets and cold storage solutions, to mitigate the risks of cyberattacks and unauthorised access. These measures are designed to shield digital assets from the evolving threats in cyberspace.

- **Operational Integrity and Transparency**: Guidelines stipulate that custodial service providers maintain accurate records, undergo regular audits and provide transparent reporting to clients. This transparency is vital for building trust within the digital finance ecosystem and for ensuring that users have a clear understanding of the status and safety of their assets.

- **Risk Management Practices**: Regulatory frameworks require custodians to implement robust risk management strategies. These strategies include the assessment of operational, cyber and counterparty risks, ensuring that custodial services are prepared to address potential vulnerabilities proactively.

Case Studies in Regulation

- **United States (SEC and FINRA Guidelines)**: In the United States, the SEC and the Financial Industry Regulatory Authority (FINRA) have issued guidance outlining the expectations for broker-dealers operating as digital asset custodians. This guidance emphasises the necessity of secure storage practices and the legal obligations to protect client assets.

- **European Union (MiCA Framework)**: The Markets in Crypto-Assets (MiCA) regulation provides a comprehensive approach to the custody of digital assets within the EU. MiCA establishes clear standards for the operation of custodial services, including requirements for asset segregation, operational resilience and consumer protection.

- **Asia-Pacific (Hong Kong SFC Framework)**: The Hong Kong Securities and Futures Commission (SFC) has set forth a regulatory framework for virtual asset custodians, detailing requirements for custody operations, risk management and the safeguarding of client assets. This framework aims to enhance the regulatory oversight of digital asset custodians and protect investors.

The Path Forward

As the digital finance landscape continues to evolve, the role of custodial services and the need for effective user protection mechanisms become increasingly significant. Regulatory bodies worldwide are tasked with the challenge of adapting to technological advancements while ensuring that custodial practices are both secure and conducive to the growth of digital finance.

In conclusion, the global push towards stringent digital asset custody and user protection standards reflects a collective effort to foster a safer and more reliable digital finance ecosystem. By implementing rigorous regulatory frameworks and encouraging best practices in asset custody, regulators aim to protect investors from the inherent risks of digital asset transactions, thereby promoting confidence and stability in the market.

11.4 Navigating the Future: Regulation, Innovation and the Standardisation of Web3

As the digital era unfolds, cryptocurrencies stand at the crossroads of innovation and regulation, heralding a transformative period for global finance. This section explores the multifaceted future of cryptocurrencies, focusing on the dual engines driving their evolution: relentless innovation and the pressing need for standardisation to mitigate associated risks. By examining the trajectory of cryptocurrency markets, regulatory responses and emerging technologies, we can gain insights into the future dynamics of digital currencies.

The Emergence of Bitcoin ETFs:[9] Bridging Traditional and Digital Finance

One of the most pivotal developments at the intersection of traditional finance and the digital asset world is the emergence of Bitcoin Exchange-Traded Funds (ETFs). Bitcoin ETFs represent a significant leap forward in the institutional acceptance of cryptocurrencies, offering a regulated, transparent and efficient vehicle for investing in Bitcoin through traditional stock exchanges. This section explores the implications of Bitcoin ETFs for the future of cryptocurrencies, highlighting their role in innovation, risk mitigation and standardisation efforts.

Bitcoin ETFs are innovative financial products that track the price of Bitcoin and trade on traditional stock exchanges, offering investors an indirect exposure to Bitcoin's price movements without the complexities of managing digital wallets or directly trading cryptocurrencies on exchanges. This innovation bridges the gap between the burgeoning world of digital assets and the established realm of traditional finance, making Bitcoin accessible to a broader range of investors, including institutional investors who are subject to stringent regulatory and compliance requirements.

Mitigating Risks with Regulated Instruments

The introduction of Bitcoin ETFs addresses several risks associated with direct cryptocurrency investments:

- **Regulatory Oversight**: Bitcoin ETFs are subject to the regulatory frameworks governing traditional financial markets, offering a layer of protection and oversight that direct cryptocurrency investments lack.

- **Security and Custody**: Investors in Bitcoin ETFs do not need to worry about the security of digital wallets or the risks of hacking and theft. Custody of the underlying Bitcoin assets is managed by professional custodians, reducing the risk of asset loss.

- **Market Stability**: By providing a regulated and standardised way to invest in Bitcoin, ETFs can contribute to the stability of the cryptocurrency market. They offer a transparent and liquid investment option, potentially reducing volatility by smoothing the entry of institutional capital into the Bitcoin market.

Bitcoin ETFs represent a step towards the standardisation of cryptocurrency investments. They operate within the regulatory and operational frameworks established for ETFs in traditional financial markets, ensuring a consistent and standardised approach to investing in digital assets. This standardisation is crucial for integrating cryptocurrencies into the broader financial system, making them more accessible, understandable and appealing to a wide range of investors.

The success of Bitcoin ETFs could pave the way for the introduction of ETFs based on other cryptocurrencies or digital asset classes, further integrating digital assets into the traditional financial ecosystem. As regulatory bodies around the world continue to evolve their approaches to digital assets, the potential for more diversified and sophisticated cryptocurrency investment products grows. This evolution will likely spur further innovation in the financial sector, offering investors new ways to engage with digital assets within a regulated and secure framework.

However, the journey of Bitcoin ETFs is not without its challenges. Regulatory approval processes can be lengthy and complex, reflecting the cautious stance of regulatory bodies towards rapidly evolving digital asset markets. The future growth of Bitcoin ETFs and similar investment vehicles will depend on ongoing dialogue between regulators, financial institutions and the cryptocurrency community, aiming to balance innovation with investor protection and market integrity.

Bitcoin ETFs mark a significant milestone in the convergence of digital assets and traditional financial markets. They offer a regulated, innovative and accessible means of investing in Bitcoin, contributing to the standardisation and stability of the cryptocurrency market. As the landscape of digital finance continues to evolve, Bitcoin ETFs will play a pivotal role in shaping the integration of cryptocurrencies into the global financial system, heralding a new era of investment opportunities.

The Innovation Horizon

Cryptocurrency innovation continues to disrupt traditional financial systems, challenging conventional notions of money, value transfer and investment. This relentless innovation is embodied in several key trends:

- **Decentralised Finance (DeFi)**: DeFi platforms are redefining financial services, offering decentralised lending, borrowing and trading without traditional intermediaries. As DeFi ecosystems mature, they promise to enhance financial inclusivity and democratise access to financial services.

- **Non-fungible Tokens (NFTs)**: NFTs have introduced novel concepts of digital ownership and value, enabling the tokenisation of art, collectibles and even real estate. This trend underscores the expanding utility of blockchain technology beyond simple value transfer.

- **Blockchain Interoperability**: The development of cross-chain technologies aims to enable seamless interaction between disparate blockchain networks. This interoperability is crucial for realising the full potential of blockchain technology, facilitating a more integrated and efficient digital asset ecosystem.

Navigating the Risks

The rapid growth of cryptocurrencies brings with it a spectrum of risks, necessitating vigilant regulatory and technological responses:

- **Market Volatility and Speculation**: The high volatility of cryptocurrency markets poses significant risks to investors, often exacerbated by speculative trading. Addressing this challenge requires improved market oversight, investor education and the development of risk mitigation tools.

- **Security Vulnerabilities**: Despite the inherent security features of blockchain technology, the cryptocurrency landscape is fraught with risks of hacks, fraud and scams. Strengthening security protocols, enhancing custody solutions and fostering collaboration among stakeholders are critical for mitigating these risks.

- **Regulatory Uncertainty**: The evolving regulatory landscape for cryptocurrencies remains a significant challenge for both innovators and investors. The development of clear, consistent and coherent regulatory frameworks is essential for fostering a stable and secure cryptocurrency market.

The Quest for Standardisation

The path to mitigating the risks associated with cryptocurrencies and unlocking their full potential lies in standardisation:

- **Global Regulatory Standards**: The establishment of global regulatory standards for cryptocurrencies is pivotal for harmonising regulatory approaches, combating illicit activities and protecting investors. Efforts by international bodies such as the Financial Action Task Force (FATF) and the Global Financial Innovation Network (GFIN) are instrumental in this regard.

- **Technical and Operational Standards**: Beyond regulatory harmonisation, the standardisation of technical and operational aspects of cryptocurrencies is crucial for ensuring interoperability, security and user protection. Initiatives like the ISO/TC 307 standard for blockchain and distributed ledger technologies exemplify these efforts.

- **Stablecoins and CBDCs**: The rise of stablecoins and the exploration of Central Bank Digital Currencies (CBDCs) reflect a move towards stable and regulated forms of digital currency. These developments signal a convergence between innovation and the traditional financial system, offering a glimpse into a future where digital currencies are both innovative and standardised.

Future Projections

The trajectory of cryptocurrencies into the next decade and beyond paints a complex landscape, where the pace of technological innovation intersects with the evolving frameworks of global finance. This convergence is not merely a trend but a transformative shift that holds the promise of reshaping the financial services industry. As cryptocurrencies continue to gain momentum, their journey from niche digital phenomena to mainstream financial instruments hinges on achieving a delicate balance between fostering innovation and implementing effective regulation.

The advance of blockchain technology and the proliferation of cryptocurrencies are set to redefine the infrastructure of the financial sector. Innovations such as decentralised finance (DeFi) platforms, smart contracts and tokenisation of assets are breaking new ground, offering unprecedented opportunities for efficiency, transparency and accessibility in financial transactions. Moreover, the exploration and potential adoption of Central Bank Digital Currencies (CBDCs) by numerous countries signify a leap towards integrating digital currencies into the traditional banking system, promising a future where digital and fiat currencies coexist and complement each other.

CHAPTER 11 LEGAL FRAMEWORKS FOR WEB3

The global regulatory landscape for cryptocurrencies is at a critical juncture. The next few years will likely see an intensified effort towards establishing a harmonised regulatory framework that can accommodate the borderless nature of digital currencies while safeguarding the financial system against risks such as fraud, money laundering and market manipulation. The role of international regulatory bodies and agreements will be paramount in forging global standards that ensure a level playing field, preventing regulatory arbitrage and fostering international cooperation in oversight and enforcement.

The sustainable integration of cryptocurrencies into global finance requires more than just regulatory responses; it necessitates a paradigm of collaborative governance involving regulators, industry participants, technologists and consumers. This collaborative approach aims to cultivate an ecosystem where innovation can thrive within a context of security, fairness and transparency. Engaging in open dialogue, sharing best practices and developing technology-neutral regulatory approaches will be crucial for adapting to the rapidly changing landscape of digital finance.

As the digital asset space matures, the industry is poised to develop more sophisticated solutions to address the inherent risks of cryptocurrencies. Innovations in cybersecurity, fraud detection and risk management will play a critical role in enhancing the resilience of the cryptocurrency ecosystem. Moreover, the advent of more advanced and user-friendly custodial services, insurance products and investment vehicles will further mitigate risks for both retail and institutional participants, enhancing trust and participation in the market.

Looking ahead, the potential of cryptocurrencies to empower financial inclusion remains one of their most compelling value propositions. By providing accessible financial services to underserved populations around the globe, digital currencies can play a pivotal role in driving economic growth and reducing inequality. Furthermore, the continuous evolution of the cryptocurrency space is expected to spur innovation across various sectors, from finance to supply chain management, healthcare and beyond, heralding a new era of digital solutions to traditional challenges.

The future of cryptocurrencies stands at the dynamic confluence of innovation and regulatory foresight, steering towards a seamless integration with the global financial system. This path is illuminated by the rapid pace of technological progress, regulatory evolution and the spirit of collaborative governance. As the digital age progresses, the amalgamation of these elements underpins a collective endeavour to unlock the revolutionary promise of cryptocurrencies. In doing so, it aims to secure a financial landscape that is not only stable and secure but also broadly inclusive and trustful. The journey ahead is lined with both immense potential and notable challenges, necessitating a unified effort to nurture innovation within a framework of stability and trust. By fostering global cooperation and dedicating efforts towards the establishment of common standards, the domain of digital currencies is on the cusp of a transformative era. Such strides promise to redefine the contours of global finance, ensuring that the future of cryptocurrencies contributes to a robust, equitable and forward-looking financial world.

11.5 Summary

This chapter offers a comprehensive analysis of the evolving legal frameworks governing Web3 and digital assets across major global jurisdictions. It explores how regulatory bodies such as the U.S. Securities and Exchange Commission (SEC), the U.K. Financial Conduct Authority (FCA), and the European Union's Markets in Crypto-Assets (MiCA) approach the classification and regulation of tokens. Each jurisdiction takes a distinct approach to defining and regulating digital assets, balancing the need for innovation with investor protection.

The chapter also examines global regulatory strategies, highlighting both convergence and divergence in how digital assets are treated. Through the comparison of different legal structures, the chapter sheds light on the complexities of navigating cross-border regulations and the implications for market participants. It discusses the role of custodial services in securing digital assets and the critical need for strong user protection mechanisms.

Finally, the chapter addresses future regulatory trends, including the rise of Bitcoin ETFs, the importance of standardisation in the cryptocurrency space, and the potential for further global collaboration on digital asset regulation. The discussion underscores the dynamic relationship between innovation and regulation as the Web3 ecosystem continues to mature.

11.6 Notes

1. U.S. Securities and Exchange Commission. (2021). Framework for 'Investment Contract' Analysis of Digital assets. In U.S. Securities and Exchange Commission Guidance [Guidance]. www.sec.gov/files/dlt-framework.pdf (Accessed: 9 April 2024).

2. Financial Conduct Authority. (2019). Guidance on Cryptoassets.

3. Financial Conduct Authority. (2019). Guidance on Cryptoassets Feedback and Final Guidance to CP 19/3.

4. Hallak, I. & European Parliamentary Research Service. (2023). Markets in crypto-assets (MiCA). In Stefan Berger, Eero Heinäluoma, Ondřej Kovařik,

Ernest Urtasun, Andżelika A. Możdżanowska, Antonio Maria Rinaldi, & Chris MacManus, European Parliamentary Research Service (Report PE 739.221). www.europarl.europa.eu/RegData/etudes/BRIE/2022/739221/EPRS_BRI(2022)739221_EN.pdf (Accessed: 9 April 2024).

5. FINMA. (2018). FINMA publishes ICO guidelines, www.finma.ch/en/news/2018/02/20180216-mm-ico-wegleitung/ (Accessed: 9 April 2024).

6. FINMA. (2018). Guidelines for enquiries regarding the regulatory framework for initial coin offerings (ICOs). www.finma.ch/en/~/media/finma/dokumente/dokumentencenter/myfinma/1bewilligung/fintech/wegleitungico.pdf (Accessed: 9 April 2024).

7. Monetary Authority of Singapore. (2024). Guidelines on the provision of consumer protection safeguards by digital payment token service providers.

8. HKMA. (2024). Provision of custodial services for digital assets. www.hkma.gov.hk/media/eng/doc/key-information/guidelines-andcircular/2024/20240220e4.pdf (Accessed: 9 April 2024).

9. SEC.gov | Statement on the Approval of Spot Bitcoin Exchange-Traded Products. (2024). www.sec.gov/newsroom/speeches-statements/gensler-statement-spot-bitcoin-011023 (Accessed: 9 April 2024).

Index

A

Aave, 151, 156, 161–163
AGI, *see* Artificial General Intelligence (AGI)
AI, *see* Artificial intelligence (AI)
AMMs, *see* Automated Market Maker (AMMs)
Application-Specific Integrated Circuits (ASICs), 38
Artificial General Intelligence (AGI)
    automated efficiency *vs.* ethical boundaries, 283
    future-proofing labour and automation, 284
    groundbreaking technologies, 281
    immutable record-keeping, 284
    intersection, 282
    intrinsic complexity, 281
    ledger/decentralised architecture, 282
    operations, 283
    smart contracts, 284
    symbiosis, 285
    symbiotic relationship, 282
Artificial intelligence (AI), 10, 11
    blockchain, 286
    educational sector, 292–194
    environmental sustainability, 298–300
    healthcare landscape, 290–292
    integration, 291
    interaction, 286
    predictive analytics/DeFi, 288, 289
    supply chain management, 296–298
    transparent and secure voting systems, 294–296
    venn diagram, 286
    Web3 ecosystem, 300
        cultural impact/directions, 302
        digital currency communities, 301
        generative technologies, 301
        make it more movement, 302
ARTs, *see* Asset-referenced tokens (ARTs)
ASICs, *see* Application-Specific Integrated Circuits (ASICs)

INDEX

Asset-referenced tokens (ARTs), 309, 310
Automated Market Makers (AMMs), 149, 157, 239, 240

B

Bitcoin, 27
    Blocksize War, 44
    cryptographic methodologies, 30
    currencies, 32
    diverse wallet types, 45–47
    financial technology, 27
    genesis block, 30
    gold jewellery (inscriptions)
        cultural/memetic value, 49
        decentralisation/security, 48
        definition, 46
        economic implications, 48
        network integrity, 48
        novel concept, 46
        ordinals protocol, 47
    mining, 34–42
    Nakamoto, Satoshi, 28–30
    properties, 33
    technical aspects, 32–34
    theoretical threat/51% attack, 43, 44
    transaction mechanism, 33
    whitepaper, 28
Bitcoin Exchange-Traded Funds (ETFs), 322–324
Blockchain technology

AGI (*see* Artificial General Intelligence (AGI))
artificial intelligence (AI), 10, 11
Bitcoin, 3, 7, 29
blocks definition, 4
Byzantine Generals' problem, 8
centralised *vs.* decentralised *vs.* distributed, 5–7
consensus algorithms, 21–24
consensus mechanism, 7
decentralisation, 4
definition, 3
digital signatures
    algorithms, 16
    binding, 16
    definition, 16
    handwritten signatures, 16
    key generation, 16
    multi-signature, 17
    properties, 17
    signing method, 17
    uniqueness, 16
    verification method, 17
double-spending problem, 7
encryption, 14, 15
enterprise-level systems, 8
EVM (*see* Ethereum Virtual Machine (EVM))
evolution/diversity, 5
foundational aspects, 3
hash functions, 12–14
information *vs.* value transfer, 10
Internet, 9, 10

NETs (*see* Non-fungible Tokens (NFTs))
projections, 327–329
proof of work (PoW), 7
Python libraries, 18–21
Real-World Assets (RWA), 177, 178
secure/reliable method, 9
smart contracts, 8

C

CDPs, *see* Collateralised debt positions (CDPs)
Centralised exchanges (CEXs), 239
Centralised *vs.* Decentralised *vs.* Distributed, 5–7
CEXs, *see* Centralised exchanges (CEXs)
CFMM, *see* Constant Function Market Maker (CFMM)
Collateralised debt positions (CDPs), 151, 164
Consensus algorithms
    double-spending problems, 22
    DPoS, 23
    fundamental design, 21–24
    implementation, 22
    participants/nodes, 22
    PBFT, 24
    Proof of Stake (PoS), 23
    Proof of Work (PoW), 22
    representative project, 24
Constant Function Market Maker (CFMM), 251–253
Conversion methodology, 33

D

DAOs, *see* Decentralised autonomous organisations (DAOs)
DApps, *see* Decentralised applications (DApps)
Decentralisation, 4
Decentralised applications (DApps), 8, 57, 58, 121
Decentralised autonomous organisations (DAOs), 8, 57, 245, 268
Decentralised exchanges (DEXs), 148–150, 239
    core operations, 240–242
    decentralised identity (DID), 248
    democratic governance model, 245
    development, 248
    JIT liquidity attacks, 250
    liquidity providers (LPs), 239, 240, 249, 253
    market capitalization
        algorithmic trading, 247
        burn-and-mint equilibrium, 248
        distribution strategy, 248
        liquidity provision, 246

INDEX

Decentralised exchanges
    (DEXs) (cont.)
  mechanism/fiscal policy
      design, 247
  partnerships/
      integration, 247
  strategies, 246
  token burn, 246
  MetaMask wallet, 122
  security/governance, 245
  token/liquidity pools, 242–244
  traditional finance, 249
  TWAMM vs. CFMM, 251–253
  working process, 239, 240
Decentralised Finance (DeFi), 83,
    324, 327
  Aave, 161–163
  artificial intelligence, 288, 289
  collateralisation, 150
  concepts, 143
  decentralisation, 145
  decentralised exchanges
      (DEXs), 148–150
  financial transactions, 143, 144
  functional differences, 145
  insurance protocols, 154, 155
  interoperability, 170
  interoperability and
      composability, 145
  intrinsic characteristics, 145
  leading platforms, 150, 151
  MakerDAO, 163–166
  market risks/volatility, 170
  operational differences, 145
  permissionless, 144
  prediction markets/
      oracles, 156–158
  protocols, 156
  Real-World Assets (RWA), 178
  regulations, 168, 169
  regulatory framework, 145
  scalability, 170
  security protocols, 168
  smart contracts/blockchain, 144
  stablecoins, 151–153
  Total Value Locked (TVL),
      166, 167
  Traditional Finance
      (TradFi), 146–148
  Uniswap, 157–161
Decentralised identity (DID), 168
Decentralised Physical
    Infrastructure
    Networks (DePIN)
  analytical comparison, 183
  asset valuation and
      liquidity, 192
  blockchain/smart contracts, 181
  components, 181
  data privacy and security, 192
  flywheel concepts, 185–187
  fundamental distinctions, 185
  interoperability, 191, 193
  interoperability protocols, 182
  off-chain/on-chain
      applications, 195
  opportunities/complexities, 189
  Oracle networks, 193, 194

privacy-preserving
technologies, 193
properties, 181
real-world
applications, 182–185
regulatory compliance, 192
regulatory hurdles, 191
RWA (see Real-World
Assets (RWA))
scalability, 192, 193
scalability/sustainability,
187, 188
Solana's architecture, 189–191
telecommunications, 182
tokenisation, 189
tokenomics and incentives, 182
transportation, 182
urban development, 183
widespread tokenisation, 195
DeFi, see Decentralised
Finance (DeFi)
Delegated Proof of Stake
(DPoS), 23
DePIN, see Decentralised Physical
Infrastructure
Networks (DePIN)
DEXs, see Decentralised
exchanges (DEXs)
DID, see Decentralised
identity (DID)
Digital assets
convergence/divergence, 318
custody/user protection, 319
FCA's regulatory framework, 317

global approaches, 316
horizons, 318
path forward, 321
regulation, 320
regulatory approaches, 319, 320
regulatory coherence/
enforcement, 317
SEC's regulatory compass, 316
secure storage/
management, 319
Digital payment token (DPT), 312
Digital Resource Networks
(DRNs), 183
Distributed ledger technologies
(DLTs), 175
DLTs, see Distributed ledger
technologies (DLTs)
DPoS, see Delegated Proof of
Stake (DPoS)
DPT, see Digital payment
token (DPT)
DRNs, see Digital Resource
Networks (DRNs)

E

Electronic Money Regulations
(EMRs), 307
E-money tokens (EMTs), 309
EMRs, see Electronic Money
Regulations (EMRs)
EMTs, see E-money tokens (EMTs)
ENS, see Ethereum Name
Service (ENS)

INDEX

EOAs, *see* Externally Owned Accounts (EOAs)
ERC, *see* Ethereum Request for Comment (ERC)
Ethereum Name Service (ENS), 168, 203
Ethereum Request for Comment (ERC)
   digital ecosystem, 106
   ERC20 standard, 83–90
      components, 84
      constructor, 85
      contract declaration, 85
      contract functions/queries, 88, 89
      deployment, 85, 86, 88
      import statement, 84
      low-level interactions, 90
      smart contract, 86
   ERC20 standardtoken contract, 84
   ERC721
      awardItem function, 93
      components, 91–94
      deployment, 95
      elements, 94, 95
      non-fungible tokens, 95–100
      token contract, 90
   ERC1155 standard
      code explanation, 101–103
      deployment, 103, 104
      HGCollections smart contract, 104–106
      minting tokens, 103
      multi-token standard, 101
   evolution, 106
   overview, 83
   types, 83
ETFs, *see* Bitcoin Exchange-Traded Funds (ETFs)
Ethereum Virtual Machine (EVM), 136
   centralised systems, 56
   core component, 55
   data blobs, 60
   decentralised computing infrastructure, 57, 58
   development journey, 58–61
   features, 55
   IDE, 65
   smart contract
      access control mechanisms, 78, 79
      addPerson function, 80
      boolean variable, 75
      constructor, 77
      contract constructor, 80
      definition, 74
      deployment and interaction, 62
      enumeration declaration, 77
      ERC (*see* Ethereum Request for Comment (ERC))
      execution environment, 62
      general architecture, 61
      integer variables, 75
      internal function, 81
      key differences, 64

INDEX

modification, 74
onlyOwner modifier, 79–81
programming language, 62
solidity, 75
source code, 64
specific types, 76
state manipulation/
query, 76
state query function, 78
state variable, 77
string variable, 75
structure/components, 61
time-based modifier, 82
time-based modifier/
mapping/structure, 81, 82
visibility specifiers, 63, 64
turing-complete language, 57
Ethereum Web3 technologies, 127
EVM, *see* Ethereum Virtual
Machine (EVM)
Externally Owned Accounts
(EOAs), 112

F

Faucets
dripping resources, 127
features, 128
operation, 128
smart contract, 128
Ethereum test network, 130
MetaMask wallet, 132, 133
sepolia network, 130, 131
Sepolia Testnet Etherscan, 134

source code, 128
websites, 132
FCA, *see* Financial Conduct
Authority (FCA)
Financial Conduct Authority
(FCA), 307, 308
Financial Industry Regulatory
Authority (FINRA), 320
Financial Market Supervisory
Authority (FINMA), 310, 311
FINMA, *see* Financial Market
Supervisory
Authority (FINMA)
FINRA, *see* Financial Industry
Regulatory
Authority (FINRA)

G

GDPR, *see* General Data Protection
Regulation (GDPR)
General Data Protection
Regulation (GDPR), 276
GFC, *see* Global Financial
Crisis (GFC)
Global Financial Crisis (GFC), 27

H

Hash functions
characteristics, 12
collision resistance, 12
hiding feature, 13
puzzle friendliness, 13

339

HKMA, *see* Hong Kong Monetary Authority (HKMA)
Hong Kong Monetary Authority (HKMA), 313–316

I

IDE, *see* Integrated development environment (IDE)
Integrated development environment (IDE)
  key features, 66, 67
  Remix development, 65
  smart contract
    compilation, 69
    debugging, 71
    deployment, 71
    interaction, 72, 74
    solidity, 68
    step-step process, 67
    testing, 70
Internet of Things (IoT), 181
Internet *vs.* blockchain, 9, 10
IoT, *see* Internet of Things (IoT)

J, K, L

JIT, *see* Just-in-Time (JIT)
Just-in-Time (JIT), 249, 250

M

MakerDAO project, 163–166
Markets in Crypto-Assets (MiCA), 309, 310

MAS, *see* Monetary Authority of Singapore (MAS)
Maximum Extractable Value (MEV), 159
MetaMask
  account details, 123
  backup, 117
  cryptographic key, 125
  download page, 114, 115
  Etherscan, 126
  functionalities, 121
  interface, 121, 122
  landing page, 116
  password setting, 116, 117
  private key, 124–126
  recovery phrase, 119
  securing option, 118
  wallet creation, 120
  warning screen, 124
  12-word recovery phrase, 125
Metaverse
  augmented reality (AR), 261
  Decentraland, 273
  digital economy, 264
  economic models/ opportunities, 266
  collaborative work/ innovation, 270, 271
  decentralised economic models, 266–268
  economic models/ opportunities, 272
  monetisation strategies, 269

tokenisation/incentives, 272, 273
value creation/distribution, 268, 269
evolution, 262
foundational elements, 264–267
immersive technologies, 264
interoperability, 265
JPMorgan Foray, 274, 275
limitations, 261
platforms, 273
preparation/ challenges, 276–278
progressive enhancement, 263
regulatory/ethical considerations, 276
spatial technologies, 265
technical and social directions, 277
Web1, Web2 and Web3 comparison, 262
MEV, *see* Maximum Extractable Value (MEV)
MiCA, *see* Markets in Crypto-Assets (MiCA)
Mining mechanisms
block creation, 35
block reward/transaction fees, 36
concept of, 34
events, 34
evolution, 38
hash rate distribution, 40
key details, 37, 38
mining pools, 39–42
table summarization, 34
traditional currency, 34
transaction validation, 35
Monetary Authority of Singapore (MAS), 312, 313

N, O

Nakamoto, Satoshi, 28–30
NFTs, *see* Non-fungible tokens (NFTs)
Non-fungible tokens (NFTs), 8, 90, 94, 95, 264
application, 201–203
authenticity, 200
constructor, 228
controlling contract behaviour, 232
creation/trading, 209
definition, 199
development environment, 222–235
digital art, 209
digital identities, 202
distribution models, 203–205
distribution strategies, 207, 208
dutch auctions, 204
evolution, 207
functions/modifiers, 228
helper functions, 229
inclusivity and integrity, 205, 206

INDEX

Non-fungible tokens (NFTs) (*cont.*)
  integration, 201
  market dynamics, 206, 207
  market volatility/liquidity, 208
  metadata, 234
  metadata standards, 220
  MetaMask transaction, 237
  minting, 228
  OpenSea's standards, 219–222
  OpenSea's testnet, 235–238
  owner-only functions, 229
  ownership, 200
  post-deployment steps, 231
  properties, 200–202
  provenance, 200
  random images, 210–214
  real estate, 202
  removeWhitelistUser function, 232
  setBaseExtension function, 234
  smart contract, 230, 233
  standardisation, 325
  standard mints, 204
  storage solution
    centralised solutions, 215
    disadvantages, 218
    IPFS node setting, 215
    methods, 215
    Pinata, 216, 217
    third-party services, 216–219
  variables, 228
  whitelistUser function, 232
  withdraw function, 229

P, Q

PBFT, *see* Practical Byzantine Fault Tolerance (PBFT)
Physical Resource Networks (PRNs), 183
PoS, *see* Proof-of-stake (PoS)
PoW, *see* Proof-of-work (PoW)
Practical Byzantine Fault Tolerance (PBFT), 24
Proof-of-stake (PoS), 23, 59
Proof-of-work (PoW), 22, 29, 36, 59
PRNs, *see* Physical Resource Networks (PRNs)
Python libraries
  Bitcoin Address, 19
  cryptographic operations, 18
  foundational elements, 21
  multi-signature address, 19
  private/public keys, 18
  transaction history, 20

R

RAO, *see* Regulated Activities Order (RAO)
Real-World Assets (RWA)
  blockchain technology, 177, 178
  computational finance, 179
  computational systems, 177
  cryptocurrency perspective, 176
  inherent transparency and security, 179
  liquidity/global accessibility, 178

INDEX

non-computational systems, 177
operational efficiency/cost reduction, 179
programmability/transparency, 180
tangible/intangible assets, 175
tokenisation, 178–180
TradFi viewpoint, 176
Regulated Activities Order (RAO), 307
Remix, *see* Integrated development environment (IDE)
RWA, *see* Real-World Assets (RWA)

S

SEC, *see* Securities and Exchange Commission (SEC)
Securities and Exchange Commission (SEC), 305
Self-sovereign identity (SSI), 168
SSI, *see* Self-sovereign identity (SSI)
Supply chain management, 296–298

T

Time-Weighted Average Market Maker (TWAMM), 159, 250–253
Token definitions
 comparative analysis, 305
 different jurisdictions, 315

Hong Kong, HKMA, 313–316
MiCA framework, 309, 310
Singapore, MAS, 312, 313
Switzerland, FINMA, 310, 311
United Kingdom, FCA, 307, 308
United States, SEC, 305
Total Value Locked (TVL), 157, 166, 167
Traditional Finance (TradFi), 146–148
Real-World Assets (RWA), 176
TVL, *see* Total Value Locked (TVL)
TWAMM, *see* Time-Weighted Average Market Maker (TWAMM)

U, V

Uniswap, DeFi
 evolution, 157, 158
 redefining access/efficiency, 160–162
 swap hook flow, 159

W, X, Y

Web3 technologies
 AI (*see* Artificial intelligence (AI))
 coinbase operates, 112, 113
 crypto brokerage (contract account), 113
 EOA *vs.* contract account, 112

INDEX

Web3 technologies (*cont.*)
   Ethereum blockchain, 127
   Ethereum hosts, 112
   faucet serves, 127–134
   Layer 2 solutions
      blockchain trilemma, 135
      cost/transactions, 136
      Ethereum network, 134
      key factors, 135
      optimistic rollups, 135
      optimistic rollups *vs.* ZK-Rollups, 136, 137
      security, 136
   MetaMask (*see* MetaMask)
   metaverse (*see* Metaverse)
   wallet types, 111
Web3 technology
   regulation/innovation/standardisation, 322
      Bitcoin ETFs, 322–324
      cryptocurrencies, 328
      cryptocurrency innovation, 324
      projections, 327–329
      risk navigation, 325
      sustainable integration, 328
   standardisation, 326

Z

Zero-knowledge proofs (ZKPs), 135, 193
ZKPs, *see* Zero-knowledge proofs (ZKPs)

SPRINGER NATURE

GPSR Compliance

The European Union's (EU) General Product Safety Regulation (GPSR) is a set of rules that requires consumer products to be safe and our obligations to ensure this.

If you have any concerns about our products, you can contact us on ProductSafety@springernature.com

In case Publisher is established outside the EU, the EU authorized representative is:

Springer Nature Customer Service Center GmbH
Europaplatz 3
69115 Heidelberg, Germany

The manufacturer's authorised representative in the EU is Springer Nature Customer Service Centre GmbH, Europaplatz 3, 69115 Heidelberg, Germany. If you have any concerns regarding our products, please contact ProductSafety@springernature.com

Printed and bound by CPI Group (UK) Ltd, Croydon, CR0 4YY